Preußens Glanz
The Splendor of Prussia

Königsschlösser in Berlin und Brandenburg
Text von Hans-Joachim Giersberg
Fotos von Leo Seidel

The Royal Palaces of Berlin and Brandenburg
Text by Hans-Joachim Giersberg
Photographs by Leo Seidel

Prestel
München · Berlin · London · New York

Inhalt

Vorwort 4

Einführung 5

Kurfürst Joachim II. **8**
Jagdschloss Grunewald, Berlin 10

Kurfürst Friedrich Wilhelm **14**
Schloss Oranienburg, Brandenburg 16
Schloss Caputh, Brandenburg 22

Kurfürst und König Friedrich III.–I. **28**
Schloss Charlottenburg, Berlin 30

König Friedrich Wilhelm I. **36**
Schloss Königs Wusterhausen, Brandenburg 38
Jagdschloss Stern, Potsdam 44

König Friedrich II. **46**
Schloss Rheinsberg, Brandenburg 48
Der Neue Flügel des Schlosses Charlottenburg – Die Wohnungen Friedrichs II., Berlin 60
Schloss Sanssouci mit Neuen Kammern und Bildergalerie, Potsdam 66
Das Neue Palais im Park von Sanssouci. Das Belvedere und das Drachenhaus, Potsdam 86

Königin Elisabeth Christine **100**
Schloss Schönhausen, Berlin 102

Preface 4

Introduction 5

Joachim II Elector of Brandenburg **8**
Grunewald Hunting Lodge, Berlin 10

Elector Frederick William **14**
Oranienburg Palace, Brandenburg 16
Caputh Palace, Brandenburg 22

Elector and King Frederick III–I **28**
Charlottenburg Palace, Berlin 30

King Frederick William I **36**
Königs Wusterhausen Palace, Brandenburg 38
Stern Hunting Lodge, Potsdam 44

King Frederick II **46**
Rheinsberg Palace, Brandenburg 48
The New Wing of Charlottenburg Palace – The Apartments of Frederick II, Berlin 60
Sanssouci Palace with the New Chambers and Picture Gallery, Potsdam 66
New Palace in Sanssouci Park. Belvedere and Dragon House, Potsdam 86

Queen Elizabeth Christina **100**
Schönhausen Palace, Berlin 102

Contents

König Friedrich Wilhelm II. 106
Das Marmorpalais im Neuen Garten, Potsdam 108

Die Pfaueninsel, Berlin 114

Die Wohnungen Friedrich Wilhelms II. im Schloss Charlottenburg, Berlin 124

König Friedrich Wilhelm III. und Königin Luise 128
Schloss Paretz, Brandenburg 130

Das Mausoleum und der Neue Pavillon im Park von Schloss Charlottenburg, Berlin 136

König Friedrich Wilhelm IV. 142
Schloss Charlottenhof und Römische Bäder. Die Wohnung Friedrich Wilhelms IV. im Schloss Sanssouci. Die Friedenskirche. Die Orangerie, Potsdam 144

Das Belvedere auf dem Pfingstberg, Potsdam 160

Schloss Lindstedt, Potsdam 164

Schloss Sacrow, Potsdam 166

Prinz Carl 170
Schloss Glienicke, Berlin 172

König und Kaiser Wilhelm I. 178
Schloss und Park Babelsberg mit Flatowturm und Gerichtslaube, Potsdam 180

Kronprinz Wilhelm und Kronprinzessin Cecilie 186
Schloss Cecilienhof im Neuen Garten, Potsdam 188

King Frederick William II 106
Marble Palace in the New Garden, Potsdam 108

Peacock Island, Berlin 114

Frederick William II's Apartments in Charlottenburg Palace, Berlin 124

King Frederick William III and Queen Louise 128
Paretz Palace, Brandenburg 130

The Queen Louise Mausoleum and the New Pavilion in the Park of Charlottenburg Palace, Berlin 136

King Frederick William IV 142
Charlottenhof Palace and Roman Baths. Frederick William IV's Apartment in Sanssouci Palace. The Church of Peace. The Orangery, Potsdam 144

Belvedere on the Pfingstberg, Potsdam 160

Lindstedt Palace, Potsdam 164

Sacrow Palace, Potsdam 166

Prince Charles of Prussia 170
Glienicke Palace, Berlin 172

King and Emperor William I 178
Babelsberg Palace and Park with the Flatow Tower and the Court Loggia, Potsdam 180

Crown Prince William and Crown Princess Cecilia 186
Cecilienhof Palace in the New Garden, Potsdam 188

Preußens Glanz – lebendig wie nie

The Splendor of Prussia – Alive as Never Before

Wenn ein talentierter Fotograf und ein ausgewiesener Kenner der preußischen Kunst- und Kulturgeschichte gemeinsam ein Buch realisieren, sind die Erwartungen des Publikums berechtigterweise hoch. Um es gleich vorweg zu nehmen: In diesem Fall werden sie nicht enttäuscht, sondern eher noch übertroffen, denn als Ergebnis der Zusammenarbeit liegt nun ein prächtiger Band über die preußischen Schlösser und Gärten vor, der im Zusammenspiel von wunderbaren Fotos und profunden Texten Maßstäbe setzt.

Auch wenn man glaubt, die Schlösser und Gärten der Hohenzollern in Berlin, Potsdam und in Brandenburg bereits in- und auswendig zu kennen: Die Fotos von Leo Seidel belehren uns eines Besseren. Ungewöhnliche Blickwinkel, überraschende Lichtführung und unbekannte Perspektiven lassen die Gärten, die Bauwerke und die kostbar ausgestatteten Innenräume in einem verblüffend anderen, neuen Glanz erstrahlen. Dazu erzählen die Texte Hans-Joachim Giersbergs, des langjährigen Generaldirektors der Stiftung Preußische Schlösser und Gärten, mit gewohnter Kennerschaft von den einstigen Bewohnern und den Architekten, Malern, Bildhauern und Dekorationskünstlern, die am preußischen Hof tätig waren und die aktuell fotografierten Meisterwerke einst schufen.

Alle hier vorgestellten Schlösser und Gärten werden heute von der Stiftung Preußische Schlösser und Gärten Berlin-Brandenburg erhalten, gepflegt und wissenschaftlich erforscht, damit sich ein breites Publikum in diesen weltbekannten Anlagen bilden, erfreuen und erholen kann. Seien auch Sie herzlich eingeladen, sich von Preußens Glanz verzaubern zu lassen. Tauchen Sie ein in eine Zeit, die zwar vergangen, aber Dank der erhaltenen Schlösser, Gärten und Kunstwerke lebendig geblieben ist und uns heute eindrucksvolle und spannende Einblicke in die Epoche der preußischen Könige und deutschen Kaiser gewährt.

Hartmut Dorgerloh
Generaldirektor der Stiftung Preußische Schlösser und Gärten Berlin-Brandenburg

When a talented photographer and a proven authority on Prussian art and cultural history produce a book together, then the public justifiably has high expectations. To get right to the point, in this case the book does not fall short but surpasses all expectations, as this collaboration has resulted in a magnificent work about Prussian palaces and gardens. The combination of wonderful photos and profound texts sets new standards.

Even if you believe that you already know the Hohenzollern palaces and gardens in Berlin, Potsdam, and Brandenburg inside out, Leo Seidel's photos will be a revelation. His unusual angles of vision, surprising ways of directing light, and new perspectives allow the gardens, the buildings, and the luxuriously appointed interiors to shine with a new, astonishingly different splendor. In the accompanying texts, Hans-Joachim Giersberg, the long-time General Director of the Prussian Palaces and Gardens Foundation Berlin-Brandenburg, tells with his customary expertise of the former occupants and the architects, painters, sculptors, and decorators who were once active at the Prussian court and created the masterpieces shown in the photographs.

All of the palaces and gardens presented here are preserved, maintained, and researched by the Prussian Palaces and Gardens Foundation Berlin-Brandenburg, so that a wide audience can find edification, pleasure, and recreation at these world-renowned sites. We warmly invite you to be enchanted by the splendor of Prussia. Immerse yourself in a time that, although past, has remained alive through the preserved palaces, gardens, and works of art, which today afford us impressive and exciting insights into the era of the Prussian kings and German emperors.

Hartmut Dorgerloh
General Director of the Prussian Palaces and Gardens Foundation Berlin-Brandenburg

Die Stadtschlösser in Berlin und Potsdam

The City Palaces in Berlin and Potsdam

Das Stadtschloss in Berlin war die Hauptresidenz der Hohenzollern und Verwaltungssitz des Königreiches Preußen. Das Schloss in Potsdam entwickelte sich seit der Zeit des Kurfürsten Friedrich Wilhelm – ab 1675 der »Große Kurfürst« genannt – zu einer beliebten Nebenresidenz.
Beide Schlösser wurden 1945 zerstört und die Ruinen 1950 bzw. 1951/60 abgerissen.
Wenn die in Berlin und Brandenburg gelegenen und erhaltenen bzw. wiederhergestellten Schlösser präsentiert werden, so muss doch anfangs auf die Bedeutung und die Geschichte der beiden zerstörten Stadtschlösser in den genannten Städten eingegangen werden.
Das Berliner Schloss war 1443 bis 1451 unter dem Kurfürsten Friedrich II. auf der Spreeinsel der Stadt Cölln unter Einbeziehung mittelalterlicher Bauteile, wie der Stadtbefestigung und des Rundturmes (der sogenannte »Grüne Hut«) errichtet worden. Unter dem Kurfürsten Joachim II. wurde es ab 1538, vermutlich nach einem Entwurf von Conrad Krebs, durch Caspar Theiß zu einem stattlichen Renaissance-Bau, beeinflusst von den sächsischen Schlössern, umgestaltet. In der folgenden Zeit, besonders während der Regierungszeit des Kurfürsten Friedrich Wilhelm wurde es durch die Baumeister Johann Arnold Nering und Johann Gregor Memhardt mehrfach verändert und erweitert. Am Ende des 17. Jahrhundert hatte es dadurch ein sehr uneinheitliches Aussehen erhalten mit Baulichkeiten, die sich um zwei große Höfe gruppierten. Im Nordwesten schloss sich der Lustgarten an. Unter dem Kurfürsten Friedrich III. (als König Friedrich I.) wurde es zwischen 1698 bis 1716 mehrfach umgebaut und erhielt eine einheitliche Gestalt. Daran war zwischen 1698 bis 1706 Andreas Schlüter beteiligt, der den nordöstlichen Teil mit dem inneren Schlosshof gestaltete. Ihm folgte Johann Friedrich Eosander, der die Anlage um das Doppelte erweiterte. Besonders hervorragend und reich gestaltet waren die Wohn- und Festräume Friedrichs I., die zu den besten des deutschen Barock um 1700 zählten. Den Umbau schloss Martin Heinrich Böhme unter Friedrich Wilhelm I. zwischen 1713 und 1716 ab.
Die Innenräume wurden im 18. und 19. Jahrhundert mehrfach verändert. Daran waren vor allem Georg Wenzeslaus von Knobelsdorff und Johann August Nahl um 1745 beteiligt. Carl von Gontard und Friedrich Wilhelm von Erdmannsdorff schufen die Königskammern für Friedrich Wilhelm II. von 1787 bis 1790. Der Pfeilersaal war ein Werk von Carl Gotthard Langhans d. Ä. 1791 für den gleichen König. Auch der Kronprinz Friedrich Wilhelm (IV.) ließ durch Karl Friedrich Schinkel ab 1825 Räume verändern. Nach seinem Entwurf schufen von 1843 bis 1853 Friedrich August Stüler und Albrecht

The City Palace in Berlin was the principal residence of the Hohenzollerns and the administrative center of the Kingdom of Prussia. Since the time of Frederick William, Elector of Brandenburg – known as the Great Elector after 1675 – the palace in Potsdam had developed into a favorite second residence. Both palaces were destroyed in 1945, and the ruins were demolished in 1950 and between 1951 and 1960.
In order to introduce the surviving and restored palaces in Berlin and Brandenburg, the significance and history of the two destroyed palaces in these cities must be discussed first.
The Berlin City Palace was constructed from 1443 to 1451 under Elector Frederick II on an island in the Spree which was part of the town of Cölln. It incorporated medieval components such as the town fortifications and the Round Tower (the "Green Hat"). Under Elector Joachim II, it was rebuilt beginning in 1538 by Caspar Theiss as an imposing Renaissance building influenced by the palaces in Saxony, presumably according to a design by Conrad Krebs. In the following years, especially during the reign of Elector Frederick William, it was altered and extended a number of times by the architects Johann Arnold Nering and Johann Gregor Memhardt. By the end of the 17th century it had gained a very irregular appearance, with buildings grouped around two large courtyards. To the north-west it adjoined the pleasure gardens. It was repeatedly remodeled under Elector Frederick III (later King Frederick I) between 1698 and 1716, and given a uniform appearance. Andreas Schlüter was involved from 1698 to 1706, and designed the north-east portion with the inner palace courtyard. He was followed by Johann Friedrich Eosander, who doubled the size of the buildings. Frederick I's richly decorated residential rooms and halls of state are particularly outstanding and are numbered among the best German Baroque rooms of around 1700. Martin Heinrich Böhme finished the remodeling under Frederick William I between 1713 and 1716.
The interior was repeatedly altered in the 18th and 19th centuries, above all by Georg Wenzeslaus von Knobelsdorff and Johann August Nahl in about 1745. Carl von Gontard and Friedrich Wilhelm von Erdmannsdorff created the royal chambers for Frederick William II from 1787 to 1790. The Hall of Pillars was the work of Carl Gotthard Langhans the Elder in 1791 for the same king. From 1825, while he was still crown prince, Frederick William IV had the rooms altered by Karl Friedrich Schinkel. From 1843 to 1853, following Schinkel's designs, Friedrich August Stüler and Albrecht Dietrich Schadow built the dome over the Eosander portal with the palace chapel beneath. Between 1844 and 1857, Stüler laid out a succession of imposing rooms and created the stair-

Berliner Stadtschloss von Osten, Luftbild, um 1930, Landesarchiv Berlin
Berlin City Palace from the east, aerial photo, c. 1930, Landesarchiv Berlin

Berliner Stadtschloss, ausgebrannte Südseite, 1950, SPSG Fotothek
Berlin City Palace, burnt-out south side, 1950, SPSG Fotothek

Dietrich Schadow die Kuppel über dem Eosander-Portal mit der darin befindlichen Schlosskapelle. Stüler legte von 1844 bis 1857 eine repräsentative Raumfolge an und schuf das Treppenhaus, den Weißen Saal und die Schlosskapelle unter maßgeblicher Beteiligung König Friedrich Wilhelms IV.
Auch während der Regierungszeit Kaiser Wilhelms II. zwischen 1888 und 1914 sind durch Ernst von Ihne Veränderungen der Schlossausstattungen und Umbauten vorgenommen worden. Das Schloss, das nach 1918 zu einem Museum wurde, brannte 1945 aus und die durchaus noch aufbaufähige Ruine wurde 1950/51 gesprengt und abgetragen.
Das Portal IV des Südwestflügels, auf dem Karl Liebknecht 1918 die Deutsche Republik ausgerufen hatte, wurde 1962 bis 1964 nach einem Entwurf von Roland Korn in das ehemalige Staatsratsgebäude der DDR eingefügt. Es ist ursprünglich von Johann Friedrich Eosander 1706 bis 1713 als Wiederholung des Gartenportals V von Andreas Schlüter gebaut worden. Die Atlantenhermen waren Werke von Baltharsar Permoser; sind zwischen 1706 und 1708 entstanden und gelten als Anregung für seine Dekoration des Wallpavillons am Dresdner Zwinger 1716 bis 1718 und auch für die Gartenfassade des Schlosses Sanssouci von Friedrich Christian Glume 1745 bis 1747.

Die Geschichte des Potsdamer Stadtschlosses lässt sich bis in das 13. Jahrhundert zurückverfolgen. Die im Landbuch Kaiser Karls IV. 1375 genannte Burg ist nach Ergebnissen von Grabungen schon im 13. Jahrhundert angelegt worden. Aus ihr entwickelte sich ein Schloss, besonders nach der Übernahme 1593 durch die Kurfürstin Katharina. Der Kurfürst Friedrich Wilhelm machte Potsdam nach 1660 zu seiner zweiten Residenz neben Berlin und ließ 1662 bis 1669 an der Stelle des alten Bauwerks ein neues Schloss errichten. Dieses orientierte sich in seiner Außenarchitektur an holländischen Vorbildern. In den Jahren 1679 bis 1682 wurde das Schloss nach Plänen von Michael Mathias Smit und Johann Arnold Nering erweitert, indem man die Seitenflügel bis zum Alten Markt, dem städtischen Zentrum, verlängerte. Auch unter Friedrich I. sind weitere Umbauten vorgenommen worden und die Schlossanlage bekam durch das Fortunaportal (1701 von Jean de Bodt) einen wirkungsvollen Eingangsbau. Georg Wenzeslaus von Knobelsdorff gab dem Schloss 1744 bis 1752 sein endgültiges Aussehen. An der künstlerischen Gestaltung des Außenbaus sowie der Innenräume waren Johann August Nahl, Friedrich Christian Glume, Johann Peter Benckert und Johann Gottfried Heymüller maßgeblich beteiligt. Um 1800 wurden eine Wohnung für die Königin Luise sowie für König Friedrich Wilhelm III. die Blaue

case, the White Hall and the palace chapel with considerable involvement by King Frederick William IV.
Changes in the palace furnishings and building alterations were also carried out between 1888 and 1914, during the reign of Emperor William II, by Ernst von Ihne. The palace, which became a museum after 1918, burned down in 1945. The ruins, which could certainly have been restored, were dynamited and carried away in 1950/51.
Portal IV of the south-west wing, from which Karl Liebknecht proclaimed the German Republic in 1918, was incorporated into the former state council building of the GDR according to a design by Roland Korn between 1962 and 1964. It was originally built by Johann Friedrich Eosander from 1706 to 1713 as a replica of garden portal V by Andreas Schlüter. The atlantis figures, the work of Balthasar Permoser between 1706 and 1708, are regarded as the inspiration for his decorations of the wall pavilions of the Zwinger Palace in Dresden from 1716 to 1718, and also for the garden façade of Sanssouci Palace by Friedrich Christian Glume from 1745 to 1747.

The history of the Potsdam City Palace can be traced back to the 13th century, when the castle mentioned in Emperor Charles IV's land book of 1375 already existed, according to excavations. A palace developed from it, particularly after Electress Catherine took it over in 1593. Elector Frederick William made Potsdam his second official residence after Berlin and had a new palace constructed from 1660 to 1669 on the site of the old one. Its exterior architecture was inspired by Dutch models. In the years between 1679 and 1682, the palace was enlarged to plans by Michael Mathias Smit and Johann Arnold Nering by extending the side wings to the old marketplace, the town center. Further rebuilding was carried out under Frederick I, and the palace received an imposing entrance, the Fortuna Portal (1701 by Jean de Bodt). Georg Wenzeslaus von Knobelsdorff gave the palace its final appearance between 1744 and 1752. Johann August Nahl, Friedrich Christian Glume, Johann Peter Benckert, and Johann Gottfried Heymüller played key roles in designing the exterior as well as the interior. Around 1800 the living quarters for Queen Louise as well as for King Frederick William III, the Blue and the Yellow Chambers of State and the Etruscan Room, were furnished. Frederick William IV and his consort Elizabeth also lived in the palace. Ferdinand von Arnim's plans of 1856 for rebuilding were never carried out, however. The Palace Theater, incorporated in 1745 to a design by von Knobelsdorff, was removed in 1801, but was copied in Frederick the Great's era in the New Palace. After 1918, the palace became

Stadtschloss Potsdam, Luftbild, um 1935, SPSG
Potsdam City Palace, aerial photo, c. 1935, SPSG

Stadtschloss Potsdam, ausgebrannte Südseite, um 1950, SPSG
Potsdam City Palace, burnt-out south side, c. 1950, SPSG

und die Gelbe Paradekammer und das »Etruskische Zimmer« eingerichtet. Auch Friedrich Wilhelm IV. und seine Gemahlin Elisabeth bewohnten das Schloss. Umbaupläne von Ferdinand von Arnim 1856 wurden jedoch nicht ausgeführt. Das 1745 nach einem Entwurf von Knobelsdorff eingebaute Schlosstheater wurde schon 1801 ausgebaut, hatte aber seine Wiederholung in friderizianischer Zeit im Neuen Palais gefunden. Nach 1918 wurde das Schloss zu einem Museum. In den letzten Kriegstagen des Jahres 1945 brannte es aus und die durchaus wiederherstellbare Ruine wurde 1959/60 abgetragen.
Erhalten blieb die 1685 von Johann Arnold Nering erbaute Orangerie, die 1714 unter Friedrich Wilhelm I. zu einem Stall für die königlichen Reitpferde verändert wurde. Knobelsdorff gab 1746 dem Bau seine heutige Gestalt, indem er ihn um zwölf Achsen nach Westen verlängerte. Die Pferdegruppen auf den zwei Risaliten schuf Friedrich Christian Glume. Nach leichten Zerstörungen 1945 konnte der Marstall wieder aufgebaut werden. Nach mehreren, meist musealen Nutzungen wurde dort zwischen 1977 und 1980 ein Filmmuseum eingerichtet, das im April 1981 eröffnet werden konnte.

a museum. In 1945, in the last days of the war, it burned down and the ruins, which could undoubtedly have been restored, were demolished in 1959/60. The orangery built by Johann Arnold Nering in 1685 survived. It had been converted in 1714 under Frederick William I into stables for the royal horses. Knobelsdorff gave the building its present form in 1746, extending it by twelve bays to the west. The two groups of horses were created by Friedrich Christian Glume. Following slight damage in 1945, the royal stables were rebuilt and used for various purposes, mostly as a museum. Finally a film museum, which opened in April 1981, was established there between 1977 and 1980.

Lucas Cranach d. J. | Lucas Cranach the Younger

Joachim II., Kurfürst von Brandenburg, um 1555, SPSG
Joachim II, Elector of Brandenburg, c. 1555, SPSG

Kurfürst

Joachim II.

Joachim II, Elector of Brandenburg

reg. 1535–1571

Jagdschloss Grunewald
Berlin

Grunewald Hunting Lodge
Berlin

Ansicht des Schlosses von Südosten mit dem Küchenbau. Beide Gebäude stammen aus der Mitte des 16. Jahrhunderts.
View of the palace from the south-east with the kitchen building. Both buildings date from the mid-16th century.

Jagdschloss Grunewald
Berlin

Grunewald Hunting Lodge
Berlin

Das Jagdschloss Grunewald ist nach der Zerstörung des Berliner Stadtschlosses 1945 und der Sprengung der verbliebenen Reste des Baus 1950 das älteste Schloss in Berlin. Von seinem Erbauer, dem brandenburgischen Kurfürsten Joachim II., wurde es »Zum grünen Wald« genannt, da es in dem heute zu Berlin gehörenden und damals vor den Toren der Stadt gelegenen Forstgebiet »Grunewald« lag.

Das auf einer künstlichen Insel am Ufer des Grunewaldsees gelegene Schloss ist im Jahre 1542 in den Formen der sächsischen Renaissance errichtet worden. Der vermutliche Baumeister war Caspar Theiß, der aus dem sächsischen Raum stammte und am Umbau des Berliner Schlosses und an den Schlössern in Dresden und Torgau beteiligt war.

Kleinere Umbauten erhielt das Jagdschloss Grunewald im 17. und frühen 18. Jahrhundert. Durch ein einheitliches Mansarddach, die Vergrößerung der Fenster und die Neuverputzung durch Martin Grüneberg und Georg Heinrich Behr um 1700 wurde aus dem Renaissance-Schloss ein barockes Haus.

König Friedrich Wilhelm I. richtete vor 1734 im Schloss eine Wohnung für den Oberjägermeister Georg Christoph Graf von Schlieben ein und Friedrich der Große ließ dann 1770 die südlichen Nebengebäude als Magazin für das Hofjagdzeug umbauen, das zu dieser Zeit vom ehemaligen Jägerhof in Berlin hierher verlegt wurde. Außerdem erhielt der Jagdzeugmeister eine Wohnung im Schloss.

1794 wurden in der zweiten Etage Räume für die Gräfin Lichtenau, die Mätresse König Friedrich Wilhelms II., eingerichtet.

1828 nahm man die Tradition der Parforcejagd im Grunewald wieder auf und das Jagdschloss erhielt somit seine alte Bestimmung zurück. Im Jahr 1907 fand die letzte Hofjagd im Grunewald statt. Vorher hatte jedoch der Kaiser Wilhelm II. einige den modernen Wohnbedürfnissen angepasste Veränderungen im Schloss durchführen lassen. Nach dem Ersten Weltkrieg wurde das Schloss Bestandteil der ehemals Preußischen Schlösserverwaltung und diese stattete 1932 das Haus mit Gemälden aus dem 15. bis 19. Jahrhunderts und mit wenigen Einrichtungsgegenständen aus. Da das Haus im Zweiten Weltkrieg kaum zerstört worden war, konnte es 1949 als erstes Museum in Berlin wiedereröffnet werden. Damals wie heute beherbergt das Schloss Gemälde des 15. bis 19. Jahrhunderts und nur einige Einrichtungsgegenstände. 1973/74 konnte im Erdgeschoss die alte Hofstube aus der Zeit Joachims II. freigelegt werden.

Südlich des Schlosses befindet sich das Jagdzeugmagazin. Der kurfürstliche Jägerhof lag ursprünglich am Rand des Tiergartens und wurde ab 1765 von

Grunewald Hunting Lodge is the oldest palace in Berlin, after the destruction of the Berlin City Palace in 1945 and its subsequent demolition in 1950. Its builder, the Elector of Brandenburg Joachim II, named it "greenwood" because it was located in the Grunewald area of forest that today belongs to Berlin and in those days was outside the city gates.

The palace was constructed in 1542 in the Saxon Renaissance style on an artificial island on the banks of Lake Grunewald. The probable architect was Caspar Theiss, who originally came from the Saxony area and was involved in rebuilding the Berlin Palace and the palaces in Dresden and Torgau.

Minor alterations to Grunewald Hunting Lodge were carried out in the 17th and early 18th century. A uniform mansard roof, the enlargement of the windows, and new plastering by Martin Grüneberg and Georg Heinrich Behr turned the Renaissance building into a Baroque house around 1700.

King Frederick William I set up an apartment in the lodge for his Grand Master of the Hunt, Georg Christoph Graf von Schlieben, prior to 1734, and in 1770 Frederick the Great had the southern annex reconstructed as a store for the royal hunting equipment, which was then transferred there from the former hunting store in Berlin. Furthermore, the keeper of the hunting equipment was given an apartment in the lodge.

In 1794, rooms on the second floor were furnished for Countess Lichtenau, the mistress of King Frederick William II.

In 1828, the tradition of coursing was revived in Grunewald, and the hunting lodge regained its old purpose. The last royal hunt in Grunewald took place in 1907. Before this, however, Emperor William II had some changes carried out to adapt the lodge to the requirements of modern living. After the First World War, it became a part of the Prussian Palace Administration, which in 1932 furnished the house with paintings from the 15th to the 19th century and a few pieces of furniture. Because the house had hardly been damaged during the Second World War, in 1949 it was the first museum to be reopened in Berlin. Then as now, the palace contains paintings from the 15th to the 19th century and only a few articles of furniture. In 1973/74, the old Great Hall on the ground floor from the time of Joachim II was uncovered.

The hunting store lies to the south of the palace. The electoral hunting store was originally on the edge of Tiergarten park, and was used by Frederick the Great after 1765 as a banking house. The storehouse at Grunewald was built for the hunting paraphernalia from the Berlin storehouse. Older buildings on the site had to be reconstructed for this purpose, and a large 40-meter-long hall resulted. In the 1960s an attempt was made to revive the old hunting store, but nothing existed of the former equipment. Articles from the collection of the

Wilhelm Barth

Schloss Grunewald, 1832, SPSG
Grunewald Hunting Lodge, 1832, SPSG

Friedrich dem Großen als Bankhaus genutzt. Für das Jagdzeuginventar des Berliner Jägerhofes wurde am Jagdschloss Grunewald das sogenannte Jagdzeugmagazin errichtet. Ältere Gebäude beim Jagdschloss mussten zu diesem Zweck umgebaut werden und eine große, 40 Meter lange Halle entstand. In den 60er Jahren des 20. Jh. war man bemüht, das alte Jagdzeugmagazin wieder zu revitalisieren, doch von der früheren Ausstattung war nichts mehr vorhanden. Bestände aus der Sammlung der Stiftung Preußischer Kulturbesitz und des ehemaligen Zeughauses wurden als Leihgaben für eine Ausstellung verwendet. Hinzu kamen Trophäen aus den Revieren des ehemals preußischen Königshauses und eine Gemäldesammlung mit jagdlichen Motiven. Mit Unterstützung eines Fördervereins, der Stiftung Deutsche Klassenlotterie und einiger privater Mäzene konnte die Einrichtung komplettiert werden. Am 29. Januar 1977 wurde das Jagdmuseum Grunewald eröffnet.

Prussian Cultural Heritage Foundation and the former Armory were loaned for an exhibition. Trophies from the hunting grounds of the former Prussian royal families and a painting collection with hunting scenes were added. The support of a sponsor, the Stiftung Deutsche Klassenlotterie, and some private patrons made it possible to complete the furnishings. On January 29, 1977 Grunewald Hunting Museum was opened.

Links: Der aus der Renaissance stammende Saal wurde 1973 bei Renovierungsarbeiten wieder in seinen ursprünglichen Zustand versetzt.
Left: The hall dates from the Renaissance and was restored to its original condition in 1973.

Unten: Raum im Obergeschoss des Schlosses mit Gemälden von Lucas Cranach d. Ä. mit der Darstellung von »Adam und Eva« (1557) und »Lucretia« (1529).
Bottom: Room on the upper floor of the palace with paintings by Lucas Cranach the Elder portraying "Adam and Eve" (1557) and "Lucretia" (1529).

Rechts: Blick in das 1977 wiedereröffnete Jagdzeugmagazin. Es war 1770 eingerichtet worden; die ursprünglichen Bestände verschwanden in den 1960er Jahren. Die heutige Ausstattung mit Trophäen, Jagdgewehren und sogenannten »Lappen« vermittelt einen jagdlichen Eindruck.
Right: View inside the hunting storehouse, which reopened in 1977. It was equipped in 1770; the original collections disappeared in the 1960s. The collections featured today with trophies, hunting rifles, and so-called sewelling flags provide an impression of the hunt.

GWMZB
17 17

Pieter Vason

Kurfürst Friedrich Wilhelm, genannt »Der Große Kurfürst« und seine Gemahlin Louise Henriette von Nassau-Oranien, um 1666, SPSG
Elector Frederick William, named "The Great Elector" and his Consort Louise Henrietta of Nassau-Orange, c. 1666, SPSG

Kurfürst (»Der Große Kurfürst«)

Friedrich Wilhelm

Elector Frederick William "The Great Elector"

reg. 1640–1688

Schloss Oranienburg Brandenburg

Oranienburg Palace
Brandenburg

Schloss Caputh Brandenburg

Caputh Palace
Brandenburg

Ansicht der südlich zur Stadt gewandten Fassade von Schloss Oranienburg, die nach 1699 von Johann Arnold Nering errichtet wurde.
View of the façade of Oranienburg Palace facing south toward the city, constructed after 1699 by Johann Arnold Nering.

Schloss Oranienburg
Brandenburg

Oranienburg Palace
Brandenburg

Oranienburg, in der Nähe Berlins gelegen, zählte früher zu den prächtigsten Residenzen der Hohenzollern in Brandenburg.
Der brandenburgische Kurfürst Joachim II. hatte in der Mitte des 16. Jahrhunderts anstelle der mittelalterlichen Burganlage ein Jagdschloss errichtet, das im Dreißigjährigen Krieg in einen sehr desolaten Zustand geriet. Als 1650 der brandenburgische Kurfürst Friedrich Wilhelm, der ab 1675 der »Große Kurfürst« genannt wurde, seiner Frau Louise Henriette, einer Prinzessin aus dem Haus Oranien-Nassau, das Anwesen schenkte, ließ diese durch den Baumeister Johann Gregor Memhardt zusammen mit Michael Mathias Smit bis 1655 ein neues Schloss errichten, das bereits 1652 den Namen Oranienburg erhalten hatte. Später nahm auch der bei dem Schloss gelegene Ort Bötzow diesen Namen an.
Nach dem Tod der Kurfürstin Louise Henriette 1667 wurde es still um das holländisch anmutende Schloss. Erst ihr Sohn, Kurfürst Friedrich III., ab 1701 erster preußischer König Friedrich I., ließ es 1689, anfangs von Johann Arnold Nering durch Anfügen von Seitenflügeln in H-Form, in eine französisch anmutende Anlage verwandeln, die er seiner Mutter, wie die Inschrift bezeugt, widmete. Sein Sohn allerdings, König Friedrich Wilhelm I., hatte wenig Interesse am Schloss und dem dazugehörigen Garten. Eine Renaissance erlebt die Anlage noch einmal unter dem Bruder Friedrichs des Großen, August Wilhelm, zwischen 1744 und 1758. Dieser ließ im Inneren neue Räume einrichten und den Garten durch neue Alleen und Bauten verschönern. Nach dem Tod des Prinzen wohnte niemand mehr im Schloss, und es geriet bald in einen Zustand, dass »man in einigen Jahren wohl nicht mehr wagen dürfte hineinzugehen«, wie der Hofmarschall Valentin von Massow im August 1801 an Friedrich Wilhelm III. schrieb.
In der Memoirenliteratur wird berichtet, dass der König Friedrich Wilhelm II. Oranienburg seiner Schwiegertochter Luise von Mecklenburg-Strelitz zu ihrem 18. Geburtstag am 10. März 1794 geschenkt habe. Es gibt zwar keine Belege dafür, aber der König hatte im Herbst 1793 entsprechende Umbaupläne in Auftrag gegeben, die zwar ausgearbeitet, aber nicht verwirklicht wurden. Das große Schloss entsprach wohl kaum dem gewandelten Zeitgeschmack nach ländlicher Zurückgezogenheit. Im abgeschiedenen Paretz fand man nach 1797 das entsprechende Ideal und »auf ein Jahrhundert voller Glanz und lachender Farben folgte ein anderes voll Öde und Verwahrlosung. Andere Zeiten kamen; der Geschmack ging andere Wege. Schloss Oranienburg war vergessen« schrieb Fontane im Jahre 1861.
Das Schloss wurde an den Berliner Arzt und Apotheker Dr. J. G. Hempel verkauft, nachdem vorher das wertvolle Inventar nach Berlin und Charlot-

Oranienburg, near Berlin, was at one time one of the most magnificent residences of the Hohenzollern family in Brandenburg.
In the mid-16th century, Elector Joachim II of Brandenburg erected a hunting lodge on the site of a medieval castle, which fell into a ruinous state during the Thirty Years' War. When in 1650 Elector Frederick William of Brandenburg, who was called the Great Elector after 1675, gave the estate to his wife, Louise Henrietta, a princess from the House of Orange-Nassau, she had the architects Johann Gregor Memhardt and Michael Mathias Smit build a new palace. Construction lasted until 1655 but already in 1652 it was known as Oranienburg. Later, the village of Bötzow near the palace adopted this name.
After the death of Electress Louise Henrietta in 1667, not much was heard of the palace, which was reminiscent of Dutch architecture. It was not until 1689 that her son, Elector Frederick III, who became the first Prussian king as Frederick I, had it transformed – at first by Johann Arnold Nering – into a structure in the French style through the addition of side wings in the form of an "H." He dedicated it to his mother, as documented by an inscription. His son, King Frederick William I, however, had little interest in the palace and the garden that belonged to it. The palace and grounds experienced a renaissance under the brother of Frederick the Great, Augustus William, between 1744 and 1758.
He had new rooms constructed inside and the garden beautified through promenades and buildings. No one else lived in the palace after the death of the prince, and it was soon in such a condition that "probably in a few years no one will any longer dare to go inside," as the major-domo, Valentin von Massow, wrote to Frederick William III in August 1801.
Memoirs record that King Frederick William II gave Oranienburg to his daughter-in-law, Louise of Mecklenburg-Strelitz, on her 18th birthday, March 10th, 1794. Although there is no documentary evidence supporting this, the king commissioned appropriate building plans in the autumn of 1793, which were prepared but never implemented. The large palace probably no longer complied with the changing taste of the time for country seclusion. After 1797, the suitable ideal was found in the isolated village of Paretz and, "following a century full of glory and laughing colors came another full of desolation and neglect. Other times came, tastes went other ways. Oranienburg was forgotten," wrote Fontane in 1861.
The palace was sold to a Berlin physician and apothecary, Dr. J. G. Hempel, after its valuable contents had first been transferred to Berlin and Charlottenburg. With the installation of a weaving-mill and later a chemical factory to produce sulphuric acid, its decline and fall was sealed. Fires in 1833 and 1842

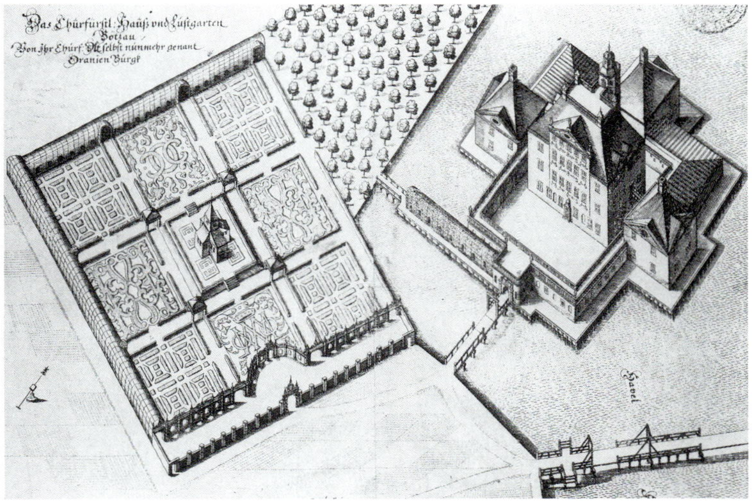

Johann Gregor Memhardt

Schloss und Garten Oranienburg, 1652, SPSG
Oranienburg Palace and Garden, 1652, SPSG

tenburg überführt worden war. Mit der Einrichtung einer Weberei und später einer chemischen Fabrik, speziell für Schwefelsäure war der Niedergang besiegelt. Brände von 1833 und 1842 dezimierten die Bausubstanz und führten zum Abriss des Südostflügels. Der Konservator der Kunstdenkmäler in Preußen, Ferdinand von Quast, hatte aber schon 1845 festgestellt, dass »das ganze Schloss eine kunstmäßige Gesamtanlage« war und wiederhergestellt werden müsse, denn zwischenzeitlich war es in den Besitz der Königlichen Seehandlung übergegangen. Nach 1851 übernahm der Intendant der Königlichen Schlösser und Gärten wiederum das Schloss und nach Umbauten zog 1860 ein Lehrerseminar ein, das bis 1925 blieb. Im Hauptgeschoss des Nordwestflügels einschließlich der Porzellankabinette blieben bis 1918 einige Räume dem König vorbehalten.

Auch der einst so prächtige Garten, der schon unter Friedrich Wilhelm I. durch Abbruch der Menagerie, der Orangerie, der Grotte sowie durch die Beseitigung der Röhren der Wasserkunst Einbußen erlitten hatte, war unter August Wilhelm durch die Erweiterung des Lustgartens, den Bau einer neuen Grotte, einer Lindenallee u. a. noch einmal zur Blüte gelangt. Doch der Garten geriet mangels allgemeiner Pflege mehr und mehr in Missachtung und Verfall. Eine Ausnahme bildete die 1792 vollendete Orangerie.

1920 gingen Schloss und Park in Staatsbesitz über. Von 1933 bis 1937 war das Schloss Kaserne der Wachgruppe Brandenburg der SS. Der sich 1938/39 anschließende Umbau zur Polizeischule brachte Wanddurchbrüche, neue Treppenanlagen, Zwischenstufen, Einrichtung von Sanitäranlagen und vieles andere mehr, aber auch denkmalpflegerische Maßnahmen in den Räumen, die Reste künstlerischer Substanz früherer Jahrhunderte aufwiesen. An der Nordseite wurde zur gleicher Zeit axial zum Schloss eine zweigeschossige Dreiflügelanlage hinzugefügt. Da Oranienburg ein besonderer Schwerpunkt der Rüstungsindustrie war, wurde die Stadt 1944/45 durch Bomben schwer beschädigt. Das Schloss selbst war vornehmlich durch die Sprengung der Havelbrücke in Mitleidenschaft gezogen worden. Erhalten geblieben waren jedoch das Porzellankabinett mit der stuckierten und bemalten Decke sowie kleinere Kabinette mit Stuckdekorationen im Nordwestflügel. 1947 bezog eine sowjetische Fliegerdivision den Neubau von 1939 hinter dem Schloss. Die militärische Nutzung bestand nach deren Auszug fort, denn bis 1990 war das Schloss Kaserne, anfangs der kasernierten Volkspolizei, dann der Grenztruppen der Nationalen Volksarmee der DDR.

Von 1997 bis 1999 wurde das Schloss umfassend restauriert. In die östliche Hälfte zog die Oranienburger Stadtverwaltung ein, im südwestlichen Flügel befindet sich das Kreismuseum Oranienburg, der nordwestliche sowie die

decimated the fabric of the building and led to the demolition of the south-east wing. The curator of artistic and cultural monuments in Prussia, Ferdinand von Quast, had already determined by 1845 that "the complete palace is artistically of a piece" and must be restored, because in the meantime it was in the possession of the royal maritime trading enterprise. After 1851, the Intendant of Royal Palaces and Gardens took it over in turn and in 1860, following reconstruction, a college for teachers moved in and remained until 1925. Some rooms on the main floor of the north-west wing, including the Porcelain Cabinet, remained reserved for the king until 1918.

The garden, once so magnificent, which had already suffered losses under Frederick William I through the abandonment of the menagerie and the orangery, the demolition of the grotto, as well as the removal of the pipes for the water works, once again blossomed under Augustus William through the expansion of the pleasure garden, the construction of a new grotto, and an avenue of lime trees, among other things. But the garden fell more and more into neglect and decay for lack of general care. An exception was the orangery, completed in 1792.

In 1920, the palace and park became state property. From 1933 until 1937, the palace was the barracks of the Brandenburg guard detachment of the SS. Subsequent remodelling into a police school between 1938 and 1939 brought breaches in the walls, new staircases, intermediate landings, the installation of sanitary facilities, and much more, but also restoration and preservation measures in rooms that had remnants of artistic work of earlier centuries.

At the same time on the north side, a two-storey, three-winged complex was added on an axis to the palace. As Oranienburg had a particular concentration of the armaments industry, the town was heavily damaged by bombing in 1944/45. The palace itself was most affected by the blasting of the Havel Bridge. However, the Porcelain Chamber with its stuccoed and painted ceilings as well as smaller rooms with stucco decorations in the north-west wing remained undamaged. In 1947, a Soviet air division moved into the new building of 1939 behind the palace. Military use continued after its departure, as the palace was a barracks until 1990, at first for the barracked People's Police and then for the border guards of the People's Army of the GDR.

The palace was fully restored from 1997 until 1999. Oranienburg city council moved into the eastern half and the Oranienburg District Museum is in the south-west wing, while the north-west wing as well as half of the main building of the palace are reserved for the Prussian Palaces and Gardens Foundation Berlin-Brandenburg. The reopening of the palace took place from August until November 1999, with the exhibition "Onder den Oranje boom. Dutch

Johann David Schleuen

Schloss Oranienburg, Ansicht von Nordwesten, um 1760, SPSG
Oranienburg Palace, view from the north-west, c. 1760, SPSG

Hälfte des Hauptbaus des Schlosses ist der Stiftung Preußische Schlösser und Gärten Berlin-Brandenburg vorbehalten. Von August bis November 1999 fand mit der Ausstellung »Onder den Oranje boom. Niederländische Kunst und Kultur im 17. und 18. Jahrhundert an deutschen Fürstenhöfen« die Wiedereröffnung des Schlosses statt.
Im Januar 2001 wurde das Schlossmuseum als 27. Haus der Stiftung Preußische Schlösser und Gärten Berlin-Brandenburg mit einer ständigen Ausstellung eröffnet. Gezeigt werden Kunstwerke, vornehmlich Gemälde und Gobelins aus der Zeit des Kurfürsten und Friedrichs I. sowie aus der Zeit des Prinzen August Wilhelm.
Im Jahre 2005 konnte im Erdgeschoss die Silberkammer wieder eingerichtet werden, die sich ursprünglich an dieser Stelle befand. Halten wir es abschließend mit Fontane, wenn er schrieb: »Es ist nicht alles hin, es existieren noch Spuren, gerettete Überbleibsel aus alter Zeit her und ihnen gilt zum Schluss unser Besuch.«

Art and Culture in the 17th and 18th Centuries at German Royal Courts."
In January 2001, the palace museum was opened with a permanent exhibition as the 27th house of the Prussian Palaces and Gardens Foundation Berlin-Brandenburg. On display are works of art, primarily paintings and tapestries from the period of the Great Elector and Frederick I, as well as from the time of Prince Augustus William.
In the year 2005 the silver chamber was refurnished on the ground floor in the place that it originally occupied. To conclude, let us think of it as Fontane did when he wrote: "Not everything is gone, there exist yet traces, remnants of times gone by and in the end, it was for these we paid the visit."

Ansicht des nördlichen Schlosshofes mit den 1697 entstandenen Seitenflügeln.
View of the northern palace courtyard with the wings built in 1697.

Links oben: Ehemalige Schlafkammer mit zwei Gemälden des niederländischen Malers Franz Post (um 1650) sowie Möbeln aus Elfenbein aus dem Besitz Johann Moritz von Nassau-Siegen stammend.
Top left: Former bedchamber with two paintings by the Dutch artist Franz Post (c. 1650) as well as furniture made of ivory owned by Johann Moritz of Nassau-Siegen.

Links unten: In der ehemalige Porzellangalerie sind jetzt Tapisserien ausgestellt, die Taten des Großen Kurfürsten zeigen, hergestellt um 1695 in der Manufaktur Pierre Mercier in Berlin.
Bottom left: Tapestries created about 1695 in the Pierre Mercier workshop in Berlin depicting the deeds of the Great Elector are now on display in the former porcelain gallery.

Rechts oben: Stuckdecke der Porzellankammer mit einem von Augustin Terwesten 1697 signierten Deckengemälde, das eine »Allegorie auf die Einführung des Porzellans in Europa« zeigt.
Top right: Stucco ceiling in the porcelain chamber with a ceiling painting signed by Augustin Terwesten, 1697, portraying an "Allegory of the Introduction of Porcelain to Europe".

Rechts unten: Die Porzellankammer wurde 1695–97 eingerichtet. Die Stuckaturen stammen vermutlich vom Hofbildhauer Johann Michael Döbel, das Deckenbild schuf der Hofmaler A. Terwesten.
Bottom right: The porcelain chamber was furnished 1695–97. The stucco work was presumably fashioned by the court sculptor Johann Michael Döbel; the ceiling painting is by the court painter A. Terwesten.

Schloss Caputh Brandenburg

Caputh Palace Brandenburg

Zum ersten Mal wird Caputh 1450/51 als im Besitz der Familie von Rochow erwähnt. 1594 erwarb es die Kurfürstin Katharina als Sommerresidenz und nach ihrem Tode im Jahre 1602 wurde es von ihrer Nachfolgerin Eleonore, der zweiten Frau des Kurfürsten Joachim Friedrich, vollendet. Der Freiherr von Raith, Otto von Beylandt, erhielt für seine Verdienste 1604 Caputh als Geschenk. Nach dessen Tode 1608 fiel der Besitz wieder an den Kurfürsten zurück. Der Dreißigjährige Krieg fügte auch dem Schloss Caputh schwere Schäden zu. Erst 1662 schenkte der Kurfürst Friedrich Wilhelm von Brandenburg seinem Bau- und Quartiermeister Philipp de Chieze das Anwesen, der unter Verwendung der noch vorhandenen Reste des einstigen Baus ein schlichtes Gebäude errichtete, zu dem auch eine Gartenanlage gehörte. Es ist nicht ganz eindeutig, wann das Anwesen wieder an den Kurfürsten zurückfiel. De Chieze starb 1673, jedoch schon 1671 wird erwähnt, das Haus und Garten Caputh wieder zurückgefordert wurden, um es der zweiten Gemahlin des Kurfürsten, der Kurfürstin Dorothea, »auf Lebzeiten« zu schenken. Es begann nun ein größerer An- und Umbau am Schloss, dessen Architekt leider nicht bekannt ist. Das Haus wurde um vier Achsen nach Osten erweitert, dadurch entstanden der heutige Saal und die Zimmer des Kurfürsten. Hinzugefügt wurde eine geschwungene Freitreppe, die aus dem nunmehr in der Mitte des Schlosses liegenden Treppenhaus in den Garten führte. Die beiden südlichen Pavillons wurden in den 1680er Jahren angefügt. Bis auf den seitlichen westlichen Anbau aus dem Anfang des 20. Jahrhunderts ist diese äußere Gestalt des Schlosses bis heute erhalten geblieben und damit ein wichtiges Beispiel für die brandenburgische Baukunst des späten 17. Jahrhunderts aus der Zeit vor Andreas Schlüter.

Das repräsentative Äußere wurde noch von der prächtigen Ausstattung der Innenräume übertroffen. Schon 1686 bezeichneten ausländische Besucher das Schloss als »besonders sehenswert, besonders angenehm für jeden Besucher und zu einem Vergnügen für jeden Mann, der sich dort befindet«. Die Innenräume des Schlosses sind klar gegliedert, östlich des in der Mitte gelegenen kleinen Treppenhauses und des Vestibüls befinden sich der Festsaal, der die ganze Tiefe des Hauses einnimmt, sowie die Wohnräume des Kurfürsten. Die westliche Schlosshälfte war der Kurfürstin vorbehalten.

Im Pavillon dieser Seite befand sich ein Porzellankabinett, über dessen Ausstattung bisher nur wenig bekannt ist. Lediglich das vorhandene Deckenbild gibt Auskunft über die Verwendung des Raumes. In der schon erwähnten Beschreibung von 1686 ist auch die Ausstattung der Schlossräume erwähnt: »Im allgemeinen sind alle Gemächer mit schönen Möbeln, Spiegeln, Gemälden, Porzellan von großer Kostbarkeit und großen Vasen geschmückt und

Caputh is first mentioned in 1450/51 as the property of the von Rochow family. In 1594 it was acquired by Electress Catherine as a summer residence and after her death in 1602 was completed by her successor, Eleanor, the second wife of Elector Joachim Frederick. Baron Raith, Otto von Beylandt, received Caputh in 1604 as a gift for his services. After his death in 1608, the property reverted to the elector. The Thirty Years' War also brought severe damage to Caputh Castle. It was not until 1662 that Elector Frederick William of Brandenburg made a present of the estate to his architect and quartermaster, Philip de Chieze, who erected a simple building making use of the remains of the former structure, to which a garden also belonged.

It is not clear when the estate again reverted to the elector. De Chieze died in 1673, but already in 1671 it is mentioned that the return of the Caputh house and garden was being demanded so that it could be presented to the elector's second wife, Electress Dorothea, "for life." Large-scale remodeling and enlargement of the palace now began, but unfortunately the name of the architect responsible is unknown. The house was expanded to the east by four bays, creating the present-day hall and the rooms of the electress. A curving flight of steps was added, leading from a staircase in what was now the middle of the house out into the garden. The two southern pavilions were added in the 1680s. With the exception of the early 20th-century extensions on the western side, this exterior design of the palace has survived to the present and is thus an important example of late 17th-century architecture in Brandenburg before the time of Andreas Schlüter.

The imposing exterior was even surpassed by the magnificent decoration of the rooms inside. As early as 1686, foreign visitors described the palace as "particularly worth seeing, particularly pleasant for every visitor and to the pleasure of everyone there." The palace has a clear interior layout. East of the vestibule and the small staircase in the middle were the residential chambers of the elector and the hall that took up the whole depth of the house. The western half of the palace was reserved for the electress. The pavilion on this side included a porcelain chamber, about whose decoration little is known to date. Only the surviving ceiling painting provides information about the use of this room. In the above-mentioned description from 1686, the decoration of the palace rooms was also mentioned, "In general, all of the rooms are decorated with beautiful furniture, mirrors, porcelain of great value and large vases and I know of no other prince that can boast of possessing better." In the estate inventory that was completed after the death of Electress Dorothea in 1689, a large number of works of art were yet again listed, including precious wall coverings of gilded cordwain, brocade and atlas. It is today difficult to imagine

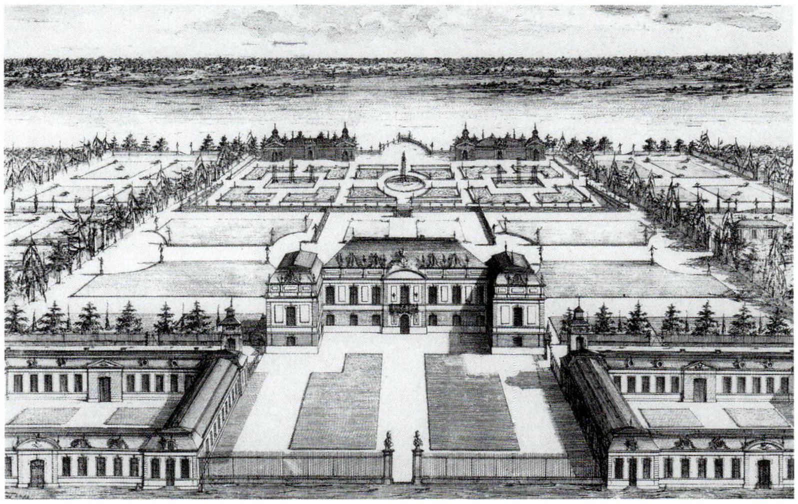

Jean Baptiste Broebes

Schloss und Garten Caputh, aus: »Prospect der Palläste und Lust-Schlösser seiner Mayestät in Preussen«
Caputh Palace and Garden, from "Aspects of the Palaces and Summer Residences of his Majesty in Prussia", Augsburg 1733, SPSG

ich weis nicht, welch andere Fürsten sich rühmen könnten, schöneres zu besitzen.« Im Nachlassinventar, das nach dem Tode der Kurfürstin Dorothea im Jahre 1689 angefertigt wurde, ist noch einmal die Vielzahl von Kunstwerken aufgeführt, dazu gehören u. a. kostbare Goldledertapeten sowie Brokat- und Atlasbespannungen der Wände. Es ist heute kaum zu glauben, dass sich in dieser Zeit über 300 Gemälde, meist holländische Stillleben und Landschafts- und Genredarstellungen im Schloss befanden.
Da Schloss und Garten an die Erben der Kurfürstin Dorothea gefallen waren, kaufte der Kurfürst Friedrich III. 1690 Caputh von diesen zurück und schenkte es seiner zweiten Gemahlin Sophie Charlotte. Ihr gefiel das schöne, aber etwas abgelegene Schloss nicht sonderlich, sie gab es deshalb ihrem Gemahl bereits 1694 zurück und widmete sich fortan dem neuen Schloss in Lietzenburg, das nach ihrem Tode 1705 den Namen Charlottenburg erhielt.
Kurfürst Friedrich III., ab 1701 preußischer König Friedrich I., behielt jedoch Caputh und gestaltete es immer weiter mit kostbaren Einrichtungsgegenständen sowie ledernen und textilen Wandbespannungen und Gemälden aus, wovon die Inventare aus den Jahren 1698 und 1710 Auskunft geben. Es verwundert deshalb nicht, dass im Juni 1709 das Schloss Caputh zum festlichem Rahmen des Treffens der »drei Friedrichs« wurde, des preußischen Königs Friedrich I., Friedrich August von Polen und Friedrich IV. von Dänemark. Die königliche Gesellschaft war mit dem Schiff vom Potsdamer Stadtschloss nach Caputh gekommen.
Zum Schloss gehörte auch ein prächtiger, nach holländischen Vorbildern angelegter Lustgarten, der, von einem Absatz unterbrochen, bis zur Havel reichte. Von hier aus konnte man das Stadtschloss in Potsdam sehen. Den Garten schmückten nicht nur Broderien, sondern auch Skulpturen und regelmäßig angelegte Wege. Auch eine Orangerie ist belegt, denn im Jahre 1713 sind Myrthen, Orangen- und Feigenbäume nach Potsdam abgegeben worden.
Der Tod Friedrichs I. 1713 beendet die wohl glänzendste Periode von Schloss und Garten Caputh. Im Gegensatz zu den anderen Lustschlössern blieb Caputh im königlichen Besitz, da es am Rande eines großen Tiergartens lag und nun Friedrich Wilhelm I. als Jagdschloss diente. Diesem König verdankt das Schloss eine besondere Ausstattung, die des Fliesensaales im Souterrain, der bereits unter Friedrich I., noch ohne Fliesen, als Sommerspeisesaal entstanden war. Die annähernd 7500 blauweißen holländischen Fayencefliesen, mit denen um 1720 Wand- und Deckenflächen vollständig verkleidet wurden, verleihen dem gewölbten Raum eine eindrucksvoll Wirkung. Dieses besondere Beispiel der Fliesenmode in der ersten Hälfte des 18. Jahrhunderts

that at that time over 300 paintings, mostly Dutch still-lifes, landscapes and genre pictures, were to be found in the palace.
As the palace and gardens fell to the heirs of Electress Dorothea, Elector Frederick III bought Caputh back from them in 1690 and gave it to his second wife, Sophie Charlotte. She did not particularly like the beautiful but somewhat remotely situated palace, so she returned it to her husband in 1694 and dedicated herself from then on to the new palace in Lietzenburg, which was given the name Charlottenburg after her death in 1705.
Elector Frederick III, after 1701 King Frederick I, kept Caputh, however, and continued to decorate it with expensive pieces of furniture, leather and fabric wall-coverings, and paintings, about which the inventories from the years 1698 and 1710 provide information. It is no wonder then that, in July 1709, Caputh Palace was the festive venue for the meeting of the "three Fredericks;" the Prussian King Frederick I, Frederick Augustus of Poland, and Frederick IV of Denmark. The royal party had come by ship to Caputh from the Potsdam City Palace.
Within the palace grounds was a magnificent pleasure garden inspired by Dutch gardens. It extended down to the Havel River, interrupted by a terrace. From there the City Palace in Potsdam was visible. The garden was adorned with not only broderie, but also statues and a regular network of paths. An orangery is also documented, because in 1713 myrtle, orange, and fig trees were delivered to Potsdam.
The death of Frederick I in 1713 ended the most brilliant period for the palace and garden of Caputh. In contrast to other summer residences, Caputh remained in royal possession because it was on the edge of a large hunting park and now served Frederick William I as a hunting lodge. The palace owes a unique feature to this king: the Tiled Room in the basement, which Frederick I had built – without the tile – as a summer dining hall. Close to 7,500 blue and white Dutch faience tiles were used to completely cover the walls, floor, and ceiling in around 1720, imparting an impressive effect to the vaulted room. This particular example of tile fashion in the first half of the 18th century contributes considerably to the art-historical significance of the whole palace of Caputh. Along with its assumed model, the room of the same name in Oranienbaum Palace, the Tiled Room of Caputh is an exceptional manifestation of Baroque tile fashion in Germany.
Frederick the Great showed no interest in this small Baroque palace. He leased the estate in 1765 to a commercial counselor named Schmidt, who set up a dye works for Turkish yarn. In 1788, the French Chevalier de Grosset attempted to operate a leather factory there, but seems to have had little success, because

trägt wesentlich zur kunsthistorischen Bedeutung des gesamten Schlosses Caputh bei. Neben seinem vermutlichen Vorbild, dem gleichnamigen Raum im Schloss Oranienbaum, gehört der Fliesenkeller von Caputh zu den außerordentlichsten Raumschöpfungen der barocken Fliesenmode in Deutschland.

Friedrich der Große zeigte für dieses kleine barocke Schloss kein Interesse. Er verpachtete das Anwesen 1765 an einen Kommerzienrat Schmidt zur Einrichtung einer Färberei für türkisches Garn. 1788 versuchte der Franzose Chevalier de Grosset eine englische Lederfabrik zu betreiben, doch scheint das nicht ganz gelungen zu sein, denn er wurde 1794 des Landes verwiesen. Danach ging das Schloss wieder in königliche Verwaltung über und man errichtete 1796 im Schlossgarten eine Baumschule. Da die Krone kein Interesse mehr an Schloss und Garten Caputh hatte, wurde es im März 1813 an den Amtmann Julius Wilhelm Belche versteigert. Nach jahrelangen Streitigkeiten wurde der Kaufvertrag wieder rückgängig gemacht, und 1820 erwarb der pensionierte Generalleutnant August von Thümen das Anwesen, nachdem Friedrich Wilhelm III. einen Tag vor dem beabsichtigten Auktionstermin dem Kauf zugestimmt hatte.

Es scheint für Peter Joseph Lenné ein reizvoller Auftrag gewesen zu sein, den kleinen, nur etwa vier Hektar großen Park, dessen Barockgestaltung in dieser Zeit kaum noch zu erkennen war, nach 1828 in einen Landschaftsgarten umzuwandeln und ihn nun wieder, die Idee des 17. Jahrhunderts aufnehmend, in die große Landschaftskonzeption um Potsdam einzugliedern. So war auf engem Raum ein landschaftliches Kleinod entstanden, dessen besonderer Reiz seine Öffnung zum Wasser hin ist, was den Garten viel größer erscheinen lässt. Von hier aus geht der Blick wie im 17. Jahrhundert bis nach Potsdam.

In der zweiten Hälfte des 19. Jahrhunderts lag die Glanzzeit des Schlosses weit zurück. Das Äußere war zwar noch erhalten, aber im Inneren war von dem einstmals reichen Inventar kaum noch etwas übrig geblieben. »Wohin die Hand der Zerstörung buchstäblich nicht reichen konnte – die hohen Deckengemälde sind übrigens geblieben und sprechen zu uns von jener Morgenzeit brandenburgischer Macht und brandenburgischer Kunst« (Fontane). Nach dem Tod des Generals August von Thümen im Jahre 1826 ging der Besitz an seinen Sohn Wilhelm über, in dessen Zeit auch die Neuanlage des Parkes von Lenné fällt. Wilhelm von Thümen starb 1856 und der Nachfolger war August von Thümen, der 1898 seinen Neffen Alfred von Willich zum Mitbesitzer ernannte, der nach Thümens Tod 1908 Schloss und Park Caputh übernahm. Er ließ umfangreiche Arbeiten im Inneren des Schlosses

he was banished from the country in 1794. Thereafter, the palace was placed under royal administration and a tree nursery was set up in the palace garden in 1796. As the crown no longer had an interest in the palace and garden of Caputh, it was auctioned off to the district magistrate, Julius William Belche, in March 1813. After years of dispute, the sale agreement was retracted and in 1820 a retired lieutenant-general, August von Thümen, acquired the property, after Frederick William III had given his approval to the sale one day before the intended date of auction.

It seems to have been an appealing assignment for Peter Joseph Lenné to turn this small park, which had an area of only about four hectares and a Baroque design that had become almost indiscernible with time, into a landscape garden. Picking up a 17th-century idea, in 1828 he began to integrate it into the grand landscape scheme of Potsdam. In this way a jewel of landscaping was created in a small space. Its special appeal is that it opens to the water, which gives the garden the impression of being much larger. From there, the view extends all the way to Potsdam, as it did in the 17th century.

In the second half of the 19th century, the palace's heyday was long over. Although the exterior was still preserved, hardly anything remained of its former rich interior decoration and fittings. "There, where the hand of destruction literally could not reach – the high ceiling paintings, incidentally, remain and speak to us of the dawn of Brandenburg's power and Brandenburg's art," (Fontane). After the death of General August von Thümen in 1826, the property went to his son Wilhelm, in whose time Lenné redesigned the garden. On the death of Wilhelm von Thümen in 1856, Caputh passed to August von Thümen, who declared his nephew Alfred von Willich to be co-owner in 1898. After Thümen's death in 1908, von Willich took over the palace and park. He had extensive work carried out inside the palace and had a side wing added onto the western pavilion in order to make living conditions more comfortable. Some alterations were also carried out in the park, including the construction of a tennis court, a flower garden near to the so-called Cavalier House built between 1836 and 1843, a nursery with greenhouses and a rose garden surrounded by a pergola. Alfred von Willich died in 1941 in Caputh and his wife was forced to leave the palace in 1945.

After occupation by the Red Army in 1946, the palace was turned over to the mayor of Caputh, who used it as an agricultural school and later as a central vocational school. In 1987, a Teltow electronic firm took it over to use the palace, park and additional buildings as a company educational center. The political events of 1989 put a stop to the building work that had been going on for two years and the property came under the supervision of a trust agency.

Ansicht der Südseite des 1671 erbauten Schlosses mit dem erst 1908 errichteten hofseitigen Anbau.
View of the south side of the building constructed in 1671 with the extension on the courtyard side first built in 1908.

durchführen und am westlichen Schlosspavillon einen Seitenflügel anfügen, der bequemere Wohnbedingungen ermöglichte. Auch im Park wurden einige Veränderungen durchgeführt, so wurde ein Tennisplatz gebaut und nahe dem zwischen 1836 und 1843 entstandenen sogenannten Kavalierhaus ein Blumengarten, eine Gärtnerei mit Gewächshäusern sowie ein von einer Pergola umgebener Rosengarten geschaffen. Alfred von Willich starb 1941 in Caputh und seine Frau Hertha musste 1945 das Schloss verlassen.
Nach der Besetzung des Schlosses durch die Rote Armee wurde es 1946 an den Caputher Bürgermeister übergeben, der es danach als Landwirtschafts- und später als zentrale Berufsschule nutzten ließ. 1987 übernahm ein Teltower Elektronikbetrieb Schloss und Park sowie die dazu gehörigen Gebäude, um eine Betriebsakademie einzurichten. Die politische Wende 1989 stoppte die bereits zwei Jahre laufenden Bauarbeiten und das Anwesen kam unter die Aufsicht der »Treuhand-Gesellschaft«. Um die Bedeutung von Schloss und Garten Caputh wissend, hatte sich die Potsdamer Schlösserverwaltung seit 1990 intensiv um die Übernahme dieser Anlage bemüht. Doch erst 1995 kamen Schloss und Garten Caputh in die Stiftung Preußische Schlösser Berlin-Brandenburg. Ziel war es, Haus und Garten zu restaurieren und ein Schlossmuseum für die Zeit des Großen Kurfürsten und Friedrich I. einzurichten. Da die Hauptwerke barocker Schlossarchitektur und Dekorationen in Brandenburg/Preußen, die beiden Residenzschlösser in Berlin und Potsdam 1945 vernichtet und die Ruinen später abgetragen wurden, kommt dem Schloss Caputh als einem der wenigen erhaltenen Beispiele vorschlüterscher Baukunst um 1700 eine besondere Bedeutung zu.
Im September 1998 wurde der erste Teil des Schlosses nach umfangreicher Restaurierung wiedereröffnet und im September 1999 konnten die Wiederherstellungsarbeiten von Schloss und Garten Caputh abgeschlossen werden. Das Kavalierhaus ist nach umfänglichen zweijährigen Wiederherstellungsarbeiten im April 2002 als Hotel und Gaststätte eröffnet worden.

Cognizant of the significance of the palace and garden in Caputh, the Potsdam Palace Administration made great efforts to take over the property from 1990, but not until 1995 were Caputh Palace and its garden made over to the Prussian Palaces and Garden Foundation Berlin-Brandenburg. The goal was to restore the house and garden and to open a palace museum devoted to the period of the Great Elector and Frederick I. Because the major works of Baroque palace architecture and decoration in Brandenburg-Prussia, the two residences in Berlin und Potsdam, were destroyed in 1945 and the ruins later demolished, Caputh Palace is specially significant as one of the few surviving examples of pre-Schlüter architecture around 1700.
In September 1998, after extensive restoration, the first section of the palace was re-opened and in September 1999 the restoration work on Caputh Palace and its garden was concluded. The Cavalier House, after two years of major restoration work, was opened as a hotel and restaurant in April 2002.

Links: Festsaal mit reicher Ornamentik des späten 17. Jahrhunderts. Das Deckengemälde, wohl vom Hofmaler Jacques Vaillant, zeigt die Göttin Minerva als Beschützerin der Künste und Wissenschaften. Die Gemälde an den Wänden sind Bildnisse der Kinder des Kurfürstenehepaares. Die Marmorgruppe stellt den »Raub der Proserpina« dar und entstand vermutlich um 1680.

Left: Banquet hall with lavish late 17th-century ornamentation and the ceiling painting, probably by the court painter Jacques Vaillant, depicting the goddess Minerva as protectress of the arts and science. The paintings on the walls are portraits of the children of the elector and his consort. The marble group portrays the "Abduction of Persephone" and is presumed to originate from about 1680.

Unten: Das Kabinett der Kurfürstin ist als Gemäldekabinett mit Bildern aus der niederländischen Schule des 17. Jahrhunderts eingerichtet. Der vermutlich englische Kabinettschrank stammt vom Ende des 17. Jahrhunderts.

Bottom: The electress' room is decorated as a picture gallery with paintings from the Dutch school of the 17th century. The cabinet, assumed to be English, dates from the 17th century.

Rechts: Der sogenannte Fliesensaal mit ca. 7.500 blau-weißen holländischen Fliesen ist um 1720 entstanden und diente als Sommerspeisesaal. Angeregt wurde er von einem ähnlichen Raum des Fürsten Leopold von Anhalt-Dessau im Schloss Oranienbaum bei Wörlitz.

Right: The so-called Tile Room with c. 7,500 blue-and-white Dutch tiles was built around 1720 and served as a summer dining room. It was inspired by a similar room in Prince Leopold of Anhalt-Dessau's Oranienbaum Palace near Wörlitz.

Antoine Pesne

König Friedrich I. in Preußen auf dem Thron, um 1710, SPSG
King Frederick I in Prussia on the Throne, c. 1710, SPSG

Friedrich Wilhelm Weidemann

Königin Sophie Charlotte in Preußen, um 1702/05, SPSG (erworben mit Mitteln der Stiftung Deutsche Klassenlotterie Berlin)
Queen Sophie Charlotte in Prussia, c. 1702/05, SPSG (acquired with funds from the German Class Lottery Foundation Berlin)

Kurfürst, ab 1701 König

Friedrich III.–I.

Elector Frederick III–I, from 1701 King

reg. 1688–1713

Schloss Charlottenburg
Berlin

Charlottenburg Palace
Berlin

Südseite des Schlosses, errichtet von Johann Arnold Nering nach 1695, und Erweiterung mit dem Kuppelbau von Johann Friedrich Eosander, genannt Göthe. In der Mitte des Ehrenhofes steht das Reiterstandbild Friedrich Wilhelms, des Großen Kurfürsten, geschaffen von Andreas Schlüter um 1700.
The south side of the palace, erected by Johann Arnold Nering after 1695, and the extension with a dome by Johann Frederick Eosander, named Göthe. In the middle of the cour d'honneur stands the equestrian statue of Frederick William, the Great Elector, by Andreas Schlüter c. 1700.

Schloss Charlottenburg Berlin

Charlottenburg Palace Berlin

Am 1. Juli 1699, dem Geburtstag des brandenburgischen Kurfürsten Friedrich III., wurde das nach dem Tod der ersten preußischen Königin Sophie Charlotte 1705 in Charlottenburg umbenannte Schloss Lietzenburg eingeweiht. Es war ein relativ bescheidener zweigeschossiger und elf Achsen breiter Bau, den der Kurfürst Friedrich III. von Brandenburg für seine zweite Gemahlin, die aus dem Hause Hannover stammende Prinzessin Sophie Charlotte, hatte errichten lassen.

Seit 1684 mit Friedrich III. vermählt, war ihr 1690 für die persönliche Hofhaltung das in der Nähe von Potsdam gelegene Schloss Caputh übereignet worden, das bis zu ihrem Tod 1689 die zweite Gemahlin des Großen Kurfürsten, Sophie Dorothea, bewohnt hatte, und das Friedrich III. aus der Erbmasse seiner Stiefmutter zurückerwerben konnte. Doch Caputh schien für die Kurfürstin nicht so behaglich gewesen zu sein, außerdem lag es von der Residenz Berlin zu weit entfernt, so dass sie das Anwesen 1694 ihrem Gemahl zurückgab. Als »Ersatz« erhielt sie ein auf halbem Wege zwischen Berlin und Potsdam bei dem Dorf Lietze (Lietzow) befindliches Gelände für ein neu zu errichtendes Schlösschen und einen anzulegenden Garten. Schon im gleichen Jahr entstanden erste Entwürfe von dem schwedischen Hofarchitekten Nicodemus Tessin d. J., doch wählte man dann den Plan des Berliner Baumeisters Johann Arnold Nering für die Ausführung. Da dieser schon 1695 starb, übernahm bis April 1699 Martin Grünberg die Bauleitung. Der Grundstein war nach der Mitte des Jahres 1695 gelegt worden; das genaue Datum ist nicht bekannt. Die Ausführung zog sich bis 1699 hin.

Aus dem Kurfürstentum Brandenburg war 1701 das Königreich Brandenburg/Preußen geworden, denn der Kurfürst Friedrich III. hatte sich am 18. Januar 1701 in Königsberg selbst zum König Friedrich I. gekrönt. Sophie Charlotte war somit die erste preußische Königin. Schon im Vorgriff auf die mit allen Mitteln erstrebte Rangerhöhung war am Berliner Schloss vor allem durch Andreas Schlüter intensiv gebaut worden. Natürlich erwies sich auch Lietzenburg sehr schnell als zu klein und die neuen repräsentativen Anforderungen bedingten geradezu zwangsläufig eine Vergrößerung bzw. Erweiterung des Schlosses. Pläne dazu fertigte der schwedische Architekt Johann Friedrich Eosander an, der sich auf Reisen in Italien und Frankreich weiterbildete und um 1699 zurückkehrte. Wenn auch bis zum Tod Friedrichs I. 1713 nicht alles fertig wurde, so entwickelte sich Charlottenburg doch bald zu einer repräsentativen Anlage mit einer breiten Gartenfassade, einem dominierenden Turm und reich ausgestatteten Innenräumen, wie die Wohnräume für das königliche Paar, die Eichengalerie und das Porzellankabinett. Von den beiden geplanten Orangerien war nur die westliche bereits 1702

On July 1, 1699, the birthday of Elector Frederick III of Brandenburg, Lietzenburg Palace in Charlottenburg was inaugurated. In 1705, following the death of the first Prussian queen, Sophie Charlotte, it was renamed after her. It was a relatively modest, two-storey building, eleven bays wide, which Elector Frederick III of Brandenburg constructed for his second wife, Princess Sophie Charlotte of the House of Hanover.

Married to Frederick III since 1684, she had been given Caputh Palace near Potsdam in 1690 for her personal court. The second wife of the Great Elector, Sophie Dorothea, had occupied it until her death in 1689, and Frederick III had been able to reacquire it from the estate of his stepmother. However, Caputh seems not to have suited the electoral princess; besides, it was too far from the residence in Berlin, so she gave it back to her husband in 1694. As a "substitute," she received land halfway between Berlin and Potsdam near the village of Lietze (Lietzow) on which to erect a new palace and lay out a garden. Initial building plans were drawn up in the same year by the Swedish court architect, Nicodemus Tessin the Younger, but the plans chosen were by the Berlin architect Johann Arnold Nering. Nering died in 1695, and Martin Grünberg took over supervision of the work in April 1699. The foundation stone was laid after mid-1695; the exact date is unknown. Construction lasted until 1699.

The Electorate of Brandenburg became the Kingdom of Brandenburg-Prussia in 1701 when Elector Frederick III crowned himself King Frederick I on January 18, 1701, in Königsberg. This made Sophie Charlotte the first Queen of Prussia. In anticipation of this elevation in standing, which had been pursued by every means, intensive building work had already been carried out on the Berlin Palace, primarily by Andreas Schlüter. Naturally, Lietzenburg very soon proved to be too small, and the new demands of official representation almost inevitably required an enlargement or extension of the palace. The Swedish architect Johann Frederick Eosander, who had furthered his studies on trips to Italy and France and returned around 1699, drew up plans for it. Although not everything was completed by Frederick I's death in 1713, Charlottenburg soon developed into a palace to match his royal status, with a wide garden façade, a dominating tower, and richly decorated interiors, such as the residential rooms of the royal couple, the Oak Gallery and the small Porcelain Room. Of the two orangeries planned, only the western one had been completed by 1702. After 1740, the "New Wing" was built for Frederick the Great on the eastern side as its counterpart to plans by Georg Wenzeslaus von Knobelsdorff.

Naturally, the Baroque palace had to have a garden that appropriately represented the new royal status. The French gardener Siméon Godeau began it in 1697. As a student of Le Nôtre, he derived most of his inspiration from the gardens

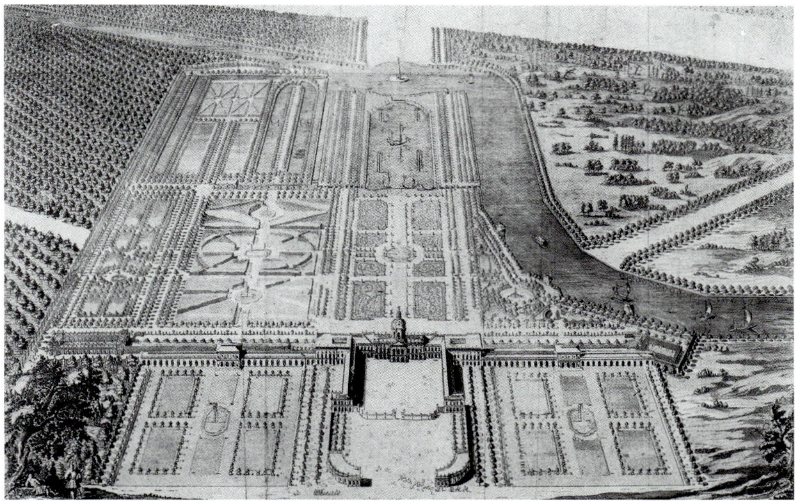

Johann August Corvinus nach/after
Johann Friedrich Eosander

Schloss Charlottenburg, Ansicht aus der Vogelschau, um 1720, SPSG
Charlottenburg Palace, Bird's-Eye View, c. 1720, SPSG

fertig gestellt worden. Auf der östlichen Seite entstand nach 1740 als Pendant nach Entwürfen von Georg Wenzeslaus von Knobelsdorff für Friedrich den Großen der »Neue Flügel«.
Natürlich gehörte zu dem barocken Schloss, das den neuen königlichen Anspruch repräsentierte, auch ein entsprechender Garten. Dieser wurde von dem Franzosen Siméon Godeau ab 1697 angelegt. Als Schüler von Le Nôtre waren für ihn vor allem die Anlagen von Versailles von vorbildhafter Wirkung. So erstreckte sich in Charlottenburg nach Norden ein breites Broderieparterre bis zu einem Wasserbassin, das durch eine Verbindung zur Spree auch als Hafen für Gondeln und Lustschiffe gedacht war. Heckenquartiere bildeten schattenspendende Bereiche. Da Charlottenburg damals noch in unbebautem Gelände lag, kam der Sichtbeziehung zu anderen Schlössern große Bedeutung zu. Weite Blickachsen verbanden die Residenz mit den Schlössern Oranienburg, Schönhausen und der Zitadelle Spandau. Unter der Königin Sophie Charlotte entwickelte sich Lietzenburg zu einem wahren Musenhof. Philosophische Fragen wurden mit Leibniz erörtert, Opern und Schauspiele aufgeführt, bei denen man manchmal selbst mitspielte oder mitwirkte; im Garten konnte man mit freiem Blick lustwandeln. Die Größe, die das Schloss nach Plänen Eosanders im ersten Jahrzehnt des 18. Jahrhunderts angenommen hatte, ordnete das einstmals als privates Lustschloss gedachte Charlottenburg nun auch in eine allgemeine Repräsentation ein, ja es wurde sogar zeitweilig bevorzugt dafür genutzt. So trafen sich 1709 drei Könige in Charlottenburg, nämlich der preußische König Friedrich I., Friedrich August von Polen und der dänische König Friedrich IV.

of Versailles. And so a broad parterre de broderie stretched northward in Charlottenburg to a water basin, which was connected to the Spree River and conceived as a harbor for gondolas and pleasure boats. Hedged areas provided shade. As Charlottenburg was not a built-up district at that time, its visual relationship to the other palaces was of great significance. Broad prospects linked the residence with the Oranienburg and Schönhausen palaces and the Spandau Citadel. Under Queen Sophie Charlotte, Lietzenburg developed into a true court of the muses. Philosophical questions were discussed with Leibniz; operas and plays, in which sometimes even the members of the court took part, were performed; a stroll in the park offered unobstructed views. Following Eosander's plans, the palace, once planned as a summer residence, had so grown in size in the first decades of the 18th century that it was now also used for official representation; in fact, at times it was even the preferred venue. Three kings met in Charlottenburg in 1709: the Prussian king, Frederick I; Frederick Augustus of Poland; and the Danish king, Frederick IV.

Blick vom Turm auf das nach 1945 wiederhergestellte barocke Parterre.
View from the tower to the Baroque parterre that was restored after 1945.

Gartenseite des Schlosses mit der 1702–13 von J. F. Eosander verlängerten Fassade.
Garden side of the palace with the façade extended by J. F. Eosander, 1702–13.

Links: Die Alte Galerie, auch Eichengalerie genannt, von dem Engländer Charles King entstand um 1703. An den Wänden hängen Portraits brandenburgischer Herrscher, über dem Kamin ein Portrait von König Friedrich I. im Krönungsornat von Friedrich Wilhelm Weidemann.
Left: The Old Gallery, also called the Oak Gallery, was created by the Englishman Charles King around 1703. Portraits of Brandenburg rulers hang on the walls; above the fireplace is a portrait of King Frederick I in coronation regalia by Friedrich Wilhelm Weidemann.

Unten: Das Porzellankabinett am Ende der Enfilade ist einer der Höhepunkte des Schlosses. Der 1717 durch die Abgabe nach Dresden, 1760 durch die Zerstörung durch österreichische Truppen dezimierte und 1945 als Beutekunst nach Moskau verbrachte Bestand wurde bis 1977 wieder eingerichtet. Heute zählt man über 2.500, meist chinesische Porzellane aus der Zeit um 1700.
Bottom: The Porcelain Cabinet at the end of the enfilade is one of the highlights of the palace. The collection, which had been decimated by the tribute sent to Dresden in 1717, destruction by the Austrian troops in 1760, and by being taken to Moscow in 1945 as captured art, had been replenished by 1977. Today there are over 2,500 pieces, mostly Chinese porcelain, from the period around 1700.

Rechts: Schlafzimmer der Königin Sophie Charlotte mit einer Vielzahl von Gemälden vom Ende des 17. Jahrhunderts. Die Möbel sind in Berlin vor 1690 gefertigt, das Porzellan auf dem Kaminsims stammt aus China um 1700.
Right: Bedchamber of Queen Sophie Charlotte with a number of paintings from the late 17th century. The furniture was produced in Berlin before 1690, the porcelain on the mantelpiece is from China and dated around 1700.

Antoine Pesne

König Friedrich Wilhelm I., um 1729, SPSG
King Frederick William I, c. 1729, SPSG

Antoine Pesne

Königin Sophie Dorothea, 1737, SPSG
Queen Sophie Dorothea, 1737, SPSG

Carlo Francesco Rusca

Die Söhne König Friedrich Wilhelm I., 1737, SPSG
The Sons of King Frederick William I, 1737, SPSG

König

Friedrich Wilhelm I.

King Frederick William I

reg. 1713–1740

Schloss Königs Wusterhausen Brandenburg

Königs Wusterhausen Palace
Brandenburg

Jagdschloss Stern Potsdam

Stern Hunting Lodge
Potsdam

In diesem Raum hat Friedrich Wilhelm I. während seines jährlichen Aufenthaltes auf Schloss Königs Wusterhausen sein bekanntes Tabakskollegium abgehalten.
Frederick William I held his renowned Tobacco Round in this room during his annual stays at Königs Wusterhausen Palace.

Schloss Königs Wusterhausen Brandenburg

Königs Wusterhausen Palace Brandenburg

Die erste schriftliche Erwähnung der Burg Wusterhausen geschah im Jahre 1320; auch im Landbuch Kaiser Karls IV. 1375 ist ein »castrum wusterhusen« genannt. Seit dem Ende des 14. Jahrhunderts ist der Ort im Besitz der Familie von Schlieben. Von 1475 bis 1669 war er Eigentum der Schenken von Landsberg. Im späten 16. Jahrhundert erhielt das spätere Schlossgebäude die heute noch prägende Grundstruktur eines für Landsitze der Renaissance verbindlichen Typs des »Festen Hauses«. Anschließend war es im Besitz von Friedrich von Jena, dem Geheimrat des Großen Kurfürsten. Im Jahre 1683 erwarb Kurprinz Friedrich, der spätere Kurfürst Friedrich III. und nachmalige König Friedrich I., das Amt Wusterhausen. Es folgten bauliche Veränderungen und Verschönerungen am Schloss und die Anlage eines neuen Lustgartens durch den französischen Kunstgärtner Siméon Godeau.
Der zehnjährige Kurprinz Friedrich Wilhelm (I.) erhielt das Gut Wusterhausen Weihnachten 1698 als Geschenk und 1703 wurden die beiden seitlichen Kavalierhäuser zur Unterbringung des prinzlichen Gefolges errichtet.
In Opposition zur verschwenderischen Hofhaltung seines Vaters entwickelte der Kurprinz, seit 1701 preußischer Kronprinz, in Wusterhausen schon frühzeitig seine eigenen politischen und ökonomischen Anschauungen, die nach seiner Thronbesteigung 1713 zur grundlegenden Staatsreform führen sollten. Die Vorliebe für alles Militärische, die ihn seit seiner Kindheit prägte, bestimmte auch die Kronprinzenjahre. So befehligte er in Wusterhausen ein eigenes Regiment und begann mit dem Aufbau des später berühmt gewordenen Leib-Bataillons der »Langen Kerls«. Außerdem frönte der Kronprinz hier seiner außerordentlichen Jagdleidenschaft. Von 1713 bis zum Ende seiner Regierung 1740 verbrachte Friedrich Wilhelm I. alljährlich die Herbstmonate von August bis November in Wusterhausen. In dieser Zeit war auch die gesamte königliche Familie anwesend.
Neben den groß angelegten Parforcejagden wurden hier auch wichtige politische Entscheidungen getroffen. 1717 erfolgte die Umbenennung des Ortes von Wendisch Wusterhausen in Königs Wusterhausen. Man verwendete aber in den Quellen des 18. Jahrhunderts immer nur die Bezeichnung Wusterhausen.
Nach dem Tod Friedrich Wilhelms I. 1740 wurde das Schloss zum Kronfideikommiss, d.h. zum unteilbaren und unveräußerbaren Familienbesitz erklärt. Zunächst erbte es sein Sohn, der Prinz August Wilhelm, der aber kein Interesse daran zeigte. Damit begann der Verfall. Von 1798 bis 1802 bewohnte es zeitweilig Prinz Heinrich, der Bruder Friedrichs des Großen. Danach aber begann die weitere Vernachlässigung und Demöblierung. Der Wassergraben um das Schloss wurde ab 1831 zugeschüttet. 1832 entwarf

The first written mention of Wusterhausen Castle dates from 1320; a "castrum wusterhusen" is also named in Emperor Charles IV's land book in 1375. From the end of the 14th century, the place was in the possession of the von Schlieben family, and from 1475 to 1669 belonged to the barons of Landsberg. In the late 16th century, the future palace building was given the basic structure of a fortified manor-house that still characterizes it today, the type obligatory for country residences of the Renaissance. Afterwards, it was in the possession of Frederick of Jena, the Privy Councilor of the Great Elector. In 1683 Prince Frederick, the future Elector Frederick III and thereafter King Frederick I, acquired the administrative district of Wusterhausen. Structural alterations and embellishments to the castle followed and the laying out of a new pleasure garden by the French nurseryman Siméon Godeau.
The ten-year-old Prince Frederick William (later King Frederick Wilhelm I) received the Wusterhausen property on Christmas 1698 as a present, and in 1703 the two cavalier houses was erected alongside to accommodate the princely entourage.
In opposition to the extravagant way his father ran his court, the prince, who was the Prussian crown prince after 1701, began early to develop his own political and economic views in Wusterhausen that would lead to fundamental reforms of state after his accession to the throne in 1713. His preoccupation with everything military, a characteristic since childhood, also determined his years as crown prince. He commanded his own regiment in Wusterhausen and began to build up his own personal battalion of tall soldiers that would later gain fame. Besides that, it was here that the crown prince indulged in hunting, his great passion. From 1713 until the end of his reign in 1740, Frederick William I annually spent the autumn months from August to November in Wusterhausen. The whole royal family was also present during this time.
Along with the large-scale coursing hunts, important political decisions were also made here. In 1717, the name of the village was changed from Wendisch Wusterhausen to Königs Wusterhausen. In 18th century sources, however, only the name Wusterhausen was used.
After the death of Frederick William I in 1740, the palace was declared a royal entailed estate, which means it was the indivisible and inalienable property of the family. At first, it was inherited by his son, Prince Augustus William, who showed no interest it. This was the beginning of its decline and deterioration. Prince Henry, the brother of Frederick the Great, lived in it for a time from 1798 to 1802. Thereafter, however, it was further neglected and the furnishings were removed. The moat around the palace was filled in after 1831. In 1832, Lenné drew up a plan for beautifying the garden, but it was never carried out.

Selbstbildnis / Self-portrait of

König Friedrich Wilhelm I., 1737, SPSG
King Frederick William I, 1737, SPSG

Lenné einen Verschönerungsplan für den Garten, der jedoch nicht ausgeführt wurde.
Unter dem preußischen König Friedrich Wilhelm IV. begann 1855 die Instandsetzung des Gebäudes. Fontane besuchte im Jahre 1862 das Schloss, das ein Jahr später wieder durch Wilhelm I. als Jagdschloss genutzt wurde. Auch der Kaiser Wilhelm II. hielt hier Hofjagden ab. Nach der Revolution 1918 und der Abdankung des Kaisers konnte das Schloss öffentlich besichtigt werden, aber wegen mehrerer Einbrüche und Plünderungen musste es bereits 1919 wieder geschlossen werden.
Infolge der Auseinandersetzungen des preußischen Staates mit dem vormals regierenden preußischen Königshaus kam das Schloss in die 1926 gegründete Schlösserverwaltung, die es alsbald als Museum wieder öffnete. 1943 bis 1945 diente das Schloss als Auslagerungsdepot für Kunstwerke aus dem Berliner Schloss Monbijou.
1945 bis 1947 war es Sitz der sowjetischen Militäradministration und danach bis 1957 Berufsschule der Deutschen Finanzverwaltung. Ein verheerender Brand vernichtete 1951 den gesamten Dachstuhl, der wieder aufgebaut wurde. Von 1957 bis 1964 war auf dem Schlossgelände eine sowjetische Nachrichteneinheit stationiert. Im Jahre 1964 wurde die gesamte Liegenschaft, die bis dahin den Staatlichen Schlössern und Gärten Potsdam-Sanssouci zugeordnet war, dem Rat des Kreises Königs Wusterhausen übereignet, der hier seinen Verwaltungssitz einrichtete. Bis 1968 erfolgte eine Instandsetzung und Nutzbarmachung des Schlosses für diese neue Funktion. 1991 zog die Kreisverwaltung aus dem Schloss aus. Mit den Bemühungen der Schlösser und Gärten Potsdam-Sanssouci, die das Schloss-Ensemble nach 1990 wieder zurückgewinnen wollte, begannen mit Unterstützung von Fördermitteln des Landes Brandenburg erste Baumaßnahmen. 1998 wurde die Stiftung Preußische Schlösser und Gärten Berlin-Brandenburg, als Nachfolgerin der Staatlichen Schlösser und Gärten Potsdam-Sanssouci, wieder offizielle Eigentümerin des Schlosses und des Gartens Königs Wusterhausen. Die Kavalierhäuser jedoch blieben erst im Besitz des Landkreises Dahme-Spreewald und wurden später an private Nutzer abgegeben.
Nach umfangreichen Restaurierungsarbeiten konnte im Jahre 2000 das Schloss Königs Wusterhausen als Schlossmuseum mit dem Schwerpunkt der Zeit Friedrich Wilhelms I. wiedereröffnet werden. Die großzügig angelegten Schlossräume, die heute in ihrer schlichten Ausstattung ganz dem Lebensstil Friedrich Wilhelms I. entsprechen, geben vorrangig einen Überblick über das künstlerische Schaffen Brandenburg-Preußens in der ersten Hälfte des 18. Jahrhunderts. Die Gemäldeausstellung dokumentiert die Neigung des

The repair of the building began under King Frederick William IV in 1855. In 1862 Fontane visited the palace, which was used once again as a hunting lodge a year later, by William I. Emperor William II also held royal hunts here. After the revolution of 1918 and the abdication of the emperor, the public was permitted to view the palace, but because of break-ins and plundering it had to be closed again in 1919.
As a result of a dispute between the Prussian state and the former royal family, the palace was transferred to the palace administration founded in 1926, which immediately reopened it as a museum. From 1943 to 1945, the palace served as depot for works of art evacuated from the Berlin Monbijou Palace.
From 1945 until 1947 it was the seat of the Soviet military administration and thereafter until 1957 the vocational school of the German fiscal authorities. In 1951 a devastating fire destroyed the whole roof, which was rebuilt. A Soviet intelligence unit was stationed in the palace grounds from 1957 to 1964. In 1964, the complete property, which had been assigned to the State Palaces and Gardens of Potsdam-Sanssouci, was transferred to the district council of Königs Wusterhausen, which installed its seat of administration there. Renovation work for this new function lasted until 1968, and the district authority moved out of the palace in 1991. Through the efforts made after 1990 by the State Palaces and Gardens of Potsdam-Sanssouci, which wanted to re-establish the palace ensemble, the first construction measures started with development funds from the state of Brandenburg. In 1998, the Prussian Palaces and Gardens Foundation Berlin-Brandenburg, as successor to the Palaces and Gardens of Potsdam-Sanssouci, became the official owner of the palace and garden of Königs Wusterhausen. The cavalier houses, however, remained at first the property of the district of Dahme-Spreewald and were later handed over to private users.
After extensive restoration work, Königs Wusterhausen was re-opened in the year 2000 as a museum focusing mainly on the time of Frederick William I. The generously proportioned rooms of the palace that today, with their modest furnishings, completely reflect the lifestyle of Frederick William I, aim first and foremost to provide an survey of the artistic creativity of Brandenburg-Prussia in the first half of the 18th century. The exhibition of paintings documents the king's penchant for portraits, animal pictures, and hunting scenes, and shows a stag hunt by an unknown painter from around 1735. Other works worthy of mention are a series of portraits of the royal children painted by Friedrich Wilhelm Weidemann and a series of over forty officers of the regiment that Frederick William I commanded as crown prince. Most of the portraits were painted by Adám Mányoki. This "gallery of officers" regained its traditional

Unbekannter Meister / Unknown master

Hirschhetze bei (Königs) Wusterhausen, Detail mit Ansicht des Schlosses, um 1735, SPSG
Stag Hunt at (Königs) Wusterhausen, detail with view of the palace, c. 1735, SPSG

Königs zu Portrait-, Tier- und Jagddarstellungen und zeigt die Hirschjagd eines unbekannten Malers um 1735. Hervorzuheben sind die Serie mit Bildnissen der Königskinder, gemalt von Friedrich Wilhelm Weidemann und die Reihe der über vierzig Offiziere des von Friedrich Wilhelm I. als Kronprinz befehligten Regimentes. Die meisten Portraits wurden von Adám Mányoki gemalt. Diese »Offiziersgalerie« kehrte nach etwa 190 Jahren wieder an ihren angestammten Platz in Königs Wusterhausen zurück. Eine Besonderheit stellen ohne Zweifel die ca. vierzig eigenhändig gemalten Bilder des Königs dar. Diese waren 1862 aus dem Schloss Kossenblatt nach Königs Wusterhausen überführt worden und bis 1945 dort verblieben. Ein Platz in der Kunstgeschichte gebührt ihnen als frühes Beispiel naiver Malerei. Sie entstanden zwischen 1735 und 1739.

In den Wohnräumen des Königspaares werden einige qualitätvolle Beispiele der Möbelkunst aus Berlin und Potsdam um 1730/40 ausgestellt, die sich durch schlichte Eleganz auszeichnen.

Die Ausstattungsstücke, welche die Nutzung des Gebäudes in der zweiten Hälfte des 19. Jahrhunderts als kaiserliches Jagdschloss dokumentieren, haben in der Galerie der oberen Etage ihren Platz gefunden. Dazu zählen einige aus der späteren Einrichtung erhaltene Möbel und eine Sammlung von Jagdtrophäen, zumeist aus der Zeit Wilhelms II.

Mit der Restaurierung des Schlosses ergab sich auch die Möglichkeit der Neugestaltung des nur noch rudimentär erhaltenen Schlossgartens. Eine vollständige Rekonstruktion des barocken Zustandes war auf Grund der unvollständigen Quellen nicht zu realisieren. Der Schlossgarten vereint nun die ursprünglichen barocken Elemente mit den Resten der Gestaltung des 19. Jahrhunderts und der Zeit um 1969 zu einem Gesamteindruck.

place in Königs Wusterhausen after about 190 years. Without a doubt, a special feature is the approximately forty pictures painted by the king's own hand. These were transferred from Kossenblatt Palace to Königs Wusterhausen in 1862 and remained there until 1945. They earn a place in art history as early examples of naïve painting. They originated between 1735 and 1739.

In the living quarters of the royal couple a few examples can be seen of the high quality of furniture from Berlin and Potsdam from around 1730/40, distinguished by its simple elegance.

Period pieces that document the use of the building in the second half of the 19th century as an imperial hunting lodge have found a place in the gallery on the upper storey. They include some surviving pieces of furniture from the later decoration and a collection of hunting trophies, mostly from the time of William II.

The restoration presented the opportunity to redesign the garden, which had survived only in a rudimentary state. A complete restoration of the garden to its Baroque condition was not feasible because of insufficient original sources. The palace garden now forms a single ensemble, combining original Baroque elements with the remains of its design in the 19th century and the period around 1969.

Im Festsaal hängen ca. 40, von König Friedrich Wilhelm I. zwischen 1735 und 1739 im nahen Schloss Kossenblatt eigenhändig geschaffene Gemälde.
In the Great Hall hang about 40 paintings by King Frederick William I that he painted himself in nearby Kossenblatt Palace between 1735 and 1739.

Eingangsseite des Schlosses mit dem noch aus der Renaissancezeit stammenden Treppenturm, der zu den einzelnen Etagen führt.
Entrance side of the palace with the stair tower, which dates from the time of the Renaissance, leading to the individual floors.

Jagdschloss Stern Potsdam

Stern Hunting Lodge Potsdam

Rechts: Einen typisch holländischen Charakter zeigt das nach 1730 errichtete Jagdschloss Stern. Es war der »Probebau« für das spätere Holländische Viertel in Potsdam.
Right: Stern Hunting Lodge, built after 1730, has a typical Dutch character. It was a "test model" for the later Dutch Quarter in Potsdam.

König Friedrich Wilhelm I. ließ 1724 bis 1729 westlich der Stadt Potsdam ein ca. 100 km² großes Jagdgebiet, die Parforceheide, einhegen. Anregung und Unterstützung für dieses Projekt erhielt er von seinem Freund, dem Fürsten Leopold von Anhalt-Dessau, mit dem ihn die Jagdleidenschaft verband. So schickte dieser aus Wörlitz einen fürstlichen Jäger, der das Anlegen der sechzehn Sternschneisen im Wald und die Umzäunung des gesamten Gebietes beurteilen sollte.

Am Schnittpunkt von zehn breiten Schneisen wurde 1730 bis 1732 ein kleines Jagdschloss von einem unbekannten Baumeister errichtet. Dieses Gebäude, auf das die Bezeichnung »Schloss« wegen seiner geringen Größe und seines bescheidenen Äußeren nur bedingt zutrifft, ist mit seiner Ziegelbauweise, dem geschweiften Giebel und den großen Fenstern ganz holländischen Vorbildern verpflichtet. Es ist gleichsam als Probebau für das spätere »Holländische Viertel« in Potsdam anzusehen.

Im Inneren nimmt an der Giebelseite des Gebäudes ein Saal fast die gesamte Hälfte des Hauses ein. An seinen geschweiften Wänden sind zwischen den Fenstern Hirschköpfe angebracht, auf denen die abgeworfenen Geweihe des »großen Hans«, des Lieblingshirsches des Königs, befestigt sind.

An der Kaminwand sind Bilder mit Jagddarstellungen in die Vertäfelung eingelassen, die in ihrer naiven Erzählfreude mit Arbeiten von Georg Lisiewski vergleichbar sind.

Die übrigen Räume des Hauses, die Küche, der Flur, das Adjutantenzimmer und der Schlafraum mit dem Bett in der Form einer Schiffskoje, entsprechen bürgerlich-holländischer Wohnkultur.

Das daneben stehende Kastellanhaus, 1730 aus Fachwerk mit Mansarddach errichtet, ist schon seit 1750 zugleich Gaststätte, aber jetzt seit einigen Jahren, ebenso wie das Jagdschloss, geschlossen.

Das Jagdschloss Stern ist kulturgeschichtlich höchst bemerkenswert. Es ist nicht nur der einzige Schlossbau, der in der Regierungszeit Friedrich Wilhelms I. errichtet wurde, an keinem anderen Ort lässt sich heute noch seine Jagdleidenschaft und der bei aller Schlichtheit herrschende Anspruch des Soldatenkönigs besser nachweisen als an diesem Haus.

Between 1724 and 1729, King Frederick William I ordered a large hunting reserve of about 100 square kilometers, the Parforce Heath west of the city of Potsdam, to be enclosed. He was encouraged and supported in this project by his friend, Prince Leopold of Anhalt-Dessau, who shared the king's love of the hunt and sent a huntsman from his estate at Wörlitz to assess the laying out of the sixteen forest aisles radiating star-like from two points and the fencing in of the whole area.

A small hunting lodge was built by an unknown architect between 1730 and 1732 at the intersection of ten broad aisles. Because of its small size and its modest exterior, this building can hardly be described as a palace. With its brick construction, curved gable and large windows it is firmly in the tradition of Dutch architecture and can be considered an experiment for the later Dutch Quarter in Potsdam.

Inside, a hall takes up almost half of the house on the gable side of the building. Displayed between the windows on the curved wall are stags' heads, to which are attached the antlers cast off by "Big Hans," the king's favorite stag. Pictures of hunting scenes are set into the paneling on the hearth wall. Their naïve joy in narrative is comparable to the works of Georg Lisiewski.

The remaining rooms of the house, the kitchen, the entrance hall, the adjutant's chamber and the bedroom with a bed in the form of a ship's bunk correspond to the Dutch middle-class style of decor.

Next to it stands the castellan's house, a half-timbered construction with a mansard roof dating from 1730. From 1750 it was an inn, but for several years now, like the hunting lodge, it has been closed to the public.

In terms of cultural history, the Stern Hunting Lodge is most remarkable. It is not only the only royal residence built during the reign of Frederick William I; no other place attests better to the Soldier King's passion for the hunt and, despite its simplicity, his demands as a ruler.

Antoine Pesne

Kronprinz Friedrich (II.), 1738, SPSG
Crown Prince Frederick (II), 1738, SPSG

Antoine Pesne

Kronprinzessin Elisabeth Christine, 1738, SPSG
Crown Princess Elizabeth Christina, 1738, SPSG

Johann Heinrich Tischbein d. Ä. | Johann Heinrich Tischbein the Elder

Prinz Heinrich von Preußen, 1769, SPSG
Prince Henry of Prussia, 1769, SPSG

König

Friedrich II.

King Frederick II

reg. 1740–1786

Eine Kolonnade verbindet die beiden Türme der Seitenflügel von Schloss Rheinsberg und lässt den Blick auf den Grienericksee frei.
A colonnade connects the two towers of the wings of Rheinsberg Palace and leaves the view of Grienericksee lake open.

Schloss Rheinsberg Brandenburg

Rheinsberg Palace
Brandenburg

Der Neue Flügel des Schlosses Charlottenburg – Die Wohnungen Friedrichs II. Berlin

The New Wing of Charlottenburg Palace –
The Apartments of Frederick II
Berlin

Schloss Sanssouci mit Neuen Kammern und Bildergalerie Potsdam

Sanssouci Palace with the New Chambers
and Picture Gallery
Potsdam

Das Neue Palais im Park von Sanssouci. Das Belvedere und das Drachenhaus Potsdam

New Palace in Sanssouci Park. Belvedere
and Dragon House
Potsdam

Schloss Rheinsberg Brandenburg

Rheinsberg Palace Brandenburg

Der Kronprinz Friedrich (II.) gab nach seiner missglückten Flucht 1730 und der anschließenden Festungshaft in Küstrin dem Druck seines Vaters nach und stimmte der Hochzeit mit Elisabeth Christine von Braunschweig-Bevern zu.
Sein Verhältnis zum Vater wurde versöhnlicher, so dass dieser ihn 1732 zum Chef eines Regimentes in Neuruppin und Nauen ernannte. In Neuruppin bewohnte er ein einfaches Bürgerhaus. Vor den Mauern der Stadt hatte er einen Garten, in dem er 1735 von Georg Wenzeslaus von Knobelsdorff, den er schon früher kennen gelernt hatte, den sogenannten Apollotempel, sein erstes Bauwerk, errichten ließ.
Von Neuruppin war es nicht weit bis nach Rheinsberg und dort machte Friedrich Bekanntschaft mit dem Besitzer des aus der Spätrenaissance stammenden Wasserschlosses am Grienericksee, Oberleutnant de Beville. Der Vater, Friedrich Wilhelm I., hatte zwar geplant, dass er seinen Wohnsitz in Berlin nehmen solle, aber Minister Grumbkow konnte den König davon überzeugen, dass es besser wäre, wenn der Kronprinz an einem anderen Ort wohnen würde. Es käme sonst wieder zu unliebsamen Auftritten. Der König stimmte dem zu.
De Beville hatte wohl die Absicht, das Schloss sehr bald zu verkaufen, denn schon im Oktober 1733 begannen erste Kaufverhandlungen, die 1734 mit einem Kaufvertrag abgeschlossen wurden. Bereits im Juni begannen erste Umbaumaßnahmen unter der Leitung des Baudirektors Johann Gottfried Kemmeter und des Kondukteurs A. Freiherr von Wangenheim. Der Umbau war im August 1736 soweit fertig, dass der Kronprinz und die Kronprinzessin einziehen konnten. Die Bautätigkeit war aber trotzdem noch nicht beendet, denn geplant war ein Nordflügel, so dass das Schloss einen U-förmigen Grundriss erhalten sollte. Außerdem war als Pendant zum Klingenbergturm ein gleicher Turm an der Nordseite und eine zwischen den beiden Türmen den Schlosshof zum See hin abschließende Kolonnade vorgesehen. Der 1737 von einer Italienreise zurückkehrende Knobelsdorff übernahm sogleich die Bauleitung, wobei er sich an die Vorgaben der vorigen Baumeister zu halten hatte. So war bis 1740 aus der mittelalterlichen Burg eine barocke Dreiflügelanlage entstanden.
Als sich Friedrich im März 1737 bei seinem Regiment in Neuruppin aufhielt, schrieb er an den General von Grumbkow: »Ich reise jetzt nach Reinsberg zurück, es ist meyn Sanssouci.« Am Ende seines Lebens bekannte er, dass er »nur in Rheinsberg glücklich gewesen« sei. Rheinsberg war auch die Anregung für seine spätere Residenz in Sanssouci; gleich zweimal vermerkte er auf der dortigen Grundrissskizze »come à Reinsberg«.

After his failed attempt to flee in 1730 and subsequent imprisonment in the fortress of Küstrin, Crown Prince Frederick (later Frederick II) gave in to pressure from his father and agreed to marry Elizabeth Christina of Brunswick-Bevern.
His relationship to his father became more conciliatory, and so his father appointed him colonel of a regiment in Neuruppin and Nauen in 1732. In Neuruppin he lived in a simple town house. In his garden outside the city walls he commissioned Georg Wenzeslaus von Knobelsdorff, with whom he had earlier become acquainted, to construct the so-called Temple of Apollo in 1735, his first building project.
It was not far from Neuruppin to Rheinsberg, where Frederick made acquaintance with Lieutenant de Beville, the owner of the castle dating from the late Renaissance on Grienericksee lake. Although his father, Frederick William I, had planned that he should take Berlin as his residence, Minister Grumbkow was able to convince the king that it would be better if the crown prince lived somewhere else, otherwise there could be unpleasant scenes again. The king agreed.
De Beville apparently intended to sell the castle soon, because in October 1733 there began initial negotiations, which were concluded in 1734 with a contract of sale. The first remodeling measures began as early as June under the supervision of the director of works Johann Gottfried Kemmeter and A. Freiherr von Wangenheim. The reconstruction was so far completed in August 1736 that the crown prince and the princess were able to move in. Despite that, the building activities were not yet ended, because a north wing had been planned to give the palace a "U" form. In addition, another tower just like the Klingenberg Tower was planned as its counterpart. Between the two towers there was to be a colonnade bordering the palace courtyard on the side facing the lake. Georg Wenzeslaus von Knobelsdorff, who returned from a trip to Italy in 1737, immediately took over supervision of the work, but was to follow the specifications set by the previous architect. By 1740, a three-winged Baroque complex had emerged from the medieval castle.
While Frederick was staying with his regiment in Neuruppin in March 1737, he wrote to General von Grumbkow, "I travel now back to Reinsberg, it is my Sanssouci." At the end of his life, he professed that he had "only been happy in Rheinsberg." Rheinsberg was also the inspiration for his later residence in Sanssouci; twice he noted on the floor plans there, "come à Reinsberg."
There he could occupy himself with the arts and philosophy in circles of like-minded friends; it was there that he also began his correspondence with Voltaire, and there that he wrote his "Anti-Machiavel" containing his maxim

Georg Wenzeslaus von Knobelsdorff

Ansicht von Schloss und Park Rheinsberg, um 1740, SPSG Planslg
View of Rheinsberg Palace and Park, c. 1740, SPSG map collection

Hier in Rheinsberg konnte er sich im Kreis von Gleichgesinnten mit den Künsten und der Philosophie beschäftigen, hier begann auch die Korrespondenz mit Voltaire und hier schrieb er den »Antimachiavell« mit seiner Maxime als König »vom ersten Diener des Staates«.
Friedrich hatte in Rheinsberg zum ersten Mal eine eigene Wohnung, deren Lage, Anordnung der Räume und Ausstattung er selbst mitbestimmte. Sie lag im Obergeschoss des Südflügels und umfasste nach dem Inventar sieben Räume zuzüglich des in Inventaren nicht aufgeführten Bibliothekzimmers im sogenannten Klingenbergturm. Die sich anschließende Wohnung der Kronprinzessin hatte fünf Räume, obwohl der Vorsaal schon im Corps de Logis lag. In der ersten Gestaltungsphase zwischen 1734 und 1736 wurden die Räume illusionistisch ausgemalt, vermutlich aus zeitlichen und finanziellen Gründen. Für die Einrichtung der Zimmer hatte man Möbel aus den Schlössern Oranienburg und Köpenick zusammengetragen, wie Zeitzeugen berichten. Knobelsdorff übernahm ab 1737 nicht nur die Bauleitung, sondern auch die Dekoration der Innenräume. Somit entstand eine zweite Periode der Innenraumdekoration, in der die Bemalung der Räume durch Boisserien und Stuckmarmor ersetzt wurde. Während der Bauphase stand der Kronprinz ständig im Austausch mit seiner Schwester, der Markgräfin Wilhelmine von Bayreuth. Ihr schickte er Pläne, beschrieb die Zimmer und auch die erworbenen Gemälde von Watteau und Lancret. Bedingt durch die Nutzung der alten Gebäude, lag die Wohnung des Kronprinzen in Rheinsberg nach Süden. Die Ausrichtung nach Süden wird später auch in Sanssouci sowie in fast allen anderen Wohnräumen Friedrichs wieder aufgenommen.
In Rheinsberg wurde das ausprobiert, was in den folgenden Jahren, vornehmlich zwischen 1740 und 1750, zur künstlerischen Reife gelangte. Bereits in Rheinsberg zeigte sich die Zusammenarbeit zwischen Knobelsdorff und dem Kronprinzen, die sich in seiner späteren Regierungszeit noch verstärkte. In Rheinsberg dauerten die Arbeiten bis 1740, wobei das schon Fertiggestellte wieder verändert wurde.
Auch die Rheinsberger Gartenarchitekturen, besonders das von Knobelsdorff errichtete Gartenportal mit den flankierenden Statuen »Flora« und »Pomona« und dem heute nicht mehr existierenden Obelisken davor, wurden wenige Jahre später 1747 in Sanssouci wiederholt. Auch war an einen Bacchustempel gedacht, dessen »zwölf Satyrhermen in Riesengröße statt der Säulen das Dach tragen«. Dazu hatte Friedrich auch eine Zeichnung gemacht, wie wir sie später von Sanssouci her kennen.
Die ungefähr vierzig Personen umfassende Hofgesellschaft in Rheinsberg vergnügte sich bei Bällen, Konzerten und Theateraufführungen. Fried-

that the king was "the first servant of the state." For the first time in Rheinsberg, Frederick had an apartment of his own for which he himself decided the location, the arrangement of the rooms and their decoration. It was situated on the upper storey and, according to the inventory, consisted of seven rooms; in addition, in the so-called Klingenberg Tower there was the library room, which was not listed in the inventory. The adjacent apartment of the crown princess had five rooms, although the antechamber was already in the Corps de Logis. In the first stage of design between 1734 and 1736, the rooms were painted in illusionistic style, probably for reasons of time and money. According to eyewitnesses, furniture had been gathered from the palaces of Oranienburg and Köpenick to furnish the rooms. From 1737, Knobelsdorff assumed not only the supervision of construction, but also the decoration of the rooms inside. This brought about a second stage of interior decoration in which the decorative painting in the rooms was replaced by boisseries and stucco marble. During the building phase, the crown prince constantly exchanged thoughts with his sister, Margravine Wilhelmina of Bayreuth. He sent her building plans, and described both the rooms and the paintings by Watteau and Lancret that had been acquired. By making use of the old buildings, the crown prince's apartment in Rheinsberg faced south, an arrangement later adopted in Sanssouci as in almost all other rooms Frederick lived in.
In Rheinsberg ideas were tested that in subsequent years, primarily between 1740 and 1750, were to achieve artistic maturity. The collaboration between the crown prince and Knobelsdorff, already proven in Rheinsberg, became even stronger in later years. The work in Rheinsberg lasted until 1740, with things that had been completed being changed again.
The garden buildings of Rheinsberg, particularly the portal constructed by Knobelsdorff flanked by statues of Flora and Pomona and the obelisks in front of it that no longer exist, were repeated a few years later in 1747 in Sanssouci. A Bacchus temple had also been conceived, whose "twelve satyr hermes of gigantic size would support the roof instead of columns." Frederick had also made a sketch for it, as we know it later in Sanssouci.
The approximately forty people who made up the court in Rheinsberg amused themselves with balls, concerts, and theater performances. At the time, Frederick greatly valued discussions relating to his interest in classical poets and philosophers. Along with Lucretius, Horace, Virgil, Seneca, and Cicero, he read Marcus Aurelius, who seemed to him to be the ideal of a prince. Frederick's interest in the arts, on the other hand, corresponded to his search for answers to religious, philosophical, and political questions. Georg Wenzeslaus von Knobelsdorff, Antoine Pesne, and the young Friedrich Christian Glume

Johann Konrad Krüger nach / after Christian Friedrich Ekel

Ansicht des Schlosses Rheinsberg und der Kavalierhäuser vom Grienericksee, 1773, SPSG
View of Rheinsberg Palace and the Cavalier Houses of Grienericksee (lake), 1773, SPSG

rich schätzte die Gespräche in dieser Zeit sehr, die für seine Beschäftigung mit den antiken Dichtern und Philosophen von Bedeutung waren. Neben Lukrez, Horaz, Vergil, Seneca und Cicero las er besonders Marc Aurel, der ihm als Ideal des Fürsten erschien. Die Suche nach Antworten auf religiöse, philosophische und politische Fragen entsprach auf der anderen Seite die Beschäftigung mit der Kunst. Georg Wenzeslaus von Knobelsdorff, Antoine Pesne und der junge Friedrich Christian Glume schufen den künstlerischen Rahmen; vieles war noch zaghaft und stilistisch unsicher, sollte aber bald in Charlottenburg und in Sanssouci zur Meisterschaft reifen.

Mit dem Tod Friedrich Wilhelms I. am 21. Mai 1740 endeten in Rheinsberg die »ländlichen Freuden« und das anregende, aber auch behagliche Leben der »Republique de Platon«.

Friedrich II. schenkte 1744 das Anwesen seinem Bruder Heinrich, der aber erst nach der Vermählung mit der Prinzessin Wilhelmine von Hessen-Kassel im Jahre 1752 die Erlaubnis zur eigenen Hofhaltung in Rheinsberg erhielt. Bis zu seinem Tod 1802 blieb das Schloss ständiger Wohnsitz des Prinzen. Die in seiner Zeit veranlasste neue Ausstattung der Schlossräume, der Anbau von zwei seitlichen Pavillons 1786, die Erweiterung des Kavalierhauses und der Bau eines Theaters 1771–74 sowie die Gestaltung und Vergrößerung des Gartens ließen Rheinsberg neben Berlin und Potsdam zu einem Zentrum der Künste im späten 18. Jahrhundert in Preußen werden. Besonders der von Knobelsdorff angelegte Garten wurde durch Erweiterung und Umgestaltung, wie dem Bau von Tempel und Einsiedeleien, Erinnerungsstätten, Grotten, neuen Brücken und weiten, das Waldgebiet des Boberow bis zum Rheinsberger See durchziehenden Alleen, deutlich bereichert.

Als anerkannter Militär aus dem Siebenjährigen Krieg hervorgegangen, wichen die Vorstellungen und Urteile des Prinzen Heinrich mehr und mehr von denen seines Bruders Friedrich ab. Als sichtbaren Ausdruck des Gegensatzes ließ er 1791 gegenüber dem Schloss einen Obelisk zum Andenken an seinen schon 1758 verstorbenen Bruder August Wilhelm und all diejenigen Militärs errichten, die nach seiner Meinung von Friedrich dem Großen nicht die ihnen gebührende Anerkennung gefunden hatten.

Prinz Heinrich starb am 3. August 1802 im Alter von 76 Jahren und wurde in einer im Park errichten Grabpyramide, deren Spitze abgebrochen erscheint, beigesetzt.

Vier Jahre Residenz des Kronprinzen Friedrich und fünfzig Jahre Aufenthaltsort des Prinzen Heinrich haben Stadt und Landschaft in Rheinsberg geprägt. Von hier aus gingen immer wieder neue künstlerische Impulse aus, die dann in Berlin und Potsdam ihre endgültige Ausprägung erfuhren.

created artistic frameworks; much was as yet tentative and stylistically unsure, but was soon to ripen to mastery in Charlottenburg and Sanssouci.

With the death of Frederick William I on May 21, 1740, the "bucolic joys" in Rheinsberg ended, and so too the stimulating but also comfortable life of the "Republique de Platon."

In 1744, Frederick II gave the estate to his brother Henry, who was given permission to hold his own court in Rheinsberg only after his marriage to Princess Wilhelmina of Hessen-Kassel in 1752. Until his death in 1802, the palace remained the prince's permanent residence. The re-decorating of the rooms, the building of two pavilions at the sides in 1786, the extension of the cavalier house and the construction of a theater between 1771 and 1774, as well as the designing and enlargement of the garden, all of which was undertaken during his time, turned Rheinsberg into a center of art in Prussia in the late 18th century along with Berlin and Potsdam. The garden laid out by von Knobelsdorff, in particular, was significantly enriched through enlargement and redesign, such as the construction of temples and hermitages, memorials, grottoes, new bridges, and wide, tree-lined avenues that ran through Boberow forest all the way to Rheinsberg Lake.

Coming out of the Seven Years' War as a recognized high-ranking officer, Prince Henry's ideas and judgments deviated more and more from those of his brother Frederick. As a visible expression of these differences, he set up an obelisk across from the palace in 1791 commemorating his brother Augustus William, who died in 1758, and all the other officers, who in his opinion had not been given due recognition by Frederick the Great.

Prince Henry died on August 3, 1802, at the age of 76 and was interred in a pyramid sepulcher with a broken-off point that was constructed in the park. Four years as residence of Crown Prince Frederick and fifty years as the place of residence of Prince Henry left their mark on the town and landscape in Rheinsberg. Again and again, it was the source of innovative artistic stimuli that radiated and found their final forms in Berlin and Potsdam. So it is that palace and park, as well as the town rebuilt after the fire of 1740, impart an aura to the landscape that even we in our time cannot escape.

After the death of Prince Henry, his brother Ferdinand took over Rheinsberg and, in turn, after Ferdinand's death in 1813, his son Augustus. At the death of Augustus in 1843, Rheinsberg again became the property of the crown. The palace was seldom occupied; for example, in 1819 by Augusta of Prillwitz, the second morganatic wife of Prince Augustus, and her two daughters.

Der Große Saal oder Spiegelsaal ist ein Werk Knobelsdorffs von 1739/40 mit dem Deckengemälde »Der Tag vertreibt die Finsternis« von Antoine Pesne.
The Great Hall or Hall of Mirrors is a work by Knobelsdorff from 1739/40 with the ceiling painting "The Day Dispels the Darkness" by Antoine Pesne.

So haben Schloss und Park, wie auch die nach dem Brand von 1740 wieder errichtete Stadt, der Landschaft eine Aura gegeben, der sich auch die Menschen unserer Tage nicht entziehen können.
Nach dem Tod des Prinzen Heinrich übernahm sein Bruder Ferdinand Rheinsberg und nach dessen Tod 1813 wiederum sein Sohn August. Als dieser 1843 starb ging Rheinsberg wieder in königlichen Besitz über. Das Schloss wurde nur noch selten bewohnt, so zum Beispiel 1819 von Auguste von Prillwitz, der zweiten morganatischen Ehefrau des Prinzen August, mit ihren beiden Töchtern.
Nach dem Tod Heinrichs wurden Reparaturen am Schloss notwendig, die auch Veränderungen am Bau nach sich zogen. So wurden Attiken entfernt und den Türmen nach 1802 Kegeldächer aufgesetzt.
Nach 1819 ist in einem Vergleich zwischen dem Prinzen August und dem König Friedrich Willhelm III. der Rheinsberger Besitz dem Kronfideikommiss zugeordnet worden, wodurch das Königshaus die entsprechenden Kosten für die Reparaturen zu tragen hatte. Im Jahre 1825 wurde nach einem Gutachten von Karl Friedrich Schinkel der 1786 gebaute Nordpavillon wegen seines schlechten Zustandes abgerissen und wieder neu aufgeführt. Das Gutachten Schinkels über Rheinsberg fällt in diesem Zusammenhang nicht sehr gut aus: »Wenn man die ganze Architektur des Schlosses betrachtet, so kann man demselben durchaus keinen artistischen Wert beilegen, der Stil ist überall unrein und die Verhältnisse verfehlt, die Konstruktionen sind nur mittelmäßig, an vielen Teilen schlecht.« Man kann Schinkels Urteil heute wohl kaum noch zustimmen, aber das Verhältnis des Meisters zur Architektur des 18. Jahrhunderts war stets sehr kritisch.
Die Innenausstattung des Schlosses und damit der Kunstbesitz des Prinzen Heinrich ist nach seinem Tod »in alle Winde« verstreut worden. Von den 258 Gemälden des Prinzen wurden 1803 151 versteigert. 1823 verzeichnet das Inventar nur noch 38 Gemälde und im Laufe des 19. Jahrhunderts brachte man Kunstwerke des Schlosses nach Berlin und die wenigen, die noch im Schloss verblieben, sind 1945 verschwunden. Fontane, der zum ersten Mal 1853 in Rheinsberg war, stellte später 1859 und beim wiederholten Aufenthalt 1861 fest, dass sich »die Dinge zum schlimmen verändert haben«. Seine Beschreibung rückte aber Rheinsberg wieder in das Blickfeld der Öffentlichkeit. In England wurde Rheinsberg durch die Beschreibung von Andrew Hamilton 1880 (deutsch 1882/83), angeregt durch Fontane, bekannt. Nicht unwesentlich hat auch Kurt Tucholsky mit seiner 1912 erschienenen Erzählung »Rheinsberg. Ein Bilderbuch für Verliebte« zur Popularität des Ortes beigetragen. Das 1989 gegründete Tucholsky-Literaturmuseum erinnert daran.

Following Henry's death, the palace was in need of repairs, which also entailed alterations to the building; the attic was removed and cone-shaped roofs were placed on the towers after 1802.
In a settlement reached after 1819 between Prince Augustus and King Frederick William III, the Rheinsberg estate was classified as a royal entailed estate, by virtue of which the royal family was to assume responsibility for the cost of repairs. In the year 1825, in accordance with a report by Karl Frederick Schinkel, the north pavilion, built in 1786, was torn down and rebuilt. Schinkel's report on Rheinsberg did not turn out too well in this connection. "When one considers the whole architecture of the palace, one can attach to the same absolutely no artistic value, the style is impure everywhere and relationships fail, the design is not better than mediocre, in many parts bad." Today, Schinkel's judgment can hardly be accepted, but then the great architect's view of 18th-century architecture was consistently highly critical.
The interior decoration, which includes Prince Henry's art collection, was scattered "to the four winds" after his death. Of the prince's 258 paintings, 151 were auctioned off in 1803. In 1823, the inventory records only 38 paintings, and in the course of the 19th century the palace's works of art were brought to Berlin. The few that were left in the palace disappeared in 1945. Fontane, who was in Rheinsberg for the first time in 1853, found later in 1859 and during a repeat visit in 1861 that "things have changed for the worse." His descriptions, however, placed Rheinsberg in the focus of public attention again. In England, Rheinsberg became known through a description in 1880 by Andrew Hamilton, who had been inspired by Fontane. Kurt Tucholsky, too, made a significant contribution to the popularity of the place with his story "Rheinsberg – A Picture Book for Lovers," published in 1912. The Tucholsky Literature Museum founded in 1989 recalls this.
The fact remains, however, that Crown Prince Frederick's stay of just four years was the time that defined Rheinsberg most. For that reason, a statue of him was erected in front of the entrance to the park in 1903, and although it was toppled from its pedestal in 1950, it was stored in Sanssouci and returned safe and sound to its old place in 1995.
Beginning in 1942, Rheinsberg Palace was used as a storage depot for works of art from Sanssouci Palace, the Picture Gallery and the New Palace, as well as from Königsberg Palace. The palace remained undamaged until 1945; only the theater suffered damage to its roof by a bomb. Occupation by Soviet troops and the subsequent removal of the works of art stored in the palace by the Soviet army and, not least, plundering and theft after their withdrawal led in the end to the loss of the complete inventory of furnishings and fittings.

Prinz Heinrich starb am 3. August 1802 und wurde in einer Pyramide, mit abgebrochener Spitze als Zeichen der Unvollendung, beigesetzt.
Prince Henry died on August 3, 1802, and was laid to rest in a pyramid with the top broken off as a sign of being unfinished.

Nach wie vor aber war der nur vier Jahre währende Aufenthalt des Kronprinzen Friedrich für Rheinsberg die prägendste Zeit gewesen. Deshalb wurde ihm 1903 vor dem Eingang des Parks ein Standbild errichtet, das zwar 1950 vom Sockel gestürzt, aber in Sanssouci aufbewahrt wurde und 1995 wohlbehalten an den alten Ort zurückkehrte.
Seit 1942 war Schloss Rheinsberg Auslagerungsort für die Kunstwerke des Schlosses Sanssouci, der Bildergalerie und des Neues Palais in Potsdam sowie für das Schloss Königsberg. Bis 1945 blieb das Schloss unbeschädigt, nur das Schauspielhaus hat durch eine Bombe Schaden im Dach erlitten. Die Besetzung durch sowjetische Truppen sowie der anschließende Abtransport der im Schloss eingelagerten Kunstwerke durch die Sowjetarmee und nicht zuletzt Plünderungen und Diebstähle nach deren Abzug führte letztlich zum Verlust des gesamten Inventars. Das Schloss war danach Kinder-, später Lehrlingswohnheim und 1949 beabsichtigte man, es in eine Polizeischule umzubauen. Im Oktober 1949 wurde die Sozialversicherung Besitzer des Schlosses, dazu gehörten auch der Marstall, die Remise, das Kavalierhaus und die Schlossinsel. Der Park wurde zum größten Teil der Stadt übereignet. Von 1953 bis zum März 1991 waren die Schlossräume im Kavalierhaus und im Marstall ein Diabetikersanatorium, in dem jährlich 2000 Patienten betreut wurden.
Man kann sich unschwer vorstellen, dass diese Nutzung Schäden an der historischen Substanz bedingte. Für die Kureinrichtung waren zwangsläufig Umbauten notwendig, die letztlich zur Einbuße des historischen Grundrisses und einzelner Räume und der Dekoration führen musste. Das dies nicht zur endgültigen Aufgabe der historischen Substanz führte, ist dem ständigen Bemühen des Institutes für Denkmalpflege in Berlin zu danken, die immer wieder Mittel und Wege fanden, die Nutzung zu mildern und Restaurierungsmaßnahmen vorzunehmen. Nur beim Schlosstheater versagten die Bemühungen der Rettung und letzten Endes blieben nur die Umfassungsmauern übrig.
Aber was wäre ein Schloss ohne einen Garten? Schon in den 50er Jahren des 20. Jahrhunderts begannen erste Maßnahmen zur Rekonstruktion und zur Erhaltung des Parks und der Parkarchitektur. Entscheidend waren jedoch die Wiederherstellungsarbeiten ab 1975, bei denen man sich an der Struktur der Jahre 1760/70 orientierte. Geradezu eine Sensation war die Freilegung der Terrassen des Weinberges von seinem in Jahrzehnten gewachsenen Baumbestand gegenüber dem Schloss. Parkbauten, wie die Felsengrotte und die Grabpyramide des Prinzen, wurden restauriert. Obwohl schon 1986 die

Afterwards, the palace was a home for children and later for apprentices, and in 1949 the idea of remodeling it as a police training school was entertained. In October 1949, the GDR Social Security Administration became the owner of the palace, including the stables, the coach-house, the cavalier house and Palace Island. Most of the park was transferred to the municipality. From 1953 until March 1991, a sanatorium for diabetics that annually cared for 2,000 patients occupied the palace rooms in the cavalier house and the stables. It can be imagined that this use caused damage to the historic fabric. Reconstruction was necessary to instal the sanatorium furnishings and equipment, ultimately resulting in the loss of the historic floor plan and of individual rooms and decorations. That this did not lead to the final abandonment of the historic fabric is due to the unrelenting efforts of the Institute for the Preservation of Historic Monuments in Berlin, which constantly found ways and means to moderate the use of the palace and undertake restoration measures. The rescue efforts failed only with the palace theater, of which, in the end, only the outer walls remained.
But what would a palace be without a garden? The first measures for restoration and maintenance of the park and its architecture began as early as the 1950s. The decisive restoration work, however, began in 1975 and was based on the layout of the years 1760–70. The freeing of the vineyard terrace across from the palace from decades-old trees was an absolute revelation. Park structures like the rock grotto and the prince's pyramid sepulcher were restored. Although the decision to move the sanatorium had already been taken in 1986, this did not take place until April 1991. The palace was transferred to the Palace and Gardens Potsdam-Sanssouci Foundation, which became the Prussian Palaces and Gardens Foundation Berlin-Brandenburg in 1995. After a few weeks, the palace rooms were opened again. In December 1993, the municipality of Rheinsberg also presented the park to the foundation, so that palace and park are now reunited.
Since that time, a good deal of restoration work has been carried out in and around the palace, in the park and on the park's structures. Not only palace rooms have been restored, but large parts of the park have been recreated, too. The hedgerow theater was reconstructed, the palace theater rebuilt and, with a modern interior, officially opened in 1999. The Music Academy in the cavalier houses and the Chamber Opera of Rheinsberg Palace have now found a new home, and the palace and garden of Rheinsberg, with the Tucholsky Literature Museum, have again become an important cultural venue in the north of Brandenburg.

Verlagerung des Sanatoriums beschlossen worden war, wurde die Einrichtung erst im April 1991 aufgelöst und das Schloss der Stiftung Schlösser und Gärten Potsdam-Sanssouci, ab 1995 Stiftung Preußische Schlösser und Gärten Berlin-Brandenburg, übertragen. Nach wenigen Wochen konnten die Schlossräume wieder geöffnet werden. Im Dezember 1993 übergab die Stadt Rheinsberg auch den Park an die Stiftung, so dass nun Schloss und Park wieder vereinigt wurden.
Seit dieser Zeit sind im und am Schloss, im Park und an den Parkbauten viele Wiederherstellungsarbeiten durchgeführt worden. Es wurden nicht nur Schlossräume wieder restauriert, auch große Partien im Park sind wieder erstanden. Das Heckentheater wurde rekonstruiert. Das Schlosstheater wurde aufgebaut und konnte mit der modernen Innenausstattung 1999 eingeweiht werden. Somit haben die Musikakademie und die Kammeroper Schloss Rheinsberg in den Kavalierhäusern eine Spielstätte gefunden und Rheinsberg mit dem Schloss und Garten sowie dem Tucholsky-Literaturmuseum wieder zu einem wichtigen kulturellen Ort im Norden Brandenburgs gemacht.

Oben: Vom gegenüberliegenden Hügel mit dem von Prinz Heinrich 1791 errichteten Obelisk blickt man über den See auf das Schloss.
Top: From the hill with the obelisk erected by Prince Henry in 1791 there is a view across the lake to the palace.

Rechts: Die Bibliothek des Kronprinzen wurde in dem noch aus dem Mittelalter stammenden Klingenbergturm eingerichtet. Sie war das Vorbild für die Bibliothek im Schloss Sanssouci. Das Deckengemälde schuf Antoine Pesne, »Minerva als Beschützerin von Wissenschaft und Kunst«. Die heutige Gestaltung stammt aus der Zeit des Prinzen Heinrich 1769.

Right: The crown prince's library was housed in the medieval Klingenberg Tower. It was the model for the library in Sanssouci Palace. The ceiling painting by Antoine Pesne depicts "Minerva as Protectress of Art and Science". The decoration dates from the time of Prince Henry, 1769.

Das unmittelbar am Grienericksee gelegene Schloss wird durch die zwei Türme betont. Im Hintergrund ist das Theater des Prinzen Heinrich, erbaut 1771–74, zu sehen.
The palace, accented by two towers, stands directly on Grienericksee lake. The theater that Prince Henry built between 1771 and 1774 can be seen in the background.

Oben: Der Marmor- oder Muschelsaal genannte Raum entstand 1769 nach einem Entwurf von Carl Gotthard Langhans. Ursprünglich befanden sich hier die Räume der Königin Elisabeth Christine.
Top: The room named the Marble Hall or Shell Hall was constructed in 1769 to a design by Carl Gotthard Langhans. Originally, Queen Elizabeth Christina's chambers were here.

Unten: Die Schlafkammer des Prinzen Heinrich entstand 1786. Die frühklassizistische Dekorationsmalerei schuf Bartolomeo Verona. Die Wandbespannung sowie das Bett des Prinzen Heinrich wurde nach 2000 rekonstruiert.
Bottom: Prince Henry's bedchamber was built in 1786. The early neoclassical decorative painting was done by Bartolomeo Verona. The wall coverings as well as Prince Henry's bed were reconstructed after 2000.

Oben: In der von Prinz Heinrich 1763 eingerichteten Bildergalerie hingen ursprünglich fünfzig Gemälde. Diese wurden nach dem Tod des Prinzen versteigert, die heutige Sammlung stammt zum Teil aus Privatbesitz, zurückerworbenen und aus anderen Schlössern ergänzten Bildern.
Top: Originally 50 paintings hung in the picture gallery as arranged by Prince Henry in 1763. These were auctioned off after the death of the prince; the collection today was partially reacquired from private ownership and supplemented with pictures from other palaces.

Unten: Im 1786 errichteten südlichen Pavillon ließ Prinz Heinrich seine neue Bibliothek einrichten. Sie umfasste damals über 5000 Bände und wurde nach dem Tode des Prinzen 1802 versteigert. Ein Teil der Bände kam in die Staatsbibliothek Berlin (SPK), ebenso wie die jetzt wieder in dem Raum befindlichen Portraits von Gelehrten und Dichtern.
Bottom: Prince Henry installed his new library in the southern pavilion, which was built in 1786. At the time, it was composed of 5,000 volumes and was auctioned off after the death of the prince in 1802. Some volumes went to the Berlin State Library (SPK), as did the portraits of scholars and poets that are now once again in the room.

Rechts: Im Erdgeschoss des Südflügels befinden sich zwei von Friedrich Reclam 1771 ausgemalte gewölbte Kammern. Beide ursprünglich mittelalterlichen Räume wurden in italienische Grotten mit Darstellungen bekannter antiker Bauwerke und Skulpturen verwandelt. In der Zeit des Sanatoriums etwas in Mitleidenschaft gezogen, konnten sie in den letzten Jahren wiederhergestellt werden.

Right: On the ground floor of the south wing there are two vaulted chambers decorated with paintings by Friedrich Reclam in 1771. Both were originally medieval rooms transformed into Italian grottoes with depictions of well-known classical buildings and sculptures. They suffered when the palace was used as a sanatorium, but have been restored in recent years.

Das Eingangsportal zur Parkanlage, geschaffen von Georg Wenzeslaus von Knobelsdorff, mit Skulpturen von Friedrich Christian Glume, wurde wenige Jahre später in Sanssouci wiederholt.

The entrance portal to the park, created by Georg Wenzeslaus von Knobelsdorff, with sculptures by Friedrich Christian Glume, was copied a few years later in Sanssouci.

Der Neue Flügel des Schlosses Charlottenburg – Die Wohnungen Friedrichs II. Berlin

The New Wing of Charlottenburg Palace – The Apartments of Frederick II Berlin

Bald nach der Thronbesteigung Friedrichs II. am 31. Mai 1740 erhielt Knobelsdorff den Auftrag, als Pendant zur westlichen Orangerie des Schlosses Charlottenburg einen östlichen Flügel als Residenz für den König zu errichten. Bereits zwei Jahre später waren die Wohnung des Königs und der Speisesaal fertig. Der Festsaal und die Goldene Galerie konnten erst im Herbst 1746 vollendet werden. In diesem Neuen Flügel befanden sich im Erdgeschoss auf der Westseite Räume für die Königin Elisabeth Christine. Ob sie diese Zimmer überhaupt bewohnt hat, ist nicht überliefert. Die Räume sind 1760 durch österreichische Truppen und Kosaken verwüstet und nach 1800 von Friedrich Wilhelm III. umgestaltet worden. Erhalten hat sich nur in der sogenannten Japanischen Kammer eine Vertäfelung mit chinoiser Malerei, ähnlich dem Ersten Gästezimmer im Schloss Sanssouci.

Die Wohnung des Königs befand sich im Obergeschoss des Westflügels. Acht Räume lagen nach Süden der Stadt zugewandt. Vier Räume, das waren die eigentlichen Privaträume des Königs, sind zur Gartenseite angeordnet. Diese Räume wurden, bis auf die privaten Gemächer Friedrichs des Großen auf der Nordseite Versilberte Kammer, Bibliothek und Schreibkammer, durch Friedrich Wilhelm II. 1796/97 zu den sogenannten »Winterkammern« umgestaltet.

Der erste noch erhaltene friderizianische Raum ist die »Versilberte Kammer«, deren Wände mit weißgefasster Vertäfelung und versilberter Ornamentik versehen sind, die stilistisch einem älteren Meister zuzuordnen ist, während Decke und Voute von Johann August Nahl d. J. stammen. Die Boiserie blieb beim Bombenangriff 1943 erhalten, während die Decke zerstört und bis 1951 wieder rekonstruiert wurde. Die lang gestreckte »Bibliothek« ist der zweite friderizianische Raumtyp, ihm entsprachen später die Bibliotheken im Schloss Breslau (1750) und im Neuen Palais in Potsdam (1765). Gegenüber der nur einfach gestrichenen Rückwand erhielten die Seitenwände und die Fensterwand eine Vertäfelung von hellgrüner Farbigkeit mit versilberten Ornamenten verziert. Das Deckengemälde von Antoine Pesne zeigte Minerva als Beschützerin der Künste und der Wissenschaft, eine thematische Wiederholung des Gemäldes in der Rheinsberger Bibliothek. Der zweite Abschnitt des Gemäldes schilderte eine Allegorie der Dichtkunst und der Musik. 1743 wurden hier achtzehn antike Büsten aus der 1742 erworbenen Sammlung Polignac auf Konsolen an den Wänden aufgestellt. Die seit 1964 in dem Raum befindlichen Bücherschränke aus Zedernholz sind wohl schon um 1735 entstanden und vermutlich ursprünglich für das Potsdamer Stadt-schloss oder das Berliner Schloss Monbijou geschaffen worden.

Eine weißgestrichene Boiserie mit geschnitzter und vergoldeter Ornamentik bestimmt die Wände der »Schreibkammer«. Der Raum verweist in seiner

Soon after Frederick II's accession to the throne on May 31, 1740, Knobelsdorff was commissioned to build an eastern wing, a counterpart to the western orangery of Charlottenburg Palace, as a residence for the king. In as little as two years the apartment of the king and the dining room were finished. The ballroom and the Golden Gallery were finished only in autumn 1746. There were rooms for Queen Elizabeth Christina on the west side of the ground floor of this New Wing. It is not recorded whether she ever occupied these rooms, which were ravaged in 1760 by Austrian troops and Cossacks and remodeled after 1800 by Frederick William III. Only the paneling with chinoiserie painting, similar to that in the first guestroom in Sanssouci Palace, survived in the so-called Japanese Chamber.

The king's apartment was on the upper storey of the west wing, where eight rooms faced the south of the city. Four rooms, the actual private chambers of the king, were situated on the garden side. All of these rooms, except the private chambers of Frederick the Great on the north side, the Silver Chamber, the library, and the study, were recreated by Frederick William II in 1796/97 as the so-called Winter Apartment.

The first Frederician room that still exists is the Silver Chamber. Its walls are decorated with white paneling and silver-leaf ornamentation that is stylistically attributable to an earlier artist, while the ceiling and arches were done by Johann August Nahl the Younger. The boiserie survived the bombing in 1943; the ceiling was destroyed, but reconstructed by 1951. The elongated library is the second Frederician style of room, also seen in the later libraries in Breslau Palace (1750) and in the New Palace in Potsdam (1765). In contrast to the back wall, which was simply painted, the side walls and the window wall were fitted with paneling of a light green color and silver ornamentation. The ceiling painting by Antoine Pesne depicted Minerva as patron of the arts and science, a repeat of the motif in the Rheinsberg library. The second part of the painting represented an allegory of poetry and music. In 1743, eighteen classical busts acquired in 1742 from the Polignac collection were placed here on consoles along the walls. The bookcases of cedarwood, which have stood in the room since 1964, were most likely made around 1735, probably for the Potsdam City Palace or Monbijou Palace in Berlin.

A boiserie painted white with gilded carved ornamentation dominates the walls of the study. The style of ornamentation in the room is reminiscent still of the interior of Rheinsberg Palace. Again, the ceiling design was by Johann August Nahl. The wall paneling and the ceiling painting by Pesne in the oval at the centre, except for small remnants, were completely incinerated in 1943, while the original surfaces above the doors with playing putti and the doors themselves with medallions of classical heads survived. The corner cupboard,

Ornamentik stilistisch noch auf Innenräume des Schlosses Rheinsberg.
Der Deckenentwurf ist wiederum von Johann August Nahl. Während das Deckenbild von Pesne in dem ovalen Mittelfeld bis auf kleine Reste, wie auch die Wandvertäfelung, 1943 völlig verbrannte, sind die Supraporten über den Türen mit spielenden Putten und die Türflügel mit Medaillons antiker Köpfe original erhalten. Hervorhebenswert ist der Eckschrank nach einem Entwurf von Knobelsdorff, Berlin um 1745, und die um 1740 in Paris erworbene Standuhr mit Boulle-Marketerie und vergoldeten Bronzen. Der Kronleuchter wurde 1745 nach einem Entwurf Nahls gefertigt.
Im Jahre 1747 ließ sich Friedrich der Große am Ostende des Neuen Flügels eine zweite Wohnung, bestehend aus Konzertzimmer, Gris-de-lin-Kammer, Schreibkammer und Schlafkammer einrichten. Die drei ersten Zimmer waren reich mit Gemälden ausgestattet, die aber durch die Verwüstung des Schlosses im Jahre 1760 verloren gingen. Die Räume wurden bald wieder instand gesetzt und mit neuen Gemälden geschmückt. Graf Rothenburg erwarb 1744 für Friedrich den Großen in Paris das Gemälde von Watteau »Das Ladenschild des Kunsthändlers Gersaint«.
In der folgenden Gris-de-lin-Kammer hängt heute ein bekanntes Gemälde von Watteau: »Die Einschiffung nach Cythera«. Friedrich der Große erwarb das Bild zwischen 1752 und 1765 als letztes seiner Watteau-Serie. Seit 1973 schmückt es diesen Raum.
Der große, im Obergeschoss dieses Flügels gelegene Weiße Saal diente als Speise- und Thronsaal und wurde zu Ehren der Königinmutter Sophie Dorothea am 29. August 1742 eingeweiht. Pilaster gliedern die Wände und schaffen so Assoziationen zum Marmorsaal im Rheinsberger Schloss, der nur wenige Jahre zuvor fertig gestellt worden war. Der Raum wurde 1943 vollkommen zerstört, aber bis 1973 wieder aufgebaut, allerdings mit einem anderen Deckenbild von Hann Trier. Das originale Gemälde von Pesne zeigte das Hochzeitsmahl von Peleus und Thetis. In der Gedächtnisrede auf seinen verstorbenen Baumeister Knobelsdorff hat Friedrich II. am 24. Januar 1754 diesen Raum ausdrücklich als Werk dieses Baumeisters genannt, der sich aber der Mitwirkung von Nahl bediente.
Höhepunkt in der friderizianischen Raumgestaltung ist zweifellos die 1746 fertig gestellte Goldene Galerie, die Friedrich II. auch Knobelsdorff zuschreibt, die aber wohl ohne die Mitwirkung Johann August Nahls kaum denkbar wäre. Die Galerie brannte 1943 nahezu vollständig aus und wurde von 1961 bis 1973 rekonstruiert.

from a design by Knobelsdorff (Berlin about 1745), and the longcase clock acquired in Paris around 1740 with Boulle marquetry and gilt bronzes are both worthy of note. The chandelier was made in 1745 to a design by Johann August Nahl.
In 1747, Frederick the Great had a second apartment furnished for himself at the east end of the New Wing, consisting of a concert room, the Gris-de-lin Room, a study, and a bedchamber. The paintings which furnished the first three rooms were lost when the palace was sacked in 1760. However, the rooms were soon restored and adorned with new paintings. Count Rothenburg acquired Watteau's "The Shop Sign of Gersaint the Art Dealer," in 1744 in Paris for Frederick.
A well-known painting by Watteau, the "Embarkation for Cythera", hangs today in the next room, the Gris-de-lin Room. It was the last picture in Frederick the Greatís Watteau series, which he acquired between 1752 and 1765. It has hung in this room since 1973.
The large White Hall on the upper storey of this wing served as a banquet hall and throne room and was dedicated on August 29, 1742 to the Queen Mother, Sophie Dorothea. The pilasters that divide the wall spaces are reminiscent of the Marble Hall of Rheinsberg Palace, which had been finished only a couple of years earlier. The room was completely destroyed in 1943 and had been rebuilt by 1973, though with a different ceiling painting by Hann Trier. The original painting by Pesne depicted the wedding feast of Peleus and Thetis. In a speech in honor of the deceased Knobelsdorff on January 24, 1754, Frederick II specifically mentioned this room as the work of the late architect, who had, however, availed himself of the services of Johann August Nahl.
The Golden Gallery, finished in 1746, was without doubt the pinnacle of Frederician interior design. Frederick II attributed it, too, to Knobelsdorff, but without the cooperation of Johann August Nahl the work would have been almost inconceivable. The gallery was completely gutted in 1943 and reconstructed from 1961 to 1973.

Der von Knobelsdorff ab 1740 errichtete »Neue Flügel« war die Sommerresidenz Friedrichs II. in Berlin.
The New Wing constructed by von Knobelsdorff from 1740 was Frederick II's summer residence in Berlin.

Die schmale, lang gestreckte Bibliothek ließ Friedrich auf der Nordseite des Neuen Flügels einrichten. Die Bücherschränke, wie auch der Konsoltisch, stammen noch aus der Originalausstattung. In den Bücherschränken befinden sich heute Bestände der ehemaligen Potsdamer Stadtschlossbibliothek des Königs.

Frederick had the narrow, elongated library set up in the north side of the New Wing. The bookcases and console table were part of the original furnishings. In the bookcases today are book collections from the former Potsdam City Palace library of the king.

Die Schreibkammer Friedrichs II., neben der Bibliothek gelegen, weist stilistisch noch in die Rheinsberger Zeit, nur die Decke und die Krone (um 1740) sind nach einem Entwurf von Johann August Nahl gestaltet. Die Standuhr erwarb Friedrich II. in Paris um 1740.

Frederick II's study, situated next to the library, stylistically recalls his time at Rheinsberg; only the ceiling and the crown (around 1740) were fashioned after a design by Johann August Nahl. Frederick II acquired the longcase clock in Paris about 1740.

Die sogenannte »Goldene Galerie« ist zweifellos der Höhepunkt des friderizianischen Rokoko. Der von G. W. v. Knobelsdorff und J. A. Nahl 1746 beendete Raum war im Zweiten Weltkrieg fast vollständig zerstört worden und wurde von 1961–72 originalgetreu rekonstruiert.

The so-called Golden Gallery is without a doubt the high point of Frederician Rococo. The room that G. W. v. Knobelsdorff and J. A. Nahl finished in 1746 was almost totally destroyed in the Second World War and reconstructed as a copy of the original between 1961 and 1972.

Schloss Sanssouci mit Neuen Kammern und Bildergalerie Potsdam

Sanssouci Palace with the New Chambers and Picture Gallery Potsdam

Am 9. August 1744 erhielt der Baudirektor Friedrich Wilhelm Diterichs die Order, den westlich der Stadt Potsdam vor dem Brandenburger Tor gelegenen »Wüsten Berg« zu terrassieren und einen Weinberg anzulegen. Wohl wenig später wird auch der Plan entstanden sein, auf dem Weinberg ein Sommerschloss zu errichten.

Die Wahl des Ortes und die Lage des Schlosses zeugen vom Willen des Königs, hier nicht zu repräsentieren, sondern »ohne Sorge« seinen privaten Neigungen nachzugehen. Diese Grundhaltung wurde bestimmend für die ganze Anlage von Sanssouci.

Das Schloss ist nicht mehr Mittelpunkt von dem die zentralisierende Hauptachse ihren Ausgangspunkt nimmt, sondern ist eingebunden in die Gesamtgestaltung, die auch die landschaftlichen Gegebenheiten einbezieht. Die Hauptallee verläuft parallel zur Hügelkette, auf der in ansteigendem und abfallendem Rhythmus die Gebäude errichtet sind. Den Kern der Gartenanlage von Sanssouci bildet das Schloss mit den Terrassen, dem vorgelagerten Parterre und den diesen Bezirk seitlich begrenzenden Rampen. Das Schloss krönt die Höchsterhebung des Hügels, dessen Südabhang durch sechs in der Mitte parabolisch einschwingende Terrassen gegliedert ist. Eine von der Schlossmitte ausgehende Tiefenachse, deren Verlauf durch die Treppenanlage, den Mittelweg des Parterres und die südlich des Grabens anschließende Allee gekennzeichnet ist, wirkt neben der Hauptallee in diesem Bereich als beherrschendes Moment. Neu und einmalig ist die Art und Weise der Nutzung des Hügels. Die Terrassen sind nicht nur ein architektonisches Element, sondern dienten vornehmlich einem praktischen Zweck: In den verglasten Nischen und den Spalieren der Talutmauern wurden Wein und verschiedene Obstsorten gezogen. Durch die Bepflanzung – die Taxuspyramiden nehmen Bezug auf die Schlossfassade – wurde der Zusammenhang zwischen Schloss und Terrassen betont.

Der Baumeister Georg Wenzeslaus von Knobelsdorff hatte 30-jährig seinen Dienst als Offizier in der Armee aufgegeben, um sich fortan als Autodidakt künstlerischen Aufgaben zu widmen. Sein an den Bauwerken der Antike geschultes Formempfinden ist bereits in seinem Frühwerk, einem kleinen dorischen Rundtempel im Almatheagarten in Neuruppin, spürbar. Für den Kronprinzen Friedrich hatte er bereits 1737 bis 1740 das Rheinsberger Schloss umgebaut und war nach dessen Thronbesteigung 1740 Oberintendant der Schlösser und Gärten geworden.

Nachdem er bereits 1744 mit dem Umbau des Potsdamer Stadtschlosses zur Winterresidenz Friedrichs des Großen begonnen hatte, wurde für die Sommerresidenz vor den Toren der Stadt Potsdam am 14. April 1745 der

On August 9, 1744, the director of building, Friedrich Wilhelm Diterichs, received the order to terrace the "desolate hill" situated to the west of Potsdam outside the city's Brandenburg gate, and lay out a vineyard. A little later, undoubtedly, the plan was formed to build a summer palace above the vineyard. The choice of site and the position of the palace testify to the king's intention not to represent the state here, but rather pursue his private inclinations "without care." This fundamental attitude was decisive for the whole ensemble of Sanssouci.

The palace is no longer the central point from which the principal axis originates, but is instead integrated into a total design that also includes agricultural aspects. The main avenue runs parallel to a range of hills, upon which the buildings were constructed in an ascending and descending rhythm. The core of the gardens of Sanssouci is the palace with its terraces, the parterre in front of them and the flanking ramps. The hill is crowned by the palace, its southern slope segmented by six terraces which sweep inward at the center in a parabola. The dominant factor in this area, in addition to the main axis, is a further axis a right angles to it, starting at the center of the palace and corresponding to the flight of steps, the center path of the parterre and the avenue that continues south of the moat. The hill is used in an innovative and unique way. The terraces are not only architectural elements but serve a practical purpose. The walls have overhanging capstones, which protected the vines and various kinds of fruit grown in glass-covered niches and on trellises. The relationship between the palace and the terraces was stressed through the plants, the pyramids of yew making reference to the palace façade.

The self-taught architect Georg Wenzeslaus von Knobelsdorff had abandoned his 30-year service as an army officer in order to dedicate himself to artistic endeavors. His sense of form, schooled by the buildings of antiquity, is evident in his early work, a small, round Doric temple in the Almathea Gardens in Neuruppin. He had already rebuilt Rheinsberg Palace from 1737 to 1740 for Crown Prince Frederick, and after Frederick's accession to the throne in 1740 became his chief superintendent of palaces and gardens.

After he had begun the conversion of the Potsdam City Palace into Frederick the Great's winter residence in 1744, the foundation stone for the summer residence was laid on April 14, 1745, outside the gates of the city of Potsdam. Work on the exterior was finished in 1746 and, a year later, the colonnade was also completed. The southern side facing the garden is cheery and relaxed. The elongated single-storey building curves outwards in the middle in a flat bow, crowned by a dome, and ends on either side in round pavilions. Caryatids turned towards each other support the balustrade between tall windows. In

Johann Heinrich Christian Franke

Friedrich der Große, 1764, SPSG
Frederick the Great, 1764, SPSG

Grundstein gelegt. Der Außenbau war 1746 beendet, ein Jahr später auch die Kolonnade. Heiter und gelöst ist die südliche, dem Garten zugewandte Seite. Der lang gestreckte eingeschossige Bau tritt in der Mitte, von einer Kuppel überwölbt, in flachem Bogen hervor und endet beiderseits in Rundpavillons. Sich einander zuwendende Karyatiden tragen zwischen den hoch aufragenden Fenstern das Gebälk. In ihrer Heiterkeit und Lebensfülle verbinden die Bacchantinnen und Bacchanten das Bauwerk mit der Natur des Gartens. Die von Friedrich Christian Glume geschaffenen Plastiken gehören in ihrer individuellen Gestaltung, dem Reichtum der Phantasie und der meisterhaften Ausführung zu den besten Werken der Bildhauerkunst des deutschen Rokoko. Etwas zurückgesetzt und von den Laubengängen verdeckt, schlossen sich im 18. Jahrhundert niedrige Seitenflügel an, die erst 1841 von Ludwig Persius und Ferdinand von Arnim ihr heutiges Aussehen erhielten.
Ernst und zurückhaltender ist dagegen die Nordseite. Das Motiv der paarweise geordneten korinthischen Pilaster und Dreiviertelsäulen am Schlossbau wird durch die Säulen der Kolonnade weiter geführt. Schloss und Kolonnade verschmelzen so zu einem einheitlichen Bauwerk.
Vom Ehrenhof sieht man den sogenannten »Ruinenberg« mit den von Knobelsdorff und dem Bühnenmaler Innocente Bellavite entworfenen künstlichen Ruinen. Sie gruppieren sich um ein Bassin, dessen Wasser im 18. Jahrhundert die Fontänen im Park speisen sollte, was jedoch erst im 19. Jahrhundert in dieser Art funktionierte.
Die Aufteilung der Innenräume des Schlosses war durch eine Grundrissskizze Friedrich des Großen vorgegeben, nur weniges wurde geändert. In der Mitte des Gebäudes liegen die beiden Säle, östlich schließen sich die Räume des Königs, westlich die der Gäste an.
Die klare Gliederung des Vestibüls, das der Besucher im 18. Jahrhundert vom Ehrenhof her betrat, wird durch zehn korinthische Säulen bestimmt, die das an der Außenfront anklingende architektonische Motiv wieder aufnehmen und so den Innenraum mit dem Außenbau vereinen. Leicht ist dagegen der obere Abschluss durch ein Deckengemälde – »Flora mit Genien« von Johann Harper. Vergoldete Türornamente und die Thematik der Supraporten nehmen auf den Charakter des Hauses als Weinbergschloss Bezug. Die Autorschaft Knobelsdorffs ist für den Marmorsaal durch die Gedenkrede Friedrichs des Großen auf seinen verstorbenen Baumeister gesichert. Den elliptischen Raum überwölbt eine Kuppel, die sich, ähnlich dem Pantheon in Rom, in der Mitte zum Himmel öffnet. Wie im Vorsaal sind korinthische Säulen die architektonisch bestimmenden Elemente. Die inhaltliche Steigerung in der Raumfolge, vom Hof über Vestibül bis zum

their merriment and fullness of life, the male and female Bacchanalian figures form a link to the nature in the garden. The sculptures by Friedrich Christian Glume, in their individuality, rich inventiveness, and masterly execution, are among the best works of German Rococo sculpture. Set back somewhat and screened by the arcades are low wings that were added in the 18th century and finally given their present appearance in 1841 by Ludwig Persius and Ferdinand von Arnim.
The north side, on the other hand, is somber and restrained. The theme introduced on the palace, of Corinthian pilasters arranged in pairs and three-quarter columns, is continued in the colonnade, so that palace and colonnade form a unity.
From the cour d'honneur, the "hill of ruins" can be seen with its artificial ruins designed by von Knobelsdorff and the scene-painter Innocente Bellavite. They are grouped around a reservoir whose water was meant to feed the fountains in the park in the 18th century but did not function in this way until the 19th century.
The floor plan of the interior rooms, specified in a sketch by Frederick the Great, was carried out with few changes. The two state rooms are at the centre of the building, the king's apartments to the east, the guest apartments to the west.
Ten Corinthian columns dominate the clearly-structured vestibule, which visitors in the 18th century entered from the cour d'honneur, and take up the architectural theme of the façade, thus uniting the interior with the exterior. In contrast the upper part of the vestibule has a light design with a ceiling painting, "Flora with her Acolytes" by Johann Harper. Gilded door ornamentation and the themes on the walls above the doors refer to the character of the house as a vineyard palace. Knobelsdorff's authorship of the Marble Hall is confirmed through Frederick the Great's speech commemorating his architect. A dome, open to the sky in the middle like the Pantheon in Rome, arches over the elliptical room. As in the vestibule, Corinthian columns are the determining architectural elements. The ascending importance of the sequence of rooms from the court to the vestibule to the banqueting hall is reflected in the choice of materials for the columns: from sandstone blocks to stucco marble to Carrara marble. The groups of figures on the cornice symbolize architecture, music, painting, sculpture, and astronomy.
The small reception room between the Marble Hall and the Music Room is simple in design to allow the paintings decorating the peach-blossom-colored wall coverings to take full effect. On the ceiling "Zephyr and Flora" unfold their game of love in a masterpiece by the court painter Antoine Pesne.

Charles Sylva Dubois

»Ansicht des Schlosses Sanssouci vom gegenüberliegenden Flussufer«, Supraporte im Konzertzimmer des Schlosses Sanssouci, 1746/47
"View of Sanssouci Palace from the Opposite Bank of the River", supraporte in the Music Room of Sanssouci Palace, 1746/47

Festsaal, spiegelt sich auch in der Materialwahl dieses Architekturmotivs, vom Sandstein über Stuckmarmor bis zum carrarischen Marmor, wieder. Die Figurengruppen auf dem Gesims versinnbildlichen Architektur, Musik, Malerei, Bildhauerkunst und Astronomie.
Das kleine Empfangszimmer, zwischen Marmorsaal und Konzertzimmer gelegen, ist einfacher in der Gestaltung, um dem Bilderschmuck auf der pfirsichblütenfarbenen Bespannung volle Geltung zu verschaffen. An der Decke entfalten »Zephyr und Flora« in einem Meisterwerk des Hofmalers Antoine Pesne ihr Liebesspiel.
Das Konzertzimmer gehört zu den schönsten Räumen des deutschen Rokoko. Alles fügt sich hier zu einem Gesamtkunstwerk. Naturalistisches und für das Rokoko typisches Ornamentwerk, geschaffen von Johann Michael Hoppenhaupt d. Ä., überzieht die Vertäfelung und umspielt die rhythmisch in die Wandflächen eingelassenen Gemälde Pesnes, deren Thematik den »Metamorphosen« des römischen Dichters Ovid entnommen ist. Die Decke ist als Gitterlaube gestaltet, und den Fenstern sind Spiegel gegenüber gestellt, die den Innenraum weiten und den Freiraum hineintragen. Heitere Anmut und strahlende Festlichkeit sind der Grundtenor dieses Raumes.
Das folgende Arbeits- und Schlafzimmer des Königs ist nicht mehr in seinem ursprünglichen Zustand erhalten. Friedrich Wilhelm von Erdmannsdorff hat es nach dem Tod Friedrichs des Großen für dessen Nachfolger Friedrich Wilhelm II. im Stil des Klassizismus umgestaltet.
Abseits der Zimmerfolge liegt die Bibliothek, in ihrer runden Gestalt dem Turmzimmer im kronprinzlichen Schloss Rheinsberg ähnlich. Der warme Farbton der braunen Zedernholzvertäfelung und der vergoldeten Bronzeornamentik sowie die wohlausgewogene Proportion – der Durchmesser ist gleich der Raumhöhe – lassen diesen Raum zu einer Stätte geistigen Schaffens werden. Zwischen den Nischen sind Bücherschränke in die Wand eingelassen. Von den vier Büsten, die 1742 mit der Sammlung Polignac erworben worden, ist besonders der »Homer von Sanssouci« hervorzuheben. Der Entwurf zu diesem Raum stammt vermutlich von Knobelsdorff, der zusammen mit dem »Directeur des Ornements« Johann August Nahl auch in der Innenraumgestaltung die erste Phase des friderizianischen Rokoko im Wesentlichen geprägt hat.
Die Kleine Galerie an der Nordseite, der Wohnung des Königs vorgelagert, diente der Unterbringung von Gemälden, vernehmlich Werken französischer Malerei des 18. Jahrhunderts und Skulpturen aus der Sammlung Polignac. Die Dekorationen schuf Johann Christian Hoppenhaupt d. J., einer der Hauptmeister des Potsdamer Rokoko nach 1750.

The Music Room is one of the most beautiful rooms of German Rococo. Everything fits together to form a complete work of art. Naturalistic, typically Rococo ornamental work by Johann Michael Hoppenhaupt the Elder covers the paneling and plays around the paintings by Pesnes, which are rhythmically set into the wall surface, and whose theme is taken from the "Metamorphoses" of the Roman poet Ovid. The ceiling is designed as latticework, and the windows are placed opposite mirrors to extend the room and to bring in the open space. Light-hearted charm and a radiant festive spirit characterize this room.
The study and bedchamber that follows is no longer preserved in its original state. Friedrich Wilhelm von Erdmannsdorff remodeled it in the neoclassical style after the death of Frederick the Great for his successor, Frederick William II.
The library lies some distance from the other rooms; in its round form it is similar to the tower room in the crown prince's Rheinsberg Palace. The warm shade of the brown cedarwood paneling and the gilt bronze ornamentation, as well as the well-balanced proportion – the room's diameter is equal to its height – make the library a place for intellectual creativity. Bookcases have been let into the wall between the niches. Of the four busts that were acquired with the Polignac collection in 1742, "Homer of Sanssouci" is noteworthy. The design for this room is presumably by Georg Wenzeslaus von Knobelsdorff, who together with the "Directeur des Ornements," Johann August Nahl, fundamentally shaped the first phase of Frederician Rococo in interior decoration.
The Little Gallery on the north side, in front of the king's apartments, accommodated paintings, mainly French works of the 18th century and sculptures from the Polignac collection. The decorations were the work of Johann Christian Hoppenhaupt the Younger, one of the masters of Potsdam Rococo after 1750.
The guest rooms west of the Marble Hall have a unified room design. Opposite the windows in each is a bed alcove next to concealed doors that opened either into a wardrobe room or into the northern servants' quarters. After the simple design of the first three rooms, of which only the first stands out through murals painted by Friedrich Wilhelm Höder in the chinoiserie style, the wealth of decoration in the Voltaire Room comes as a surprise. The room bears the name of the famous French philosopher, who was a guest of the king in Berlin from 1750 to 1753 but apparently never occupied this room; his apartment was in the Potsdam City Palace. The walls are in the fashionable Chinese style, as is the painting in the first guest room, but it gained its present furnishings as early as 1752/53. Johann Hoppenhaupt the Younger is the master of the animals

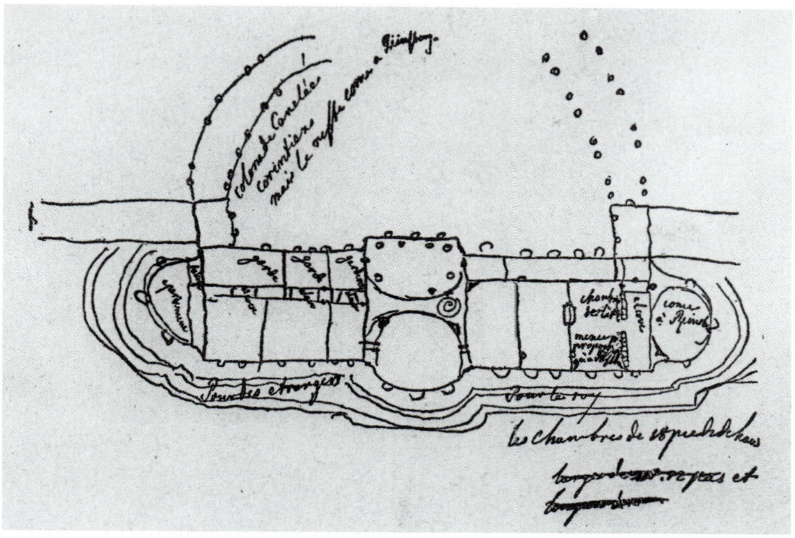

Grundriss des Schlosses Sanssouci (Zeichnung II), vermutlich Mitte des Jahres 1744 entstanden, SPSG (seit 1945 verschollen)
Floor Plan of Sanssouci Palace (drawing II), probably drawn mid-1744, SPSG (lost since 1945)

Die westlich des Marmorsaals gelegenen Gästezimmer zeigen eine einheitliche Raumdurchbildung. Den Fenstern gegenüber befindet sich jeweils die Bettnische, durch die daneben gelegene verdeckte Tür gelangt man in einen Schrankraum bzw. in den nördlichen Dienerraum. Nach der einfachen Raumgestaltung der ersten drei Zimmer, von denen sich lediglich das erste durch die Wandmalerei im Stile der Chinoiserie von Friedrich Wilhelm Höder abhebt, überrascht die Dekorationsfülle des sogenannten »Voltaire-Zimmers«. Es trägt seinen Namen nach dem berühmten französischen Philosophen, der 1750 bis 1753 Gast des Königs in Berlin und Potsdam war, dieses Zimmer aber wohl niemals bewohnt hat; seine eigentliche Wohnung befand sich im Potsdamer Stadtschloss. Die Wände waren im Stil der Chinamode, wie im ersten Gästezimmer, bemalt, aber schon 1752/53 erhielt es die heutige Ausstattung. Hoppenhaupt d. J. ist der Meister der in Holz geschnitzten und bemalten Tiere und Früchte an den Wänden. In dieser naturalistischen Dekoration wird die Besonderheit des friderizianischen Rokokos deutlich.
Auf halber Höhe wird das Schloss beiderseits von zwei im Äußeren ganz ähnlichen Gebäuden flankiert, den Neuen Kammern und der Bildergalerie. Eingeschossig, breit gelagert öffnen sie sich mit großen Fenstern zum Park. Gleich dem Schloss tritt die Mitte beider Gebäude leicht hervor und wird durch eine Kuppel betont. Nach Knobelsdorffs Plänen wurde 1747 westlich des Schlosses Sanssouci ein Orangenhaus zur Unterbringung von Kübelpflanzen, die in den Sommermonaten den Garten zierten, erbaut. Das Innere wurde 1771 bis 1774 von Georg Christian Unger, einem Schüler Gontards, in ein Gästehaus mit dem Namen »Neue Kammern« umgewandelt. Der Mittelsaal sowie die drei Räume im östlichen Teil wurden in ihrem Grundriss belassen und zu Gesellschaftsräumen umgestaltet. Von dem im Stil des späten Rokoko geschaffenen Räumen sind der ovale Buffetsaal und die Ovidgalerie hervorzuheben, deren Wände von den Gebrüdern Räntz geschaffene vergoldete Stuckreliefs aus dem Themenkreis der »Metamorphosen« des römischen Dichters Ovid zieren. Im Westen fügen sich sieben Kavalierzimmer an, von denen zwei Intarsienkabinette der Gebrüder Spindler zu den bemerkenswertesten Leistungen zählen.
Die Bildergalerie, auf der östlichen Seite des Schlosses gelegen, ist das erste für die Aufbewahrung von Gemälden bestimmte Gebäude in der Museumsgeschichte. Sie trat an die Stelle eines alten, 1746 errichteten Treibhauses. Der Landbaumeister Johann Gottfried Büring hatte in Anlehnung an das Orangenhaus (Neue Kammern) 1755 den Entwurf allerdings mit einer Kuppel gefertigt. Die Ausführung zog sich infolge des Siebenjährigen Krieges bis 1764 hin.

and fruits carved in wood and painted on the walls. The distinctiveness of Frederician Rococo is evident in this naturalistic decoration.
The palace is flanked on both sides by two buildings similar in their exteriors, the New Chambers and the Picture Gallery. Single-storey and spreading, they open with large windows to the park. As with the palace, the central parts of both buildings protrude and are accented by a cupola. According to Knobelsdorff's plans, an orangery was built west of Sanssouci Palace in 1747 to store the potted plants that adorned the garden in the summer months. The interior was converted into a guest house with the name New Chambers from 1771 to 1774 by Georg Christian Unger, a pupil of Gontard. The middle room as well as three rooms in the eastern section kept their floor plans and were remodeled as assembly rooms. Of the rooms decorated in Late Rococo style, the Oval Buffet Room and the Ovid Gallery, with walls adorned with gilded stucco reliefs by the Räntz brothers on subjects relating to Ovid's "Metamorphoses", are worthy of note. In the west, seven cavalier rooms adjoin, in which two marquetry cabinets by the Spindler brothers are among the most remarkable achievements.
The Picture Gallery to the east of the palace is the first building ever constructed specifically for keeping paintings. It took the place of the old hothouse erected in 1746. The chief architect of the province, Johann Gottfried Büring had finished the design in imitation of the orangery (New Chambers) in 1755, though with a dome. The Seven Years' War delayed its execution until 1764. The room inside almost stretches the entire length of the building; only at the east end is it divided into a cabinet for "small paintings", and at the west end a stairwell that provides direct access to the uppermost terrace. With its well-balanced proportions, its harmonious relationship between length and height, this gallery is one of the most beautiful of German museum rooms. Initially Frederick the Great preferred the works of 18th-century French masters such as Watteau, Lancret and Pater, and furnished Sanssouci Palace with large numbers of them. Later, works of the Italian Renaissance and Flemish and Italian Baroque were added. This change in taste reveals the king's efforts to demonstrate his status with a substantial and important art collection, as did many other absolutist rulers in Europe. As early as 1770, 168 paintings had been collected in the gallery. Now as then, the pictures are separated according to schools and hung close together on the wall opposite the windows. The west wing is reserved for Italian painting, the east is for Flemish. In the Cupola Room, as in the room intended for small-format pictures, works of different schools are brought together.

Skizze zu einem Bacchustempel in Rheinsberg, Anfang 1740 entstanden, Hessische Hausstiftung Eichenzell bei Fulda
Sketches for a Bacchus temple in Rheinsberg, drawn early 1740, Hessische Hausstiftung in Eichenzell near Fulda

Der Innenraum erstreckt sich fast über die ganze Länge des Gebäudes, nur am östlichen Ende sind ein Kabinett für »kleine Schildereyen«, am westlichen ein Treppenhaus, das eine direkte Verbindung zur obersten Terrasse schafft, abgeteilt. In ihrer wohlabgewogenen Proportion, in dem guten Verhältnis von Länge und Höhe, gehört diese Galerie zu den schönsten deutschen Museumsräumen. Friedrich der Große bevorzugte anfangs die Werke französischer Meister des 18. Jahrhundert, wie Watteau, Lancret und Pater, mit denen er Schloss Sanssouci in reicher Zahl ausstattete. Später kamen Werke der italienischen Renaissance sowie des flämischen und italienischen Barock hinzu. In diesem Geschmackswandel offenbart sich das Bestreben des Königs, wie viele andere absolutistische Fürsten Europas, mit einer umfangreichen und bedeutenden Kunstsammlung zu repräsentieren. Die Galerie vereinigte 1770 bereits 168 Bilder. Wie damals sind die Gemälde auch heute noch nach Schulen getrennt und an der den Fenstern gegenüberliegenden Wand in dichter Reihung ausgestellt. Der westliche Flügel ist der italienischen, der östliche der flämischen Malerei vorbehalten. Im Kuppelraum, wie in dem für kleinformatige Bilder vorgesehenen Kabinett sind Werke verschiedener Schulen vereint.
Trotz der Verluste im Zweiten Weltkrieg, die durch adäquate Bilder aus anderen Schlössern ausgeglichen werden konnten, vermittelt die Galerie auch heute noch den Eindruck einer höfischen Galerie des 18. Jahrhunderts. Unter den ausgestellten Bildern sind die Werke der italienischen Meister Bassano, Caravaggio und Reni, besonders aber die der flämischen Maler des 17. Jahrhunderts Rubens und van Dyck zu nennen.
Nach dem Tod Friedrichs des Großen hat der Nachfolger Friedrich Wilhelm II. die Räume des Schlosses Sanssouci nur kurz genutzt. Nach der Heirat mit dem späteren König Friedrich Wilhelm III. hielt sich die Königin Luise in den Jahren 1794 und 1800 im Schloss auf. Ihr Mann, der nunmehrige König Friedrich Wilhelm III., war ebenfalls gern in Sanssouci. Er hatte Friedrich den Großen noch gekannt, auf Paraden erlebt und ihn auch auf dem Totenbett gezeichnet. In einem letzten Brief an die Königin Luise schrieb er am 19. Juni 1810 er »sei im göttlichen Sanssouci zur Teestunde«.
Napoleon besuchte das Schloss im Oktober 1806 und stellte als Schutz vor Plünderungen einen kaiserlichen Schutzbrief aus. Es wurde ausdrücklich verboten, Inventarstücke mitzunehmen; ab Dezember 1806 wurden zur Bewachung des Schlosses drei französische Dragoner einquartiert, die das Schloss zu beschützen hatten.

Despite losses in the Second World War, which were made good with suitable pictures from other palaces, today the gallery still conveys the impression of a court gallery of the 18th century. Among the paintings that deserve mention are works by the Italian masters Bassano, Caravaggio, and Reni; and particularly the 17th-century Flemish paintings by Rubens and van Dyck.
After the death of Frederick the Great, his successor, Frederick William II, used the rooms of the palace only briefly. After her marriage to the future Frederick William III, Queen Louise spent the years 1794 and 1800 in the palace. Her husband, now King Frederick William III, was also fond of Sanssouci. He had known Frederick the Great, experienced him at parades and had also sketched him on his death bed. In a last letter to Queen Louise, he wrote on June 19, 1810, that he "was in divine Sanssouci at teatime."
Napoleon visited the palace in October 1806 and issued an imperial writ of protection to prevent plundering. It was expressly forbidden to take away property of the palace. From December 1806, three French dragoons were billeted for guard duty with orders to protect the palace.

Auf dem Hügel steht die Sommerresidenz Friedrichs II. in Potsdam. Davor liegen, nach Süden ausgerichtet, die sechs Weinbergterrassen. Begrenzt wird das Parterre durch einen Wasserlauf mit einer von Ludwig Persius 1833/34 entworfenen Brücke. Die Tritonen und Nereiden auf dem Geländer schuf Karl Friedrich Schinkel.

Frederick II's summer residence is on the hill in Potsdam. In front of it, facing south, are six vineyard terraces. The parterre is bounded by a watercourse with a bridge designed in 1833/34 by Ludwig Persius. The tritons and nereids in the grounds were designed by Karl Friedrich Schinkel.

Über einen Kanal, der den Hauptweg seitlich nach Süden begrenzt, blickt man auf den Weinberg. Ursprünglich waren nur die Nischen verglast, dieser Zustand wurde zwischen 1979 und 1983 wiederhergestellt, nachdem der Weinberg seit Ende des 18. Jahrhunderts vollständig verglast gewesen war.

There is a view of the vineyard from across a canal that borders the main promenade on the southern side. Originally only the alcoves were encased in glass; the vineyard was restored to this condition between 1979 and 1983, after it was completely glassed in from the late 18th century.

Das nach Skizzen Friedrichs des Großen und Entwürfen G. W. v. Knobelsdorffs errichtete Schloss wird in der Mitte durch eine Kuppel betont. 36 Hermen von F. Chr. Glume rahmen die großen Fenster.

The palace designed by G. W. v. Knobelsdorff according to sketches by Frederick the Great is accented by a dome in the middle. 36 hermes figures by F. C. Glume frame the large windows.

Unten: Nach Norden bildet eine halbkreisförmige Kolonnade einen Ehrenhof; die zwei Reihen schlanker korinthischer Doppelsäulen setzen sich auch am Hauptbau fort. Im 18. Jahrhundert standen zwischen den Säulen Orangen- oder Lorbeerbäume.
Bottom: A cour d'honneur is formed to the north by a semicircular colonnade; the two rows of slender Corinthian double columns are also continued in the main building. Orange and laurel trees stood between the columns in the 18th century.

Rechts: Im Marmorsaal, der auch als Speisesaal diente und erst 1748 fertig wurde, fanden die berühmten Tafelrunden Friedrichs des Großen statt, an denen u. a. auch der französische Philosoph Voltaire während seines Potsdamer Aufenthaltes zwischen 1750 und 1753 teilnahm.
Right: Frederick the Great's famous round tables took place in the Marble Room, which also served as a dining room and was first completed in 1748. Among others, the French philosopher Voltaire participated in them during his stay in Potsdam between 1750 and 1753.

Rechts: Das ehemalige Arbeits- und Schlafzimmer Friedrichs des Großen war noch im Todesjahr des Königs 1786 von Friedrich Wilhelm von Erdmannsdorff im klassizistischen Sinne für Friedrich Wilhelm II. umgestaltet worden.

Right: The former study and bedchamber of Frederick the Great was redesigned by Friedrich Wilhelm von Erdmannsdorff in neoclassical style for Frederick William II in 1786, the year of Frederick the Great's death.

Die Dekoration des Konzertzimmers geht vermutlich auf einen Entwurf J. A. Nahls zurück. Die Ausführung übernahm Johann Michael Hoppenhaupt d. Ä. Die Gemälde mit Motiven aus den »Metamorphosen« des Ovid stammen von A. Pesne. In den Gesamteindruck des Raumes fügen sich die vergoldete Ornamentik und auch die Stukkaturen der Decke harmonisch ein.

The decoration of the Music Room was probably based on a design by J. A. Nahl. Johann Michael Hoppenhaupt the Elder undertook its execution. The paintings with themes from Ovid's "Metamorphoses" are by A. Pesne. The gilded ornamentation and the stucco work of the ceiling harmoniously blend into the overall effect of the room.

Die mit kostbarem Zedernholz getäfelte und mit vergoldeten Bronzeornamenten verzierte Bibliothek ist ein in sich geschlossener Rundraum und wiederholt den Raumtyp von Rheinsberg. Er ist nur von den Wohnräumen des Königs durch einen schmalen Gang zugänglich.

Paneled in precious cedar wood and decorated with gilded bronze ornaments, the library is a self-contained circular room and a repeat of the room in Rheinsberg that served as a model. It is only accessible through a narrow passageway from the king's apartments.

Die lang gestreckte Kleine Galerie, die ihr Licht durch fünf große Fenster vom Ehrenhof erhält, war für die Aufbewahrung von Gemälden und Skulpturen bestimmt. Antike Bildwerke und Gemälde der französischen Rokoko-Malerei von ihren Hauptvertretern Watteau, Lancret und Pater schmücken die Wände.

The long and narrow Little Gallery, which is lit by five large windows, was intended for the display of paintings and sculptures. Classical sculptures, and paintings by Watteau, Lancret, and Pater, the major representatives of French Rococo painting, decorate the walls.

Links: Das am Ende der Enfilade gelegene Vierte Gästezimmer war ursprünglich, wie heute noch das erste Gästezimmer, im Stil der Chinamode bemalt. Bereits fünf Jahre nach seiner Fertigstellung wurde es 1752/53 mit einer von Friedrich Christian Hoppenhaupt d. J. geschaffenen Ornamentik umgestaltet.

Left: The fourth room, situated at the end of the enfilade, was originally painted in the fashionable Chinese style, as the first guest room still is today. In 1752/53, only five years after its completion, it was redesigned with decoration by Friedrich Christian Hoppenhaupt the Younger.

Die den Park von Ost nach West durchziehende Hauptallee wird durch Rondelle unterbrochen. Eins davon ist das sogenannte Musenrondell mit Skulpturen, die F. Chr. Glume nach Zeichnungen von G. W. v. Knobelsdorff schuf.

The main promenade that passes through the park from east to west is punctuated by rondels. One is the so-called Rondel of the Muses with sculptures by F. C. Glume based on sketches by G. W. v. Knobelsdorff.

Links oben: Auf halber Höhe des Berges wird das Schloss Sanssouci von zwei Gebäuden flankiert. Auf der östlichen Seite ist es die Bildergalerie, die 1755 – 64 von Johann Gottfried Büring gebaut wurde.
Top left: Sanssouci Palace is flanked by two buildings half-way up the hill. On the eastern side is the Picture Gallery, built by Johann Gottfried Büring between 1755 and 1764.

Links unten: Die Galerie beherbergt die Gemäldesammlung Friedrichs des Großen mit Werken italienischer und flämischer Barockmeister.
Bottom left: The gallery houses Frederick the Great's collection of paintings with works by Italian and Flemish Baroque masters.

Rechts: Auf der Westseite des Schlosses Sanssouci befindet sich die 1747 von G. W. v. Knobelsdorff geschaffene Orangerie. Sie wurde von 1771–74 von Georg Christian Unger im Inneren zu einem Gästehaus umgebaut.
Right: On the west side of Sanssouci Palace is the orangery, built by von G. W. v. Knobelsdorff in 1747. Between 1771 and 1774, its interior was converted into a guesthouse by Georg Christian Unger.

Links: Der Jaspissaal ist der erste große Raum, den der Besucher betritt. Wände und Fußboden sind mit Jaspis belegt und auf den Konsolen stehen antike Büsten. Das Gemälde von Johann Christoph Frisch von 1774 zeigt »Venus mit ihrem Gefolge«.
Left: The Jasper Hall is the first large room that the visitor enters. Its walls and floor are covered with jasper, and classical busts are on the consoles. The painting by Johann Christoph Frisch from 1774 shows "Venus with her Entourage".

Unten: Auf der westlichen Seite der Neuen Kammern liegen im Inneren die Gästezimmer. Eines davon ist das sogenannte »Große Intarsienkabinett«, das 1772 von den Brüdern Johann Friedrich (d. Ä.) und Heinrich Wilhelm (d. J.) Spindler geschaffen wurde.
Bottom: The guest rooms are inside the New Chambers on the west side. One of them is the so-called Large Intarsia Room built in 1772 by the brothers Johann Friedrich (the Elder) and Heinrich Wilhelm (the Younger) Spindler.

Rechts: Die lang gestreckte sogenannte Ovidgalerie ist mit vergoldeten Reliefs der Brüder Johann David und Johann Lorenz Wilhelm Räntz geschmückt, deren Thematik aus den »Metamorphosen« des Ovid entnommen ist.
Right: The long and narrow Ovid Gallery is decorated with gilded reliefs by the brothers Johann David and Johann Lorenz William Räntz, with motifs taken from Ovid's "Metamorphoses".

Das Neue Palais im Park von Sanssouci. Das Belvedere und das Drachenhaus Potsdam

New Palace in Sanssouci Park. Belvedere and Dragon House Potsdam

Am Ende der den gesamten Park von Ost nach West durchziehenden Hauptallee erhebt sich das größte Bauwerk des 18. Jahrhunderts im Park Sanssouci, das Neue Palais. Für den Sommeraufenthalt der königlichen Familie und fürstlicher Gäste bestimmt, ist es zugleich auch die bauliche Manifestation Preußens, die zeigen sollte, dass der Staat nach dem Siebenjährigen Krieg nicht am Ende seiner finanziellen Kräfte war.
Erste Pläne für einen größeren Schlossbau hatten schon 1755 Johann Gottfried Büring und Heinrich Ludewig Manger angefertigt. Sie lagen auch der späteren Ausführung ab 1763 zugrunde. Noch einmal versuchte Friedrich der Große die Vorstellung von einer barocken Königsresidenz zu verwirklichen. So wurden für die Lage als auch für die architektonische Durchbildung des Neuen Palais Kupferstiche aus dem beginnenden 18. Jahrhundert, wie der »Fürstliche Baumeister« (1711–16) von Paul Decker und die »Prospecte« der Schlösser des preußischen Königs Friedrich I. von J. B. Broebes (Augsburg 1733) zu Rate gezogen. Ursprünglich war beabsichtigt, das Neue Palais an der Havel in Verlängerung der kurzen Tiefenachse des Schlosses Sanssouci zu errichten. Aber erst nach dem Siebenjährigen Krieg konnte das Projekt ausgeführt werden. Als neuer Standort wurde das westliche Ende der Hauptallee gewählt.
Nach nur sieben Jahren war 1769 der gesamte Palais-Komplex mit den Communs und den Kolonnaden fertig gestellt. Der Landbaumeister Johann Gottfried Büring leitete bis zu seinem Weggang 1764 den Bau. Seine Stelle übernahm 1765 Carl von Gontard, der schon ein Jahr zuvor mit vielen Künstlern und Bauhandwerkern aus Bayreuth nach Potsdam gekommen war. Der Außenbau war zu diesem Zeitpunkt schon soweit fortgeschritten, dass Gontard im Wesentlichen nur auf die Dispositionen der Innenräume und deren Ausstattung Einfluss nehmen konnte.
Mit der großen Kuppel auf dem Mittelteil korrespondieren jeweils eine kleine auf den niedrigen Anbauten. Zur Auflockerung trägt der reiche Figurenschmuck vor den Pilastern und auf der Balustrade bei. Viele Figurenbildhauer haben daran ihren Anteil. Dem von seitlichen Flügeln begrenzten Ehrenhof gegenüber liegt die großartige Architekturkulisse der Communs. In diesen Gebäuden waren Küche und Wirtschaftsräume sowie Quartiere für die Dienerschaft und den Hofstaat untergebracht. Sie hatten aber auch die Aufgabe, die gesamte Schlossanlage gegen das dahinter liegende reizlose Ödland wirkungsvoll abzuschließen. Die beiden an Villenbauten Palladios erinnernden Communs verbindet eine weit ausschwingende Kolonnade mit einem Triumphbogen in der Mitte. Für die Gestaltung ist Gontard verantwortlich, der 1766 bis 1769 auch die Ausführung leitete, dies geschah auf der

The grandest 18th-century building in Sanssouci Park, the New Palace, stands at the end of the main promenade that crosses the whole park from east to west. Designed as a summer residence for the royal family and princely guests, it is at the same time an architectural manifestation of Prussia, intended to demonstrate that the state finances were not exhausted after the Seven Years' War.
Initial plans for a larger palace building had already been drawn up in 1755 by Johann Gottfried Büring and Heinrich Ludewig Manger. They were also the basis of the later work that began in 1763. Once again, Frederick the Great attempted to realize his idea of a Baroque royal residence. Copperplate engravings from the early 18th century, such as the "Royal Architect" (1711–16) by Paul Decker and the "Prospects of the castles of the Prussian King Frederick I" by J. B. Broebes (Augsburg 1733), were consulted for the positioning as well as the architecture of the New Palace. Originally, the New Palace was to be built on the Havel River as an extension of the short main axis of Sanssouci Palace, but the project could not be carried out until after the Seven Years' War. The western end of the main promenade was chosen as the new site.
In 1769, after only seven years, the whole palace complex with the Communs and the colonnades was completed. The state architect Johann Gottfried Büring was in charge of the work until he departed in 1764. Carl von Gontard, who took his place in 1765, had come from Bayreuth to Potsdam a year earlier with many artists and building craftsmen. The exterior had progressed so far by this stage that Gontard was essentially only able to influence the planning and decoration of the interior.
A small dome on each of the low annexes corresponds to the great dome on the middle section. The abundant decorative figures in front of the pilasters and on the balustrade help to make the façade lighter. Many sculptors were involved in this work. Opposite the cour d'honneur, which is bounded by the palace wings, lay the Communs, a magnificent architectural stage-set. The kitchen and utility rooms as well as quarters for the servants and members of the royal household were accommodated here. These buildings also had the task of effectively screening the whole palace complex from the unattractive, uncultivated land behind. The two Communs, reminiscent of villas by Palladio, are connected by a deeply curving colonnade with a triumphal arch at the center. From 1766 until 1769 Gontard, who was responsible for the design, was also in charge of the construction, which was carried out according to building plans of the French architect Jean Legeay.
Today the University of Potsdam occupies the Communs and the buildings behind.

Grundlage von Plänen des französischen Baumeister Jean Legeay.
In den Communs und den Gebäuden dahinter ist heute die Potsdamer Universität untergebracht.
Für die innere Anordnung des Neuen Palais waren weiterhin die Regeln des französischen Barock maßgebend. Charakteristisch für diesen Bau ist das Fehlen einer repräsentativen, in Süddeutschland besonders ausgeprägten Treppenanlage. Da das Schloss in erster Linie den Verwandten des Königs als Wohnstätte zu dienen hatte, ist es in einzelne Appartements eingeteilt, die über vier Treppen zu erreichen sind. Die Appartements besitzen Schlafräume, Schreibkabinette und Gesellschaftsräume. Hinzu kommen große Festsäle und ein Theater.
Bei der Innendekoration hielt man an den Stilelementen des Rokoko fest. Stärker noch als beim Voltaire-Zimmer im Schloss Sanssouci ist hier die besondere Eigenheit des friderizianischen Rokoko in dem wirkungsvollen Gegensatz zwischen den glatten Wandflächen und dem reichen Ornament spürbar. Blumen, Früchte, Tiere, Putten und allerlei Beiwerk verbinden sich in manchmal geradezu verwirrender Vielfalt mit der Rocaille. Allerdings sind Phantasie und Erfindungsgabe nicht mehr so reich, so dass man auf vorhandene Vorbilder zurückgriff, was auch mit den konservativen Vorstellungen des Bauherren zusammenhängt. Beim Marmorsaal wurde die Gestaltung des gleichnamigen Raumes im Potsdamer Stadtschloss aufgenommen.
Dem wahrscheinlich mit der Leitung eines großen Teils der Innendekoration beauftragen jüngeren Hoppenhaupt standen eine Vielzahl von Zieraten-Bildhauer wie Melchior Kambly und Peter Schwitzer, Stukkateure wie Merck, Pedrozzi und Sartori und Lackierer wie Martin und Chevalier zur Seite. Von hohem handwerklichen Können zeugen die Einlegearbeiten der Fußböden von den Gebrüdern Spindler. Auch viele der mit kostbaren Materialien versehenen Kommoden, zu denen Kambly in seiner Fabrik die Bronzebeschläge anfertigte, sind ihr Werk. Die große Anzahl von Gemälden, Skulpturen und Werken der Kleinkunst runden das prächtige Bild.
Der König selbst ließ sich in dem kleinen südlichen Seitenflügel einige Räume einrichten, die bereits 1765 fertig waren und zu den schönsten des Schlosses gehören. Die Festräume weisen gegenüber den Gesellschaftsräumen einen mehr architektonisch betonten Aufbau auf und sind deshalb wohl in erster Linie Gontard zuzuschreiben. Kühl und vornehm geben sich Marmorgalerie und Marmorsaal, wärmer ist dagegen die Obere Galerie (Tanzsaal) mit den in die Wände eingelassenen Gemälden italienischer Meister, wie Guido Reni, Artemisia Gentileschi und Luca Giordano. Wie sehr die

The precepts of French Baroque still set the standards for the interior layout of the New Palace. A characteristic of this building is the lack of a grand staircase for official representation of the sort particularly characteristic of southern Germany. As the palace was principally intended as a residence for the relatives of the king, it was partitioned into individual apartments accessible by four staircases. The apartments had bedrooms, a writing closet, and rooms for entertaining. In addition, there were large halls of state and a theater.
The interior decoration adhered to the elements of Rococo style. The individuality of Frederician Rococo is even more discernible here, in the effective contrast between the smooth areas of wall and the rich ornaments, than in the Voltaire Room of Sanssouci Palace. Flowers, fruit, animals, putti, and all kinds of embellishments merge with the rocaille in a diversity that can be positively bewildering. The imagination and inventiveness of the interior design, however, were not so strong that existing models could be dispensed with – a fact that can partly be attributed to the conservative views of the king. The Marble Hall was given the same design as the room of the same name in the Potsdam City Palace.
Hoppenhaupt the Younger, who was probably commissioned with a major part of the interior decorating, was assisted by a number of decorative sculptors, such as Melchior Kambly and Peter Schwitzer; stucco plasterers, including Merck, Pedrozzi, and Sartori; and varnishers and painters such as Martin and Chevalier. The inlay work in the floors by the Spindler brothers testifies to a high degree of technical skill. Their work includes many chests of drawers fashioned in precious materials, for which Kambly produced the bronze fittings in his factory. A large number of paintings, sculptures, and smaller works of art round out the magnificent ensemble.
The king himself had some rooms fitted out in the small southern side wing. They were already finished in 1765, and are among the most beautiful in the palace. In contrast to the halls for festivities, the assembly rooms exhibit a more architectural design, and for that reason should probably be ascribed first and foremost to Gontard. The Marble Gallery and Marble Hall make a cool and elegant impression; the Upper Gallery (ballroom), on the other hand, is warmer, with paintings by such Italian masters as Guido Reni, Artemisia Gentileschi and Luca Giordano set into the wall. The extent to which garden design also influenced the interior is shown in the Grotto Hall, which has large windows opening onto the park (the precious stones were added in the 19th century), and the small Oval Room with its bower design and decoration.
The theater in the main south wing is one of the few 18th-century palace theaters to survive in Germany. It was modeled on the theater in the Potsdam City

Rechts: Das Neue Palais wurde von 1763 – 69 für den Sommeraufenthalt der königlichen Familie und fürstlicher Gäste nach Plänen von Johann Gottfried Büring, Heinrich Ludewig Manger und Carl von Gontard errichtet. Es ist somit das größte Bauwerk des 18. Jahrhunderts in Sanssouci.
Right: The New Palace was constructed between 1763 and 1769 for the summer stays of the royal family and royal guests according to plans by Johann Gottfried Büring, Heinrich Ludewig Manger, and Carl von Gontard. It is thus the largest building of the 18th century in Sanssouci.

Gartenarchitektur auch Einfluss auf die Innenraumgestaltung genommen hat, beweisen der sich zum Park hin mit großen Fenstern öffnende Muschelsaal (die wertvollen Steine sind erst im 19. Jahrhundert hinzugekommen) und das kleine Ovale Kabinett mit seiner laubenartigen Raumbildung und -dekoration.

Das Theater im südlichen Hauptflügel gehört zu den wenigen erhaltenen Schlosstheatern des 18. Jahrhunderts in Deutschland. Bei der Gestaltung griff man auf das von Knobelsdorff 1748 geschaffene Theater im Potsdamer Stadtschloss zurück. Die Sitzreihen wurden dort, abweichend von der bis dahin üblichen Form des italienischen Logentheaters, ähnlich einem antiken Amphitheaters nach hinten ansteigend im Halbkreis geordnet. Beim Theater im Neuen Palais sind nur die ersten Reihen halbkreisförmig, die anderen folgen im flachen Bogen, so dass gegenüber dem Vorbild eine bessere Verbindung zwischen Zuschauerraum und Bühne erreicht wurde. Die Entwürfe für das Theater fertigte Hoppenhaupt d. J. an, er schuf auch die reichen figürlichen und ornamentalen Holzschnitzarbeiten.

Das »Zeitalter der Empfindsamkeit« kündigt sich schon in zwei kleinen Tempelbauten an, die eingebettet in die Natur vor dem Neuen Palais südlich und nördlich der Hauptallee liegen: Dem Freundschafts- und dem Antikentempel, beide 1768 von Gontard errichtet. Der Freundschaftstempel ist der Erinnerung an die 1758 verstorbene Schwester von Friedrich dem Großen, der Markgräfin von Bayreuth, gewidmet, während der Antikentempel zur Unterbringung entsprechender Münzen- und Gemmensammlungen, die 1767 erworben wurden, gedacht war.

Der im 18. Jahrhundert außerhalb des eigentlichen Gartenbereiches von Sanssouci gelegene Klausberg (Drachenberg) war 1769 auf seiner Südseite in einen Weinberg verwandelt worden. Ein Jahr später errichtete Gontard für die Winzer ein »Chinesisches Häusgen«, das heute Drachenhaus heißt. Englische Einflüsse, besonders die von William Chambers im Garten von Kew erbaute Pagode, waren wohl anregend für das nochmalige Aufleben der Chinamode, das sich schon im Chinesischen Haus von 1754 bis 1757 von Johann Gottfried Büring gezeigt hatte. Von dem höchsten Punkt des Klausberges überblickt man den ganzen Park Sanssouci. Ein idealer Standort für ein Belvedere, das Georg Christian Unger 1770 bis 1772 errichtete. Das Vorbild entnahm man einem Stich »Del Palazzo dei Cesari« von Francesco Biancini (Verona 1738). Als Vorbild diente das »Macellum des Nero« für dieses letzte und zugleich reizvolle Bauwerk des 18. Jahrhunderts in Sanssouci, das leider im Krieg zerstört, aber in den 90er Jahren des 20. Jahrhunderts mit Hilfe der Messerschmitt-Stiftung wieder aufgebaut wurde.

Palace designed by Knobelsdorff in 1748. There, in a departure from the Italian form of box theaters usual up to that time, the rows of seats were arranged in a semi-circle rising to the rear like a classical amphitheater. In the theater in the New Palace, only the first rows are arranged in semi-circular form; the others follow in a flat arc so that, in contrast to the classical model, the relationship between the auditorium and the stage is closer. The building plans for the theater were finished by Johann Christian Hoppenhaupt the Younger; he also created the rich figure and ornamental woodcarvings.

The onset of the "age of sensibility" can already be perceived in the form of two small temples in a natural setting in front of the New Palace to the north and south of the main promenade: the Temple of Friendship and the Antique Temple, both constructed in 1768 by Carl von Gontard. The Temple of Friendship was dedicated to the memory of the sister of Frederick the Great, the Margravine of Bayreuth, who died in 1758, while the Antique Temple was planned to house coin and cameo collections acquired in 1767.

The southern side of the hill named Klausberg (Drachenberg), which in the 18th century lay outside the garden of Sanssouci, was turned into a vineyard in 1769. A year later, Gontard built a "little Chinese house" for the wine-grower, known today as the Dragon House. English influences, especially the pagoda built by William Chambers in Kew Gardens, probably stimulated the revival of the Chinese style already apparent in the Chinese House built from 1754 to 1757 by Johann Gottfried Büring. The highest point on Klausberg offers a view of the whole of Sanssouci Park, an ideal spot for the belvedere that Georg Christian Unger constructed between 1770 and 1772. The model was taken from an engraving, "The Palace of the Caesars", by Francesco Biancini (Verona 1738). "Nero's Macellum" served as model for this delightful, and at the same time final, building undertaken in the 18th century in Sanssouci. It was unfortunately destroyed in the war, but was rebuilt in the 1990s with the help of the Messerschmitt Foundation.

An der Westseite bilden die Seitenflügel einen Ehrenhof, durch den man das Haus betritt. Gegenüber liegen die 1766 – 69 errichteten sogenannten Communs, Wirtschaftsgebäude mit einer entsprechenden gärtnerischen Gestaltung.

The wings form a cour d'honneur through which the house is entered. Opposite are the so-called Communs, constructed between 1766 and 1769, and the utility buildings with a matching garden design.

Der »Grotten- oder Muschelsaal« liegt in der Mitte des Schlosses. Die schlichte Grottierung des 18. Jahrhunderts wurde besonders am Ende des 19. Jahrhunderts durch Schmucksteine und seltene Mineralien bereichert. Der eingelegte schöne Marmorfußboden sowie die Grottierung schufen Johann Michael Kambly und Matthias Müller.

The Grotto Hall (or Shell Hall) is in the middle of the palace. The simple grotto effects of the 18th century were enriched through gemstones and rare minerals, especially at the end of the 19th century. The beautiful inlaid marble floor as well as the grotto effects were created by Johann Michael Kambly and Matthias Müller.

Die Marmorgalerie war der Speisesaal. Große Fenstertüren zum Garten und korrespondierende Spiegelnischen an der gegenüberliegenden Wand bestimmen die Architektur des Raumes. Das dreiteilige Deckengemälde von Bernhard Rode ist eine allegorische Darstellung der Tageszeiten.

The Marble Gallery was the banquet hall. Large French windows to the garden and matching mirrored alcoves in the opposite wall dominate the architecture of the room. The three-part ceiling painting by Bernhard Rode is an allegorical depiction of the times of day.

Der von C. v. Gontard in Anlehnung an den gleichnamigen Raum im Potsdamer Stadtschloss gestaltete »Marmorsaal« im Obergeschoss ist der Festsaal im Neuen Palais. Das große Deckengemälde von C. A. P. van Loo stellt den Olymp mit den zum Mahl versammelten Göttern dar. Die vier großen Gemälde schufen die Maler A. Pesne, B. Rode und C. A. P. van Loo. Die zwölf Marmorstatuen aus dem Berliner Stadtschloss, um 1688 von Bartholomeus Eggers geschaffen, stellen acht brandenburgische Kurfürsten sowie Julius Cäsar, Kaiser Constantin, Karl den Großen und Rudolf von Habsburg dar. Der kostbare Fußboden ist ein Werk Melchior Kamblys.

On the upper storey is the Marble Hall by C. v. Gontard, based on the hall of the same name in the Potsdam City Palace. It is the state room in the New Palace. The large ceiling painting by C. A. P. van Loo depicts Mount Olympus with the gods gathered for a feast. The four large paintings were done by the artists A. Pesne, B. Rode, and C. A. P. van Loo. The twelve marble statues from the Berlin City Palace, done around 1688 by Bartholomeus Eggers, portray eight Brandenburg electors, as well as Julius Caesar, Emperor Constantine, Charlemagne, and Rudolf von Habsburg. The lavish floor is the work of Melchior Kambly.

Links oben: Auch Friedrich der Große hatte im Neuen Palais eine Wohnung, die sich im niedrigen Südflügel befand. Das erste Vorzimmer der Königswohnung ist die »Blaue Kammer«. Als Gemäldekabinett nach einem älteren Entwurf von J. M. Hoppenhaupt d. Ä. gestaltet, befinden sich hier Bilder flämischer, italienischer und französischer Meister. Auf Konsolen in der Lisenengliederung der Wand stehen Vasen aus Meißner Porzellan, geschaffen um 1750.

Top left: Frederick the Great also had an apartment in the lower south wing of the New Palace. The antechamber of the royal apartment is the Blue Chamber. Fashioned as a picture gallery based on an earlier design by J. M. Hoppenhaupt the Elder, paintings by Flemish, Italian, and French masters are to be found here. Vases of Meissen porcelain, created around 1750, are on the consoles in the pilaster strip divisions of the walls.

Links unten: Das Konzertzimmer in der Königswohnung erinnert an den Raum im Schloss Sanssouci. Statt der Wandgemälde sind es hier reich geschnitzte Täfelungsfelder. Zur Originalausstattung gehört das Hammerklavier von Gottfried Silbermann sowie die beiden Konsoltische an der Fensterwand mit Platten vom schlesischen Chrysopras, einem Lieblingsstein Friedrichs des Großen.

Bottom left: The Music Room in the royal apartment is reminiscent of the room in Sanssouci Palace. Instead of frescoes, here there are rich carvings on the paneling. The original furnishings included the piano by Gottfried Silbermann, as well as the two console tables against the wall on the window side with tops of Silesian chrysopras, one of Frederick the Great's favorite materials.

Rechts: In dem hellen »Eckkabinett« im Oberen Fürstenquartier sind die reichen versilberten Bildhauerarbeiten mit Rocaillen und Puten hervorzuheben. Die Decke in Grisaillemalerei stellt die vier Jahreszeiten dar. Den reich eingelegten Fußboden schufen die Gebrüder Spindler. Die Räume der oberen Etage dieses Flügels wurden im 19. Jahrhundert von Kronprinz Friedrich Wilhelm (Kaiser Friedrich III.) und seiner Gemahlin Victoria und von 1888 bis 1908 von Kaiser Wilhelm II. und der Kaiserin Auguste Victoria bewohnt.

Right: A notable feature of the bright Corner Closet in the Upper Princes' Quarter are the richly silvered works of sculpture with rocailles and putti. The ceiling in grisaille painting depicts the four seasons. The sumptuous inlaid floor was the work of the Spindler brothers. The rooms of the upper storey of this wing were occupied by Crown Prince Frederick William (Emperor Frederick III) and his wife Victoria in the 19th century, and from 1888 until 1908 by Emperor William II and Empress Augusta Victoria.

Im südlichen Hauptflügel des Neuen Palais befindet sich ein Theater, das zu den wenigen erhaltenen Spielstätten dieser Art in Deutschland gehört. Die Entwürfe fertigte F. Chr. Hoppenhaupt d. J. in Anlehnung an das schon seit 1801 nicht mehr erhaltene, von G. W. v. Knobelsdorff geschaffene Theater im Potsdamer Stadtschloss an. Seit Eröffnung des Theaters 1768 wird dort bis heute ununterbrochen gespielt.

The theater in the southern wing of the New Palace is among the few surviving ones of its kind in Germany. The building plans by F. C. Hoppenhaupt the Younger were based on the theater in the Potsdam City Palace, a work by G. W. v. Knobelsdorff that was destroyed in 1801. Since the opening of the theater in 1768, performances have been staged there without interruption up to the present.

Links: Außerhalb des eigentlichen Gartenbereiches ließ Friedrich der Große einen Weinberg anlegen und 1770 durch C. v. Gontard ein Haus für den Winzer im Stil einer chinesischen Pagode errichten.
Left: Outside the actual garden grounds, Frederick the Great had a vineyard laid out and a house for the wine-grower built in the style of a Chinese pagoda in 1770 by C. v. Gontard.

Rechts: Auf dem Weinberg baute G. Chr. Unger von 1770 – 72 ein Belvedere nach dem Vorbild eines antiken Bauwerkes. Das Gebäude, das einen Überblick über die ganze Anlage von Sanssouci bietet, war in den letzten Tagen des Zweiten Weltkrieges zerstört worden und wurde in den 1990er Jahren wieder aufgebaut.
Right: Between 1770 and 1772, G. C. Unger constructed a Belvedere based on classical architecture on top of the vineyard hill. The structure, which offered a view of the whole grounds of Sanssouci, was destroyed in the last days of the Second World War and rebuilt in the 1990s.

Anton Graff

Königin Elisabeth Christine in Witwentracht, nach 1786, SPSG
Queen Elizabeth Christina in Widow's Dress, after 1786, SPSG

Königin
Elisabeth Christine
Queen Elizabeth Christina
reg. 1740–1786

Schloss Schönhausen
Berlin

Schönhausen Palace
Berlin

Schloss Schönhausen wurde 1662 als Landsitz der Familie von Dohna errichtet. Danach ist es mehrfach von J. A. Nering und J. F. Eosander umgebaut worden und kam 1691 in den Besitz des Kurfürsten Friedrich III. Von 1740 – 97 war es Wohnsitz der Königin Elisabeth Christine, der Gemahlin Friedrichs des Großen. Von 1949 – 59 war es die Residenz des Präsidenten der DDR, Wilhelm Pieck, später Gästehaus. Zurzeit wird es restauriert.

Schönhausen Palace was built in 1662 as the country residence of the von Dohna family. Thereafter, it was repeatedly remodeled by J. A. Nering and J. F. Eosander and in 1691 came into the possession of Elector Frederick III. From 1740 to 1797, it was the residence of Queen Elizabeth Christina, the wife of Frederick the Great. From 1949 to 1959, it was the residence of the president of the GDR, Wilhelm Pieck, and later a guesthouse.
At present, it is being restored.

Schloss Schönhausen Berlin

Schönhausen Palace Berlin

Schloss Schönhausen ist geschichtlich eng mit Elisabeth Christine, der Frau Friedrichs des Großen, verbunden. Sie besaß es ab 1740 bis zu ihrem Tod 1797. Der Ort, der heute ein Stadtteil von Berlin ist, wird bereits 1375 im Landbuch Kaiser Karls IV. genannt. Seit dem 16. Jahrhundert erfolgte der Ausbau des Gutes, das seit 1624 im Besitz der Familie von Dohna war. 1662 begann die Trockenlegung des Geländes, auf dem bald danach ein »petit palais« errichtet wurde. Nach dem Tod der Gräfin und des Grafen Dohna verkauften es ihre Söhne an den kurfürstlichen Geheimrat Joachim Ernst von Grumbkow. Das bestehende Schloss wird bei Nicolai (1786) wie folgt beschrieben: »Das Grumbkousche Haus war nur ein Wohnhaus, von drey Geschossen, welches in der Mitte der vollen Frontt, nach dem Platze zu, eingerückt, und mit einem Balkon, der auf zwey untermauerten Pfeilern ruhet, versehen war: der Saal ging durch alle drey Geschosse.«

Nach dem Tod Grumbkows im Jahre 1690 erwarb der Kurfürst Friedrich III. 1691 Schloss und Park. Der Baumeister Johann Arnold Nering führte Veränderungen an dem Bau durch. Das Haus bestand in dieser Zeit aus sieben Achsen mit zwei Geschossen, einem Mezzanin sowie einem Satteldach. Auf der Hofseite war ein einachsiger und auf der Gartenseite ein dreiachsiger Mittelrisalit der Fassade vorgelagert.

In diesem Haus fanden die geheimen Verhandlungen über die vom Kurfürsten Friedrich III. beabsichtigte Rangerhöhung zum König statt, die im November 1700 abgeschlossen wurden. Der brandenburgische Kurfürst musste für die österreichischen Ansprüche auf die spanische Erbfolge 8000 Mann seines Heeres zur Verfügung stellen. Er durfte sich aber nicht König »von« Preußen, sondern nur König »in« Preußen nennen. Diese Lösung fand man im Schloss Schönhausen. Am 18. Januar 1701 wurde der Kurfürst im Königsberger Schloss zum König in Preußen gekrönt.

Nach 1704 wurde Johann Friedrich Eosander, genannt von Göthe, mit Veränderungen des Schlosses beauftragt. Es entstand eine repräsentative Dreiflügelanlage mit Satteldach und seitlichen Pavillons, die aber nur ein Geschoss hoch waren. Nicolai (1786) schreibt darüber: »Eosander baute 1708 an den Seiten, in gerader Linie mit der Fronte nach dem Garten, noch zwey kleine, in halber Tiefe des Schlosses erhaltende, Pavillone, von Einem Geschoss, mit niedrigen Dächern nach italiänischer Art, mit einem Brustgeländer eingefasst, worauf kleine Statuen von Kindern standen. Jeder Pavillon war von einer Kammer und zwey Kabinetten.«

Mit dem Umbau des Schlosses ging auch eine Veränderung der Gartenanlage einher. Hinzu kamen ein Kammerhaus, ein Domestikenhaus, ein Küchen- und Stallgebäude sowie zwei Wachhäuser.

Schönhausen Palace has close historical links to Elizabeth Christina, the wife of Frederick the Great, who owned it from 1740 until her death in 1797. The village, which is today a borough of Berlin, was mentioned in Emperor Charles IV's land book of 1375. The development of the estate commenced in the 16th century. From 1624 it was the property of the von Dohna family. In 1662 began the draining of land on which a "petit palais" was erected. Following the deaths of the Count and Countess Dohna, their sons sold it to the Electoral Privy Councilor Joachim Ernst von Grumbkow. The existing house was described by Nicolai (1786) as follows: "The Grumbkovian house was but a dwelling-house, of three floors, which is indented in the middle of the front facing the square, and is provided with a balcony resting on two underpinned pillars: the hall went through all three floors."

Elector Frederick III acquired the palace and park in 1691 after the death of Grumbkow in 1690. The architect Johann Arnold Nering carried out alterations to the building. At that time the house consisted of seven bays with two storeys, a mezzanine and a pitched roof. On the courtyard side there was a single-bay middle section, on the garden side a three-bay middle section projecting from the façade.

This house was the venue for secret negotiations, concluded in November 1700, concerning the elevation of Elector Frederick III to the status of king. The Elector of Brandenburg had to make 8,000 men from his army available to defend the Austrian claims to the Spanish succession. However, Elector Frederick III was not allowed to call himself King "of" Prussia, but only King "in" Prussia. This solution was reached in Schönhausen Palace. On January 18th, 1701, the elector was crowned King "in" Prussia in Königsberg Palace.

After 1704, Johann Frederick Eosander, called von Göthe, was commissioned with the alterations to the palace. An imposing three-winged complex was built with a pitched roof and pavilions on the sides, which were, however, only one storey high. Nicolai (1786) wrote about it: "Eosander built in 1708 another two little pavilions on the sides, half as deep as the palace, in a straight line with the garden front, of one storey with a low roof in the Italian style bordered by a parapet upon which stood small statues of children. Each pavilion was of a chamber and two cabinets."

The reconstruction of the palace was accompanied by a change in the design of the garden. A store, a house for servants, buildings for the kitchen and the stable and two guardhouses were added.

Orange, cypress, pomegranate, and myrtle trees and jasmine bushes, aloe, and many other plants uncommon at the time were acquired for the garden.

Johann David Schleuen d. Ä / Johann David Schleuen the Elder

Gartenseite des Schlosses Schönhausen, um 1770, SPSG
Garden Front of Schönhausen Palace, c. 1770, SPSG

Für den Garten wurden Orangen-, Zypressen-, Granat- und Myrtenbäume, Jasminstöcke, Aloe und viele andere in der Zeit seltene Gewächse erworben.
Nach dem Tod des ersten preußischen Königs Friedrich I. am 25. Februar 1713 fiel das Schloss in einen Winterschlaf. Nur der russische Zar Peter I. hielt sich vom 10. bis 14. April 1713 darin auf. Wenig später ließ Friedrich Wilhelm I. das Inventar ins Potsdamer Stadtschloss und in die Berliner Schlösser überführen, vor allem das Porzellan und die Gläser. Der König überließ ab 1715 dem Hofmarschall und Baron Sigismund von Erlach das Anwesen als Wohnung, aber nach dessen Tod 1722 verfielen Schloss und Garten immer mehr, so dass sich der König 1730 gezwungen sah, Reparaturen an den Gebäuden vorzunehmen. Viele der Nebengebäude aber waren nicht mehr zu retten. Die alte Fasanerie war eingegangen und wurde nun als Küchengarten genutzt. Der ursprünglich mit einer Mauer umgebene Garten hatte um 1740 nur noch einen Bretterzaun. Als Baumschule dienten seit 1732 die seitlich gelegenen Küchenquartiere. Für die 1720 verkaufte und wieder erworbene Orangerie wurden 1735 neue Orangeriegewächse und Blumen angeschafft. Um 1740 gab es wieder seltene Gehölze im Garten.
Am 3. August 1740 schenkte der nunmehrige König Friedrich II. seiner Gemahlin Elisabeth Christine Schloss und Park Schönhausen. Sie kannte den Ort bereits seit 1734 und schrieb ihrem Schwiegervater Friedrich Wilhelm I., dass sie diesen Ort desto schöner und reizvoller »fände, je öfter sie ihn sehe«. Das Schloss wurde instand gesetzt und Friedrich II. schrieb ihr: »Ich will tun, was in meinen Kräften steht, um Ihnen bei der Ausschmückung ganz nach ihrem Sinne zu helfen.« Der König hat seine Frau aber später nur ein- oder zweimal in diesem Schloss besucht.
Während des Siebenjährigen Krieges musste die Königin dreimal das Schloss verlassen, am längsten in den Jahren 1760 bis 1763. In dieser Zeit war das Schloss durch Brandschatzungen und Plünderungen österreichischer Truppen verwüstet worden.
Nach der Rückkehr der Königin begannen umfangreiche Wiederherstellungs- und Erweiterungsarbeiten, die der Baudirektor Johann Boumann d. Ä. leitete. Anstelle des Ehrenhofs wurde ein Treppenhaus mit einer prachtvollen zweiarmigen Treppe eingebaut und die Flügel im Norden und Süden auf das Niveau des Mittelbaus gebracht. Auch das Innere erhielt eine prachtvolle Ausstattung mit Tapeten, geschnitzten und vergoldeten Spiegeln und ornamental geschnitzten Türen. Besonders prächtig waren der Festsaal im oberen Geschoss und die beiden Galerien an der Südseite, die marmorierte Galerie und die Zederngalerie, mit Stuckarbeiten von dem Bildhauer

After the death of the first Prussian king, Frederick I, on February 25, 1713, the palace fell into disuse. Only the Russian tsar, Peter I, lodged in the palace from April 10 to 14, 1713. A little later, Frederick William I had the palace furnishings and fittings, above all the porcelain and glassware, transferred to the Potsdam City Palace and the Berlin palaces. In 1715, the king turned the estate over to his major-domo, Baron Sigismund von Erlach, as accommodation; but after von Erlach's death in 1722, the palace and garden became more and more dilapidated, so that the king felt forced to carry out repairs on the buildings in 1730. Many of the outbuildings could no longer be salvaged. The old pheasantry fell into disuse and was now being used as kitchen garden. Around 1740, the garden, which was originally surrounded by a wall, only had a wooden fence. The kitchen quarters on the side had served as a tree nursery since 1732. New orangery plants and flowers were purchased for the orangery, which had been sold in 1720 and then re-acquired in 1735. Around 1740, there were once again rare trees in the garden.
On August 3, 1740, the Frederick II presented Schönhausen Palace and park to his wife, Elizabeth Christina. She had known the place since 1734 and wrote to her father-in-law, Frederick William I, that she found this place the more beautiful and charming "the more often I see it." The palace was restored and Frederick II wrote to her, "I will do whatever is in my power to help you decorate it completely as to your way of thinking." But the king later visited his wife only once or twice in this palace.
During the Seven Years' War, the queen was forced to evacuate the palace three times, the longest being in the years from 1760 and 1763, when the palace was pillaged and burned by Austrian troops.
The queen's return was followed by extensive restoration and enlargement work on the palace, led by the director of works, Johann Boumann the Elder. In place of a cour d'honneur, a staircase with a magnificent double flight of stairs was built and the wings in the north and south were upgraded to the standard of the main building. The interior, too, was renewed and gained superb decoration with wallpapers, carved and gilt mirrors and ornamentally carved doors. The most splendid rooms were the ceremonial hall in the upper storey and the two galleries on the south side, the Marbled Gallery and the Cedar Gallery, decorated with stucco work by the sculptor Johann Michael Graff, who, after finishing the work in Schönhausen, was employed in Rundàle Palace in Estonia.
After the death of Elizabeth Christina in 1792, the palace was seldom occupied, mostly by female members of the royal family. One of the occupants, the Duchess of Cumberland, had a keen interest in the garden and so in March

Rechts: Besonders reizvoll ist das zweiläufige Treppenhaus mit dem geschnitzten Geländer. Das Innere des Schlosses mit Festsaal und den einzelnen Räumen ist derzeit wegen Restaurierungsarbeiten nicht zugänglich.
Right: The double flight of stairs with the carved banisters is particularly charming. The interior of the palace with its Great Hall and the individual rooms is at present inaccessible because of restoration work.

Johann Michael Graff ausgestattet, der nach der Arbeit in Schönhausen in dem estnischen Schloss Rundàle (dt. Ruhental) tätig war.
Nach dem Tod der Königin Elisabeth Christine 1792 wurde das Schloss nur noch selten, meist von weiblichen Mitgliedern der königlichen Familie bewohnt. Eine der Bewohnerinnen, die Herzogin von Cumberland hatte reges Interesse an dem Garten und beantragte im März 1827 Peter Joseph Lenné, den Garten im Landschaftsstil umzuwandeln, was bis 1831 geschah.
Im Laufe des 19. Jahrhunderts verfiel das Schloss immer mehr und wurde nur noch als Manöverquartier und Bilderspeicher genutzt. Der Verfall beschleunigte sich nach dem Ersten Weltkrieg.
Da die damalige »Reichskammer der bildenden Künste« den Bau für Ausstellungszwecke nutzen wollte, begann man 1935 mit der Sanierung. Bis 1936 wurden u. a. das Dach neu gedeckt, eine Heizung eingebaut und die absinkende Haupttreppe durch Eisenkonstruktionen stabilisiert. Weiterhin wurde die dekorative Ausstattung ergänzt und denkmalpflegerisch gesichert, dabei wurden alte Rokokomalereien freigelegt. Im Erdgeschoss wurden zwei Stuckdecken des aus dem späten 17. Jahrhundert stammenden und in den 30er Jahren des 20. Jahrhunderts abgebrochenen »Hohen Hauses« in der Berliner Klosterstraße, dem früheren Quartier des ersten brandenburgischen Kurfürsten, eingebaut.
Das Schloss blieb im Zweiten Weltkrieg unzerstört. Nach 1945 war es zunächst eine Schule für die Kinder der sowjetischen Streitkräfte und nach der Gründung der DDR am 7. Oktober 1949 wurde es der Amtssitz des ersten Präsidenten Wilhelm Pieck. Nach dessen Tod 1960 war es bis zur Vollendung des Staatsratesgebäudes (1964) am ehemaligen Lustgarten in Berlin Tagungsort des Staatsrates unter der Leitung von Walter Ulbricht. Danach wurde es Gästehaus der Regierung, was mit entsprechenden Veränderungen der Räume einherging. Nach der deutschen Einheit am 3. Oktober 1990 übernahm das Bundesfinanzministerium Schloss und Park und im Oktober 1996 übergab die Bundesvermögensverwaltung das Schloss dem Land Berlin.
In der Zeit der politischen Wende 1989/90 war Schönhausen ein hochbrisanter Ort. In dem bei dem Schloss gelegenen Konferenzgebäude tagte der »Runde Tisch«. Seit 2005 gehört das Schloss zur Stiftung Preußische Schlösser und Gärten Berlin-Brandenburg.

1827 Peter Joseph Lenné was commissioned to transform it into a landscape garden, which he did by 1831.
The palace fell into increasing disrepair in the course of the 19th century and was only used as quarters for maneuvers and as a storage facility for paintings. The dereliction accelerated after the First World War.
The restoration of the building was begun in 1935, because the Reich Chamber of Fine Arts wanted to use the palace for exhibitions. By 1936, the building had a new roof, central heating had been installed, and the sagging main staircase was stabilized by iron supports. In addition, the decorations were restored, preserved and added to, a process which exposed old Rococo painting. On the ground floor, two stucco ceilings were installed that had been dismantled from the "Hohes Haus" in Klosterstrasse in Berlin, the late 17th-century former residence of the first electors of Brandenburg, which was being torn down to widen the street.
The palace remained unscathed in the Second World War. After 1945, it was at first a school for the children of the Soviet armed forces and, following the founding of the GDR on October 7, 1949, it was used as the official residence of the president of the GDR, Wilhelm Pieck. After his death in 1960, and until the completion of the Council of State building (1964) in the former Lustgarten (pleasure garden) in Berlin, it was the meeting place of the Council of State under the leadership of Walter Ulbricht. Thereafter it became the official guest house of the government, and the rooms were accordingly altered. The governing mayors of West Berlin, Richard von Weizäcker, Eberhardt Diepgen and, in July 1990, Walter Momper also met Erich Honecker in the palace. After German unification on October 3, 1990, the palace and park were taken over by the German Federal Ministry of Finance. It was managed by the Berlin State Development Corporation, a fiduciary redevelopment agency of the State of Berlin.
During the time leading up to German unification in 1989 – 90, Schönhausen was a highly charged venue. Since 2005 the palace has belonged to the Prussian Palaces and Gardens Foundation Berlin-Brandenburg.

Gottlieb Doepler

König Friedrich Wilhelm II., 1790, SPSG
King Frederick William II, 1790, SPSG

Anna Dorothea Therbusch

Wilhelmine Encke, geadelte Gräfin Lichtenau, 1776, SPSG
Wilhelmine Encke, ennobled as Countess Lichtenau, 1776, SPSG

König

Friedrich Wilhelm II.

King Frederick William II

reg. 1786–1797

Das Marmorpalais im Neuen Garten Potsdam

Marble Palace in the New Garden
in Potsdam

Die Pfaueninsel Berlin

Peacock Island
Berlin

Die Wohnungen Friedrich Wilhelms II. im Schloss Charlottenburg Berlin

Frederick William II's Apartment in
Charlottenburg Palace
Berlin

Am Ufer des Heiligen Sees liegt das Marmorpalais, die Sommerresidenz König Friedrich Wilhelms II., die 1787–92 von C. v. Gontard und C. G. Langhans errichtet wurde.
On the shores of Heiligensee lake lies the Marble Palace, the summer residence of King Frederick William II, which was built in 1787–92 by C. v. Gontard and C. G. Langhans.

Das Marmorpalais im Neuen Garten Potsdam

Marble Palace in the New Garden Potsdam

Die preußische Geschichtsschreibung hatte meist ihre heroischen Lieblinge. Der König Friedrich Wilhelm II., der Nachfolger seines Onkels Friedrich des Großen, der sechsundvierzig Jahre regierte und schon zu Lebzeiten eine historische Persönlichkeit war, wurde zwangsläufig mit diesen Maßstäben gemessen. Aber welch ein Unterschied zwischen dem wie ein Einsiedler lebenden »Philosophen von Sanssouci« und seinem den Genüssen des Lebens aufgeschlossenen Neffen, der nicht nur zweimal verheiratet, sondern von Mätressen umgeben und sogar mit zwei Damen zur linken Hand getraut war. Eine geradezu rührende Treue bewahrte er jedoch der ehemaligen Trompetertochter Wilhelmine Encke, verehelichte Madame Ritz, die 1795 zur Gräfin Lichtenau erhoben wurde. Sie nahm besonders Einfluss auf die künstlerische Entwicklung der Zeit.
Politisch bestimmend in ganz Europa war in dieser Zeit die Große Französische Revolution von 1789. Preußen beteiligte sich selbstverständlich an den Kriegen gegen die junge Republik, besaß jedoch die Klugheit, sich mit dem Frieden zu Basel 1790 aus den Kämpfen zurückzuziehen.
Bei aller Lockerheit des königlichen Lebens, wovon die Geschichtsschreiber geradezu genüsslich zu berichten wissen, ging es innenpolitisch in der Regierungszeit Friedrich Wilhelms II. nicht so frei zu. Zwar trat 1794 das schon unter Friedrich dem Großen begonnene große Gesetzeswerk, das »Allgemeine Preußische Landrecht« in Kraft, aber besondere Edikte, z. B. das über die Zensur, brachten neue Einschränkungen. Das oft getroffene pauschale Urteil der Geschichte über diesen Monarchen erfordert aber eine differenziertere Betrachtung, besonders auch der Kunst in dieser Zeit. Erst sehr spät, zu Beginn des 20. Jahrhunderts, wurde der Kunst vom Ende des 18. Jahrhundert, die bis dahin im Schatten der friderizianischen und danach Schinkels gestanden hatte, die notwendige Aufmerksamkeit gewidmet. Neben der Periode Friedrichs I. um 1700 und der Friedrichs des Großen zwischen 1740 und 1750 muss auch die Zeit Friedrich Wilhelms II. mit dem aufblühenden Frühklassizismus im letzten Viertel des 18. Jahrhunderts gewürdigt werden. Carl Gotthard Langhans und David Gilly sind die wichtigsten Künstler dieser Zeit. Leider haben Krieg und Nachkrieg viele der von ihnen geschaffenen kostbaren Räume im Berliner Schloss zerstört. Allein die Räume im Schloss und in der Meierei auf der Pfaueninsel sind ohne Schäden geblieben. Friedrich Wilhelm II. ließ Friedrich Wilhelm von Erdmannsdorff noch im Todesjahr Friedrichs des Großen 1786 dessen Arbeits- und Schlafzimmer im Schloss Sanssouci umgestalten, was programmatisch für den neuen Stil war.

Most Prussian historiography had its favorite heroes. King Frederick William II succeeded his uncle Frederick the Great, who reigned for forty-six years and was already an historical figure in his own lifetime, and the nephew was inevitably measured by the standards of the uncle. But what a contrast between the "philosopher of Sanssouci", who lived like a hermit, and his nephew, who enjoyed the pleasures of life, not only married two royal brides but was surrounded by mistresses and even entered into two further, morganatic marriages. However, he maintained a truly touching loyalty to a former trumpeter's daughter, Madame Ritz, née Wilhelmina Encke, who was ennobled as Countess Lichtenau in 1795. She had a particular influence on the artistic development of the time.
It was undoubtedly the great French Revolution of 1789 that defined politics in the whole of Europe at that time. Of course, Prussia took part in the wars against the young French republic, but had the sense to withdraw from the conflict through the Treaty of Basel in 1795.
For all the licentiousness of royal life, about which historians always report with glee, there was not much license in domestic policies during the reign of Frederick William II. Although the great body of law begun by Frederick the Great, the "Prussian General Law", came into force in 1794, special edicts, for example on censorship, brought new restrictions. The often generalized judgment of history on this monarch, however, demands a more precise and subtle assessment, particularly concerning the arts of this period. Only much later, at the beginning of the 20th century, did the art of the late 18th century, which had stood in the shadow of the Frederician style and the subsequent Schinkel style, receive the attention it merits. Alongside the periods of Frederick I around 1700, and of Frederick the Great between 1740 and 1750, the period of Frederick William II with its blossoming early neoclassicism in the last quarter of the 18th century is also worthy of appreciation. Carl Gotthard Langhans and David Gilly were the important artists of this time. Unfortunately, war and the post-war period destroyed many of the precious rooms they created in the Berlin Palace. Only the rooms in the palace and dairy on Peacock Island survived without damage. It should be mentioned that it was primarily Frederick William II who set out a program for the new style by commissioning Erdmannsdorff (1736–1800) to remodel the study and bedchamber in Sanssouci Palace in 1786, the year of Frederick the Great's death.
The early neoclassicism that blossomed under Frederick William II is counted today among the most important and richest periods of Prussian art. This especially holds true for the royal palaces.

Friedrich Ludwig Karl Krüger

Gartenseite des Marmorpalais, um 1797, SPSG
Garden Front of Marble Palace, c. 1797, SPSG

Der unter Friedrich Wilhelm II. aufblühende Frühklassizismus zählt heute zu den bedeutendsten und reichsten Epochen der preußischen Kunstgeschichte. Das gilt besonders für die Königschlösser.
Das Marmorpalais im Neuen Garten, der bedeutendste preußische Schlossbau am Ende des 18. Jahrhunderts, ließ Friedrich Wilhelm II. 1787 bis 1789 durch Carl von Gontard errichten und 1790 bis 1792 durch Carl Gotthard Langhans ausstatten. Da der würfelförmige Bau sich bald als zu klein erwies, erfolgte eine Erweiterung durch Seitenflügel, deren Ausbau aber durch den Tod des Königs unterblieb und erst nach 1840 durch Friedrich Wilhelm IV. vollzogen wurde. Das Schloss hat eine wechselvolle Geschichte: vom königlichen Sommerschloss über den Kronprinzensitz, nach 1918 Museum, während des Zweiten Weltkrieges Heerespoststelle im Nordflügel, durch Bomben beschädigt, nach 1945 sowjetisches Kulturhaus und nach 1961 Armeemuseum der DDR. 1988 kam das Haus wieder zu den Schlösser und Gärten Potsdam-Sanssouci und wurde seitdem mit viel Mühe und erheblichen finanziellen Aufwendungen des Bundes und der Länder Berlin und Brandenburg restauriert. Nach umfangreicher Wiederherstellung konnten 1997 die ersten Räume eröffnet werden; seit 2004 kann man das ganze Schloss im Innern besichtigen. Die Instandsetzung des Außenbaus dauert noch an.

King Frederick William II had the Marble Palace in the New Garden, the most important Prussian palace of the late 18th century, built by Carl von Gontard from 1787 to 1789 and decorated from 1790 to 1792 by Carl Gotthard Langhans. As the cube-shaped building soon proved to be too small, an enlargement through the addition of wings followed, but due to the death of the king, the extensions were only completed after 1840 by Frederick William IV. The palace has had a checkered history as a royal summer palace, a residence for the crown prince, and after 1918 a museum. During the war, an army mail room was in the north wing. It was damaged by bombs, served after 1945 as a Soviet arts and leisure center, and from 1961 was a GDR army museum. In 1988, the house returned to the palace and gardens administration of Potsdam-Sanssouci, and has since been restored with great effort and considerable financial expense by the federal government and the states of Berlin und Brandenburg. After extensive restoration, the first rooms were opened in 1997. Since 2004, the whole interior of the palace has been on view. The renovation of the exterior is still in progress.

Links: Der Grottensaal, der im Sommer wegen der kühlen Raumtemperatur auch als Speisesaal diente, ist als Grotte gestaltet. Die Deckengemälde von B. Rode stellen die Meeresgötter Amphitrite und Poseidon dar. Die Stühle entstanden um 1793 und standen ursprünglich in der Gotischen Bibliothek, die Hocker, um 1791, stammen aus der Orangerie des Neuen Gartens.
Left: The Grotto Room, which also served as a dining room in the summer because it is cool, is fashioned as a grotto. The ceiling painting by B. Rode portrays the sea gods Amphitrite and Poseidon. The chairs date from around 1793 and were originally in the Gothic library; the stools, from around 1791, is from the orangery of the New Garden.

Rechts oben: Der Saal im Obergeschoss war der Konzert- und Festsaal und wurde um 1790 nach einem Entwurf von C. G. Langhans dekoriert. In den ursprünglich lichtblauen Wänden sind Reliefs von Johann Gottfried Schadow mit antiken Fest- und Opferszenen eingelassen. Das Deckengemälde »Aeneas am Ufer des Tiber« fiel 1945 einem Dachstuhlbrand zum Opfer. Der von C. G. Langhans entworfene Parkettfußboden wurde 1999 rekonstruiert. Zur originalen Raumausstattung gehören auch die Kaminvasen aus Wedgwood-Porzellan.
Top right: The room was a concert and banquet hall and was decorated around 1790 based on a design by C. G. Langhans. Classical festive and sacrificial scenes are set into the reliefs by Johann Gottfried Schadow. The walls were originally light blue. The ceiling painting, "Aeneas on the Shores of the Tiber", fell victim to a fire in the attic in 1945. The parquet floor designed by C. G. Langhans was reconstructed in 1999. The fireplace vases of Wedgwood porcelain were also part of the original furnishings.

Rechts unten: Der sogenannte »Kloebersaal« im Nordflügel war ursprünglich ein Schlaf- oder Speisezimmer. Der Historienmaler August Kloeber führte 1845 – 47 die großen Wandgemälde mit mythologischen und allegorischen Darstellungen aus. Eines der Gemälde wurde 1944 bei einem Brand zerstört. Die Stuckmarmorsäulen und der Parkettfußboden wurden 2004 rekonstruiert.
Bottom right: The so-called Kloeber Room in the north wing was originally a bedroom or dining room. The historical painter August Kloeber executed the large-scale wall paintings with mythological and allegorical pictures between 1845 and 1847. One of the paintings was destroyed by a fire in 1944. The stucco marble columns and the parquet floor were reconstructed in 2004.

Links: Die Täfelung des boisierten Schreibkabinettes besteht aus Taxus-, Nussbaum-, Maulbeer- und Ahornholz sowie verschiedenen Obsthölzern und wurde 1790 nach Entwürfen von C. G. Langhans gearbeitet. Während die Deckenmalerei 1954 erneuert wurde, sind Spiegelrahmen und Supraporten erst 1996/97 rekonstruiert worden. In diesem Raum starb Friedrich Wilhelm II. 1797 nach längerer Krankheit.
Left: The paneling of the writing closet is of yew, walnut, mulberry, and maple wood, as well as the wood of various fruit trees, and was finished in 1790 according to plans by C. G. Langhans. While the ceiling painting was renewed in 1954, the mirror frames and supraportes were first reconstructed in 1996/97. Frederick William II died in this room in 1797 after a long illness.

Rechts: Der kleine dreigeschossige Pavillon wurde von C. G. Langhans 1792 – 94 in »gotischen Formen« errichtet. In ihm war die Bibliothek Friedrich Wilhelms II. untergebracht. Da er im sumpfigen Untergrund des Seeufers zu versinken drohte, wurde er 1998 restauriert.
Right: The small three-storey pavilion was erected by C. G. Langhans between 1792 and 1794 in "Gothic forms." It housed Frederick William II's library. As it was threatening to sink into the marshy subsoil, it was restored in 1998.

Die Pfaueninsel Berlin

Peacock Island Berlin

Der Nachfolger Friedrichs des Großen, Friedrich Wilhelm II., hatte nach seiner Thronbesteigung 1786 in Potsdam einen »Neuen Garten« anlegen und ein dazugehöriges Schloss, das Marmorpalais unmittelbar am Heiligen See, errichten lassen. Als die Erweiterung des Garten nach Norden mit der beabsichtigten Errichtung eines neugotischen Belvederes auf dem nahen Pfingstberg, der damals noch Judenberg hieß, aufgrund der immensen Forderungen des Besitzers 1793 scheiterte, richtete sich das Augenmerk des Königs auf die romantische Insel in der Havel, die ihm von Bootsfahrten her bekannt war.
Zum ersten Mal machte sie Ende des 17. Jahrhunderts auf sich aufmerksam, als 1683 an der Westspitze in der Nähe des späteren Schlosses ein Kaninchenjägerhaus für 800 Tiere erbaut wurde. Später wandelte sich der damalige Name Kaninchenwerder in Pfauenwerder um. 1685 schenkte der Große Kurfürst Friedrich Wilhelm die Insel dem Chemiker und Glashersteller Johann Kunkel, der hier experimentierte und die heute noch begehrten Rubingläser herstellte. Nach dem Tod des Kurfürsten im Jahre 1688 und der Vernichtung des Laboratoriumsgebäudes durch Brandstiftung ging Kunkel 1693 nach Schweden. Die Insel fiel an das Gut Bornstedt, das zum Amt Potsdam gehörte und kam mit diesem 1734 zum Potsdamer Militärwaisenhaus.
Friedrich Wilhelm II. erwarb die Insel in der Havel Ende 1793 vom Potsdamer Amt. Da im 18. Jahrhundert viele Wälder, besonders auf den Hügeln um Potsdam, abgeholzt worden waren, legte der König in einer Kabinettsorder für die Insel fest, »dass nicht das geringste an Holz – oder Buschwerk weiter gefällt werden« dürfe. So blieben die 400 Uralteichen auf der Insel erhalten.
Mit der Fassade zum entfernt stehenden Marmorpalais ausgerichtet, entstand 1794/95 das Schloss als »verfallenes römisches Landhaus« mit zwei Türmen, die durch eine Brücke verbunden sind. Das Schlösschen erhielt eine erlesene Innenausstattung. Die Architektur wurde von dem Potsdamer Zimmermeister Johann Gottlieb Brendel ausgeführt. Wichtige Anregungen zu diesem Bau gingen auf die Gräfin Lichtenau, die Mätresse des Königs, zurück. Die Insel wurde durch weitere Parkbauten, wie die um 1795 im Stil eines verfallenen gotischen Gebäudes entstandene Meierei, einen Jacobsbrunnen, ein Kastellanhaus, ein Borkenhäuschen und ein Kavalierhaus verschönert. Wie im Neuen Garten, schaffen die Bauten unterschiedlicher Stile auch hier eine romantische Wirkung. 1795 erhielt das Eiland den Namen Pfaueninsel, als man die vom benachbarten Gut Sacrow stammenden Tiere auf der Insel ansiedelte.
An der Innenausstattung des Schlosses hatte sich die Gräfin Lichtenau maßgeblich beteiligt; die Räume gelten heute als die besterhaltene Wohnung

After his accession to the throne in 1786, Frederick the Great's successor, Frederick William II, had a new garden laid out in Potsdam and a palace to go with it, the Marble Palace, erected directly on the lake named Heiligen See. When an expansion to the north of the garden with the intention of building a neo-Gothic belvedere on nearby Pfingstberg, which at the time was still called Judenberg, failed to come about in 1793 because of the immense financial demands of the owner, the king turned his attention to the romantic island in the Havel that he knew from boat trips.
It had first come to notice at the end of the 17th century, when in 1683 a rabbit breeder's hut for 800 animals was put up on its western tip near the future site of the palace. Later the name Kaninchenwerder (Rabbit Isle) was changed to Pfauenwerder (Peacock Isle). In 1685, the Great Elector Frederick William gave the island to the chemist and glassmaker Johann Kunkel, who experimented there and produced ruby glasses still coveted today. After the death of the elector in 1688 and the destruction of the laboratory building through arson, Kunkel went to Sweden in 1693. The island fell to the Bornstedt estate, which was part of the administrative district of Potsdam, and in 1734 was given with it to the Potsdam military orphanage.
Frederick William II acquired the island in the Havel at the end of 1793 from the Potsdam administrative district. Because many of the woods around Potsdam, particularly on the hills, had been deforested in the 18th century, the king prescribed in a cabinet decree for the island that "not the least of wood – nor bush shall be further felled." And so it was that the 400 ancient oaks on the island survived.
With its façade facing the Marble Palace standing in the distance, the palace was built in 1794/95 as a "dilapidated Roman country manor" with two towers connected by a bridge. The little palace was provided with choice interior decoration. The architecture was carried out by the Potsdam master carpenter Johann Gottlieb Brendel. Significant suggestions for this building originated with Countess Lichtenau, the mistress of the king. The island was brightened up with further buildings in the park such as the dairy, built around 1795 in the style of a Gothic ruin, a Jacob's well, a castellan's house, a little bark-cottage, and a cavalier's house. Here as in the New Garden, the structures created in various styles create a romantic atmosphere. In 1795, the island gained the name Peacock Island when birds from the neighboring Sacrow Estate were introduced to the island.
Countess Lichtenau played a key role in the interior decoration of the palace. The rooms are considered today to be the best-preserved residence from the time of Frederick William II. There is a great hall on the upper floor with

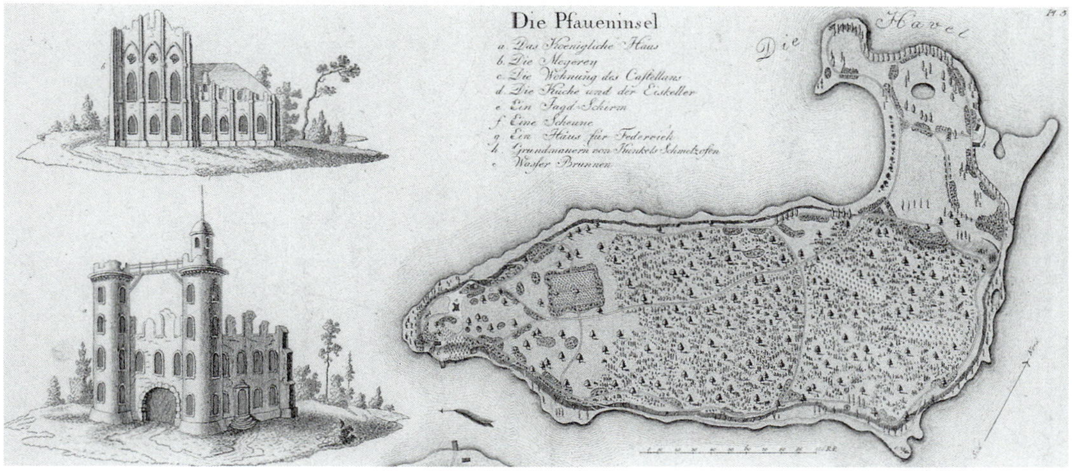

Plan der Pfaueninsel mit Ansichten der Meierei und des Schlosses, 1798, SPSG
Map of Peacock Island with Views of the Dairy and of the Palace, 1798, SPSG

aus der Zeit Friedrich Wilhelms II. Im Obergeschoss befindet sich ein großer Saal mit klassizistischen Wandtäfelungen und einem Deckengemälde von Johann Christoph Fritsch sowie Supraportenreliefs von Johann Christoph und Michael Christoph Wohler nach antiken Vorbildern. Die qualitätsvollen Möbel in den Räumen stammen von Potsdamer Kunsttischlern und orientieren sich an englischen Vorbildern.
Besonders prachtvoll ausgestattet ist ein Raum der Meierei. Während sich im Erdgeschoss eine Molkenstube befindet, öffnet sich im Obergeschoss ein prächtiger gotischer Saal nach Entwürfen von Philipp Boumann d. J. mit Stukkaturen von Constantin Sartori und Wandmalereien von Bartolomeo Verona.
König Friedrich Wilhelm II. starb schon 1797. Sein Nachfolger, Friedrich Wilhelm III., der sonst wenig Ambitionen hatte, in die Wohnungen seines Vaters zu ziehen, schätzte jedoch die Zurückgezogenheit dieser Insel. Vor allem seine Gemahlin, Königin Luise, liebte das Eiland und bevorzugte das Schloss als Aufenthaltsort.
Kurz nach 1800 begann unter dem ersten Hofgärtner Johann Anton Ferdinand Fintelmann die Umwandlung der Insel in eine »ästhetisch geprägte Landwirtschaft« (Seiler) nach dem Paretzer Vorbild. Man baute neue Wirtschaftsgebäude, wie einen Rinderstall und einen Stall für das Federvieh.
Nach dem Tod der Königin Luise 1810 genoss die Pfaueninsel auch weiter das uneingeschränkte Interesse des Königs Friedrich Wilhelm III. Es entstanden mit Schaukeln und Wippen besondere Bauten für Kinder, eine Kegelbahn mit einem russischen Rollberg für das Vergnügen der Erwachsenen. Schinkel baute ab 1823 das einstige Kavalierhaus um und setzte als repräsentative Ansicht die in Danzig von einem spätgotischen Haus abgebrochene Fassade davor.
Als der Sandsteinportikus des Luisen-Mausoleums im Charlottenburger Schlosspark 1829 durch eine Kopie aus rotem Granit ersetzt wurde, stellte man das Original auf der Pfaueninsel mit einer Büste der Königin auf.
Ein baulicher Höhepunkt war zweifellos die Errichtung des Palmenhauses nach dem Entwurf von Karl Friedrich Schinkel und die Ausführung von Albrecht Dietrich Schadow im Jahre 1830/31. Ein Großbrand im Mai 1880 vernichtete aber das ganze Bauwerk, nur die Gemälde von Karl Blechen geben noch heute einen Eindruck vom Inneren des exotisch-orientalischen Gebäudes.
Schon kurz nach 1800 begann man Tiere, einheimische und fremde, auf der Insel anzusiedeln. Diese Menagerie wurde nach 1842 der Grundstock für den späteren Zoologischen Garten. Die Insel verlor zwar dadurch eine Attrak-

classical wall paneling and a ceiling painting by Johann Christoph Fritsch, as well as supraportes with reliefs by Johann Christoph and Michael Christoph Wohler based on classical models. The high-quality furniture in the rooms was made by Potsdam cabinetmakers and inspired by English furniture.
A room in the dairy is especially splendid in its decoration. While there is a milking room on the ground floor, a magnificent neo-Gothic hall opens up on the upper storey. It was designed by Philipp Boumann the Younger with stucco work by Constantin Sartori and wall paintings by Bartolomeo Verona.
King Frederick William II died in 1797. His successor, Frederick William III, who otherwise had little inclination to move into his father's residences, appreciated the seclusion of this island. Above all his consort, Queen Louise, loved the island and made the palace her preferred place of residence.
Shortly after 1800, the first court gardener, Johann Anton Ferdinand Fintelmann, began to direct the transformation of the island into an "aesthetically defined landscape" (Seiler) along the lines of Paretz. New farm buildings were constructed, such as a cattle shed and a coop for fowl.
After the death of Queen Louise in 1810, Peacock Island continued to enjoy the undivided attention of King Frederick William III. Special equipment for the children was installed, like swings and teeter-tooters and, for the enjoyment of the adults, a bowling alley with a Russian slide, a waxed wooden hill with a wheeled sled. Schinkel began remodeling the former cavalier house in 1823 and, for a prestigious effect, gave it a façade that had been dismantled from a late Gothic house in Danzig.
When the sandstone portico of the Queen Louise Mausoleum in Charlottenburg Palace Park was replaced in 1829 with a copy in red granite, the original was placed on Peacock Island, surmounted by a bust of the queen.
An architectural highlight was without a doubt the construction of the House of Palms in the years 1830/31 to Karl Friedrich Schinkel's building plans, which were executed by Albrecht Dietrich Schadow. A major fire in May 1880, however, destroyed the whole structure, and today only a painting by Karl Blechen gives us an idea of the interior of the exotic, oriental building.
Shortly after 1800, the colonization of the island with native and exotic animals had already begun. After 1842, this menagerie became the nucleus of the future Zoological Garden. Although the island lost an attraction in this way, the design of the garden certainly profited. From 1816 to 1834, Peter Joseph Lenné had worked on it together with the court gardener Johann Arnold Ferdinand Fintelmann and created an integrated work of art that had not lost its charm even after the loss of the menagerie and the House of Palms.

Rechts: Das als »verfallenes römisches Landhaus« mit zwei Türmen 1794/95 errichtete Schlösschen wurde von dem Potsdamer Zimmermeister Johann Gottlieb Brendel nach Anregungen der Gräfin Lichtenau entworfen und gebaut.

Right: The little palace was designed and built as a "dilapidated Roman country manor" with two towers in 1794/95 by the Potsdam master carpenter Johann Gottlieb Brendel based on suggestions by Countess Lichtenau.

tion, doch für die gärtnerische Gestaltung war es durchaus ein Gewinn.
Von 1816 bis 1834 hatte Peter Joseph Lenné zusammen mit den Hofgärtner Johann Arnold Ferdinand Fintelmann daran gewirkt und ein Gesamtkunstwerk geschaffen, das auch nach der Aufgabe der Menagerie und dem Verlust des Palmenhauses seinen Reiz nicht verloren hatte.
Schon seit Anfang der 20er Jahre des 19. Jahrhunderts konnten die Berliner und Potsdamer die Pfaueninsel besuchen.
Nach der Revolution 1918 wurde die Insel durch die 1926 gegründete Verwaltung der Schlösser und Gärten übernommen. Um eine wirtschaftlich-kommerzielle Nutzung auszuschließen, wurde sie 1924 unter Naturschutz gestellt, da es ein entsprechendes Gesetz für Gartendenkmalpflege noch nicht gab. Nur wenige Male war die Insel Ort für besondere Veranstaltungen, so 1936 bei der Olympiade und ein Jahr später beim Sommerfest der Nationalsozialistischen Gemeinschaft »Kraft durch Freude«.
Am 26. April 1945, also wenige Tage vor Kriegsende, wurde die Insel durch deutsche Truppen besetzt, aber durch geschickte Verhandlungen konnte sie kampflos übergeben werden. Sie hatte zwar durch den Krieg keine nennenswerten Schäden erlitten, doch wurden nun weite Teile der Wiesen in Anbauflächen für dringend benötigte Nahrungsmittel verwandelt. Die Insel wurde außerdem für große Jugendzeltlager genutzt. Ab 1950 war sie wieder für die Öffentlichkeit zugänglich. Sie blieb bis 1995 in der Obhut der Berliner Schlösserverwaltung und gehört seitdem zu der Stiftung Preußische Schlösser und Gärten Berlin-Brandenburg.

As early as the 1920s, the citizens of Berlin and Potsdam were able to visit Peacock Island.
After the revolution of 1918, the island was taken over by the Palace and Gardens Administration founded in 1926. In order to prevent financial and commercial exploitation, it was made a nature reserve because there was as yet no legislation for the preservation of historic gardens. The island has been the venue for special events only a couple of times, once in 1936 during the Olympic Games and a year later for the summer festival of the National Socialist association "Kraft durch Freude" (Strength Through Joy).
On April 26, 1945, a few days before the end of the war, the island was occupied by German troops, but thanks to skilful negotiations they were able to surrender without a fight. Although the island had been able to survive the war without much damage to speak of, now large areas of the meadows were used to grow desperately needed food. In addition, the island was used for large youth camps. From 1950 it was once again opened to the public, remained until 1995 in the care of the Berlin Palace Administration and since 1995 has belonged to the Prussian Palaces and Gardens Foundation Berlin-Brandenburg.

Rechts: Eine Wendeltreppe führt in einem der Türme bis auf eine Plattform, von der man eine wunderbare Aussicht hat.
Right: A winding staircase in one of the towers leads to a platform with a wonderful view.

Von einem der beiden Türme, die durch eine eiserne Brücke verbunden sind, blickt man auf die Havel und das jenseitige bewaldete Ufer.
The two towers, which are connected by an iron bridge, afford a view of the Havel and the wooded shore beyond.

Der Saal im Obergeschoss ist durch hölzerne Pilaster gegliedert und bis zum Gesims vertäfelt. Verwendet wurden sogenannte »vaterländische«, d. h. einheimische Hölzer. Durch die sieben Fenster blickt man auf die Havellandschaft.

The hall in the upper storey is divided by wooden pilasters and paneled up to the cornice. "Patriotic" wood was used, i.e. native wood. Through the seven windows there is a view of the Havel landscape.

Das runde Turmzimmer im Obergeschoss des Schlosses war das Schreibzimmer des Königs. An den Wänden hängen vierzehn aquarellierte Kupferstiche von Giovanni Volpato mit Ansichten aus den vatikanischen Museen.

The round tower on the upper floor of the palace was the king's study. Fourteen copperplate engravings painted over with watercolors by Giovanni Volpato with views of the Vatican Museum hang on the walls.

Im Erdgeschoss befindet sich das sogenannte »Otaheitische Kabinett«. Der als Bambushütte gestaltete Raum zeigt Wandbilder mit dem Schloss und dem Marmorpalais im Neuen Garten in tropischer Vegetation. In der Mitte des Raumes hängt eine Glasampel in »griechischer Manier«.

On the ground floor is the so-called Otaheite Room. The room, designed as a bamboo hut, displays wall paintings of the palace and the Marble Palace in the New Garden in tropical vegetation. A glass lamp in the "Greek style" hangs in the middle of the room.

Rechts: Neben Kuhstall und Molkenstube im Erdgeschoss befindet sich im Obergeschoss der Meierei ein gotischer Saal. Die reiche Ausmalung schuf der Theatermaler Bartolomeo Verona, die Stukkaturen Constantin Sartori nach einem Entwurf von Philipp Boumann d. J. Die gewölbte Halle überrascht durch ihre phantasievolle Gliederung im Stil der Neugotik.

Right: Besides the cowshed and the milking room on the ground floor, there is a Gothic hall on the upper floor. The rich wall paintings were created by the stage designer Bartolomeo Verona, the stucco work by Constantin Sartori based on a design by Philipp Boumann the Younger. The vaulted hall is surprising in its imaginative, neo-Gothic design.

Auf der nordöstlichen Seite der Insel steht die von dem Potsdamer Zimmermeister J. G. Brendel um 1795 gebaute Meierei in Form einer gotischen Ruine.
On the north side of the island stands the dairy, built by the Potsdam master carpenter J. G. Brendel, c. 1795, in the form of Gothic ruins.

Die Wohnungen Friedrich Wilhelms II. im Schloss Charlottenburg Berlin

Frederick William II's Apartments in Charlottenburg Palace Berlin

Für gelegentliche Aufenthalte in Charlottenburg ließ sich auch Friedrich Wilhelm II. dort eine Wohnung einrichten. Die um 1788 fertig gestellten Räume an der Gartenseite des Neuen Flügels sollten von ihm nur im Sommer bewohnt werden, sie gehörten ursprünglich zur Wohnung der Königin Elisabeth Christine. Insgesamt waren es fünf Räume, wovon die drei mittleren im chinesischen Stil, die anderen in »etruskischer Manier« ausgestaltet waren. Nach der Zerstörung im Zweiten Weltkrieg wurden nur drei wiederhergestellt, wovon der mittlere Raum, das Speisezimmer, von dem italienischen Theatermaler Bartolomeo Verona ausgemalt worden war. Das sogenannte »etruskische Zimmer« war ursprünglich von dem Maler Johann Gottfried Niedlich in diesem Stil ausgemalt worden. Nach 1950 sind die drei westlichen Räume des Appartements wiederhergestellt worden.
Friedrich Wilhelm II. veränderte 1796/97 die erste Wohnung Friedrichs des Großen im Obergeschoss und gestaltete fünf Räume zu den sogenannten »Winterkammern« um. Der vom Treppenhaus erste Raum, die frühere Vorkammer Friedrich des Großen, war ursprünglich mit einer figürlichen Malerei im Stile des Pesne-Umkreises bemalt, die 1934 entdeckt, aber 1943 vollkommen vernichtet wurde. Das erste Hautelice-Zimmer ist mit Wandteppichen aus der Don Quijote-Serie, die Friedrich Wilhelm II. von seinem Onkel Heinrich geschenkt bekommen hatte, ausgestattet. Von den ursprünglich sechs Tapisserien waren vier erhalten geblieben, die man nun auf zwei Räume verteilte. Die Teppiche stammen aus der Pariser Manufaktur Le Gobelins und sind 1763 bis 1784 angefertigt worden. Ludwig XVI. hatte sie dem Prinzen Heinrich geschenkt.
Da alle Räume dieser Wohnung 1943 zerstört und bis 1962 in einem vereinheitlichenden Rokoko rekonstruiert worden waren, stellte man zwischen 1985 und 1994 auch die fünf östlichen Zimmer auf der Grundlage von Zeichnungen, Fotografien und den Bauakten im frühklassizistischen Zustand wieder her. Das originale Mobiliar war genauso erhalten geblieben wie die Deckenleuchter, die sich auslagerungsbedingt noch in Potsdam befanden.
In dem sich anschließenden Raum ließ Friedrich Wilhelm II. sein Schlafzimmer einrichten. Die Wände wurden nach der originalen Vorlage rekonstruiert und mit geblümter Tapete aus gelb und weiß gestreiftem Atlas bespannt.
Das nachfolgende Schreibzimmer ist im Krieg gänzlich ausgebrannt und wurde wie die anderen bis 1994 rekonstruiert. Die Wiederherstellung der Atlastapete ist vorgesehen.
In friderizianischer Zeit ist dieser Raum, jetzt das Ostindische Zitzzimmer, als Spiegelkammer bezeichnet worden und besaß bis zur Zerstörung 1943 ein Deckengemälde von Johann Harper mit Gruppen spielender Kinder.

Frederick William II also had an apartment fitted out for his occasional stays in Charlottenburg. His rooms on the garden side of the New Wing of the palace completed in 1788, which originally belonged to the apartment of Queen Elizabeth Christina, were meant to be occupied only in summer. Altogether there were five rooms; the middle three were designed in the Chinese fashion and the others in the "Etruscan manner." After destruction in the Second World War, only three were rebuilt, of which the room in the middle, the dining room, had been painted by the Italian stage-set designer Bartolomeo Verona. The so-called Etruscan Room had originally been painted in a corresponding style by Johann Gottfried. The three western rooms of the apartment were restored after 1950.
In 1796/97, Frederick William II altered Frederick the Great's first apartment on the upper storey and remodeled five rooms to form the so-called Winter Apartment. The first room from the stairs, Frederick the Great's former antechamber, was originally decorated with figurative painting in the style of the Pesne circle, which was discovered in 1934 but then completely destroyed in 1943. The First Hautelice Room is furnished with tapestries from the Don Quixote series that Frederick William II had received as a present from his uncle Henry. Four of the original six tapestries, now divided between two rooms, have survived. The tapestries originated in the Parisian Le Gobelins workshop between 1763 and 1784. Louis XVI had presented them to Prince Henry as a gift.
Because all of the rooms of this apartment had been destroyed in 1943 and then restored in a unifying Rococo style by 1962, the five eastern rooms were returned to their early neoclassical state between 1985 and 1994, based on drawings, photographs, and the building records. The original furniture as well as the chandeliers had survived and were still in Potsdam, having been evacuated there for safekeeping.
Frederick William II had the adjoining room fitted as his bedroom. The walls were reconstructed according to the original plans and covered with flowered wallpaper of yellow and white atlas fabric.
The adjacent study burned out completely during the war and was reconstructed like the others up to 1994. The restoration of the atlas wallpaper is planned.
In the reign of Frederick the Great, this room, which is now the East Indian Chintz Room, was termed the Mirror Chamber and until its destruction in 1943 had a ceiling painted by Johann Harper of groups of children at play. Frederick William II had the walls and even the ceiling covered in chintz, giving it the tent-like impression of a pavilion. The ceramic stove, decorated

Nach einem Entwurf von C. G. Langhans wurden 1788 im nordöstlichen Teil des Schlossparks ein Teehaus und Aussichtsturm errichtet. Das 1945 zerstörte Bauwerk wurde 1956 – 60 unter Verzicht auf die ehemalige Innendekoration wiederaufgebaut und enthält heute eine Sammlung Berliner Porzellans des 18. und 19. Jahrhunderts.

Following C. G. Langhans' design, a teahouse and an observation tower were erected in 1788 in the northeastern part of the palace park. The interior decoration was dispensed with when the structure, which was destroyed in 1945, was rebuilt between 1956 and 1960. Today it contains a collection of Berlin porcelain from the 18th and 19th centuries.

Friedrich Wilhelm II. ließ die Wände und sogar die Decke mit Zitz bespannen, so dass der zeltartiger Eindruck eines Pavillons entstand. Aus der Zeit dieses Königs stammt auch der Tonofen, der mit Hermen und einem Relief verziert ist und den eine bronzene Gruppe weiblicher Figuren abschließt. Die Neuanfertigung der charakteristischen Zitzbespannung steht noch aus.
Besonders bemerkenswert in diesen Räumen der Wohnung Friedrich Wilhelms II. sind die wiederhergestellten kostbaren Fußböden, das erhalten gebliebene originale Mobiliar sowie die originalen Kronleuchter.
Von Carl Gotthard Langhans wurde 1788 bis 1790 im Garten als Teehaus ein Belvedere errichtet. 1943 brannte es bis auf die Umfassungsmauern aus und konnte zwischen 1956 und 1960 im Äußeren wiederhergestellt werden. Im Inneren befindet sich heute eine Ausstellung mit Berliner Porzellan.

with hermes figures and a relief and crowned by a group of female figures in bronze, also originated at this time. The characteristic chintz hangings have yet to be replaced.
Particularly noteworthy in these rooms of Frederick William II's apartment are the lavish restored floors, the surviving original furniture and the original chandeliers.
A teahouse in the garden was erected by Carl Gotthard Langhans from 1788 to 1790 as a belvedere. It was gutted to the outer walls in 1943 and its exterior appearance was restored between 1956 and 1960. Today it houses an exhibition of Berlin porcelain.

Links: In den 1796/97 für Friedrich Wilhelm II. eingerichteten »Winterkammern« ist die Ausgestattung mit drei Tapisserien mit der Darstellung von Leben und Taten Don Quijotes, hergestellt in der Pariser Manufaktur Les Gobelins zwischen 1763 und 1784, hervorzuheben. Die Wandteppiche waren ein Geschenk Ludwigs XIV. an den Prinzen Heinrich, Bruder Friedrichs des Großen. Die Räume waren im Zweiten Weltkrieg zerstört und sind 1985–94 rekonstruiert worden.
Left: Notable features of the Winter Chambers, furnished in 1796/97 for Frederick William II, are the three tapestries depicting the life and deeds of Don Quixote. They were produced in the Paris Les Gobelins workshop between 1763 and 1784. The tapestries were a gift from Louis XIV to Prince Henry, the brother of Frederick the Great. The rooms were destroyed in the Second World War and reconstructed between 1985 and 1994.

Rechts: Dieser Raum war die Schlafkammer Friedrich Wilhelms II. 1943 wurde er vernichtet, von 1985–94 wiederhergestellt. Die Portraits an den rekonstruierten Wandbespannungen stammen von Johann Heinrich Schröder, Johann Georg Ziesenis u. a. und zeigen Portraits des preußischen Herrscherhauses.
Right: This room was Frederick William II's bedchamber. It was destroyed in 1943, and restored from 1985 to 1994. The portraits on the reconstructed wall coverings are by Johann Heinrich Schröder and Johann Georg Ziesenis, among others, and portray members of the Prussian ruling family.

Friedrich Georg Weitsch

König Friedrich Wilhelm III. und Königin Luise, 1791, SPSG
King Frederick William III and Queen Louise, 1791, SPSG

König
Friedrich Wilhelm III.
und Königin
Luise

King Frederick William III and Queen Louise

reg. 1797–1840/1810

Schloss Paretz Brandenburg

Paretz Palace
Brandenburg

Das Mausoleum und der Neue Pavillon im Park von Schloss Charlottenburg Berlin

The Queen Louise Mausoleum
and the New Pavilion in the Park of
Charlottenburg Palace
Berlin

Das von David Gilly 1797 errichtete Schloss Paretz ist mit seiner einfachen Formensprache und dem Rundbogen in der Mitte typisch für die Baukunst um 1800. In den 1950er und -60er Jahren entstellend verändert, erhielt es bei der Restaurierung 1999 – 2001 wieder seine alte Form.

The Paretz Palace constructed by David Gilly in 1797 is typical for architecture of around 1800 with its simple vocabulary of form and the round arch in the middle. In the 1950s and 1960s changes disfigured it, but between 1999 and 2001 it was restored to its old appearance.

Schloss Paretz
Brandenburg

Paretz Palace
Brandenburg

Nur wenige Kilometer von Potsdam entfernt liegt das Dorf Paretz. Geschichtskundige verbinden diesen Ort mit der Königin Luise. Aus dem Hause Mecklenburg-Strelitz stammend, hatte sie Weihnachten 1793 den preußischen Kronprinzen Friedrich Wilhelm (III.) geheiratet. Ihre Schwester Friderike war am selben Tag mit dessen Bruder Ludwig vermählt worden.
Der preußische König Friedrich Wilhelm II. hatte zwar 1794 dem jungen Paar anfangs das Schloss Oranienburg als Sommerresidenz überlassen, doch das Haus und die altmodische Einrichtung entsprachen nicht mehr dem Zeitgeschmack. Dem Kronprinzenpaar gefiel da schon eher das Gut Steinhöfel, welches es 1794 besucht hatte und das zu dieser Zeit kurz vor der baulichen Vollendung stand. Der Besitzer, Valentin von Massow, war mit der Tochter des Gutsherren von Paretz, das dem Minister Johann Christian Graf von Blumenthal gehörte, verheiratet. Dem Kronprinzen war zudem der Ort vom nahen Marquardt, seit 1795 Sitz des Grafen Rudolf von Bischofswerder, bekannt. So kam es Anfang Januar 1797 zum Kauf von Paretz für 80 000 Taler durch den Kronprinzen Friedrich Wilhelm (III.); das Geld hierfür hatte ihm sein Vater Friedrich Wilhelm II. geschenkt.
Der Ort, 1197 erwähnt und seit 1658 im Besitz der Familie von Blumenthal, hatte keine besondere Geschichte, lag aber in einer landschaftlich reizvollen Umgebung, in der Nähe eines märkischen Sees. David Gilly, einer der führenden Berliner Baumeister, wurde mit den Entwürfen für den Umbau des Gutshauses und bald darauf mit der Umgestaltung des ganzen Ortes Paretz betraut. Angeregt von Gut Steinhöfel, dessen Umbau Gilly für Valentin von Massow ausgeführt hatte, entstand bis 1803 mit Paretz eines der bekanntesten Architekturensembles.
Das alte Gutshaus wurde fast vollständig abgerissen und nach Gillys Entwurf neu gebaut. Im stumpfen Winkel zum Schloss öffneten sich rechts und links Stall und Scheune zur Straße hin und bildeten so einen Innenhof, von dem aus diese Gebäude keinen Zugang hatten, sondern nur flache Rundbogenfenster besaßen. Im Schlosshof waren Pappeln zu einer halbrunden »Kolonnade« angeordnet, von denen zwei vor dem Mittelrisalit des Eingangs standen. In dem sonst sehr einfachen, eineinhalbgeschossigen, durch flache Risalite auf beiden Seiten betonten Haus, markiert ein für die Architektur um 1800 charakteristisches großes Segmentbogenfenster die Mitte der Hof- und Gartenseite.
Im Inneren des Schlosses lagen traditionell in der Mitte Vestibül und Gartensaal, links in doppelter Reihe die Wohnräume des Kronprinzenpaares, rechts, durch einen Korridor getrennt, jeweils aus drei Zimmern bestehende kleine Appartements. Das Obergeschoss mit einem durchgehenden Korridor

Only a few kilometers from Potsdam lies the village of Paretz, a place associated with Queen Louise. Descended from the House of Mecklenburg-Strelitz, she married the Prussian crown prince, later Frederick William III, at Christmas 1793. Her sister Frederica was wedded to Frederick's brother, Louis, on the same day.
Although the Prussian king, Frederick William II, originally turned over Oranienburg Palace to the young couple in 1794 as a summer residence, the house and furnishings no longer complied with contemporary taste. The crown prince and his wife much preferred the Steinhöfel estate, which at the time was nearing completion and which the couple had visited in 1794. The owner, Vallentin von Massow, was married to the daughter of the lord of Paretz manor, which belonged to Minister Johann Christian Graf von Blumenthal. Moreover, the crown prince was acquainted with the nearby village of Marquardt, since 1795 the seat of Rudolf, Earl of Bischofswerder. And so in early January 1797, Paretz was bought by Crown Prince Frederick William for 80,000 thalers; the money was a present from his father.
The village, mentioned in 1197 and since 1658 in the possession of the von Blumenthal family, had an unremarkable history, but was set in charming surroundings near a lake in the Mark of Brandenburg. David Gilly (1748–1808), one of Berlin's leading architects, was entrusted with the plans for the manor house and soon thereafter with remodeling the whole of Paretz. Inspired by the Steinhöfel estate, which had been remodeled by Gilly for Vallentin von Massow, Paretz was completed by 1803 and became one of the best-known architectural ensembles.
The old manor was almost completely torn down and rebuilt according to Gilly's design. At an oblique angle to the palace, stables and barn to right and left opened onto the street and formed an inner court to which these buildings have no access, but simply flank with flat round-arched windows. Poplar trees were arranged in a semicircular "colonnade" in the palace courtyard, two of them standing in front of the middle block with the entrance. The centre of the court side and the garden side was emphasized by a large, segment-arched window typical of the period around 1800; otherwise the extremely plain, one-and-a-half-storey house was only accented by low projections on either side.
Inside the palace, the vestibule and the Garden Room lay in the middle according to tradition. To the left were the apartments of the crown prince and his wife in two rows; to the right, separated by a corridor, were small apartments, each composed of three rooms. The upper floor with a corridor running its full length served to accommodate their entourage and the children.

Franz Hillner (?)

Schloss Paretz mit Mitgliedern der Hofgesellschaft, darunter vermutlich im Vordergrund König Friedrich Wilhelm III, und Königin Luise, um 1800, SPSG, Eigentum des Hauses Hohenzollern
Paretz Palace with Members of the Court, among them in the foreground are thought to be King Frederick Wilhelm III and Queen Louise, c. 1800, SPSG, property of the House of Hohenzollern

in der Mitte diente der Unterbringung der Kinder und des Gefolges.
Die Besonderheit von Schloss Paretz sind die Tapeten in den königlichen Räumen. Zu dieser Zeit besaßen auch das Schloss in Schwedt, Haus Machnow sowie die Schlösser Freienwalde, Friedrichsfelde und Pfaueninsel ähnliche Tapeten. Während die Tapeten in den anderen Schlössern mit diesen verloren gegangen sind, haben sie sich auf der Pfaueninsel in situ und in Paretz – weil 1947 abgenommen und vor der Zerstörung gerettet – erhalten. Die königlichen Räume des Schlosses waren vorwiegend mit Tapeten ausgestattet, die in Berliner Manufakturen, u. a. von Isaac Joel, Aron Wessely und Johann Christian hergestellt wurden. Besonders reich waren der Gartensaal mit exotischen Pflanzenmotiven, der Speisesaal mit Vogeldarstellungen und das Schlafzimmer mit Landschaftsdarstellungen der Umgebung Potsdams, des Neuen Gartens und der Pfaueninsel geschmückt. Die anderen Zimmer hatten einfarbige Tapeten mit naturalistischen Bordüren.
In Paretz hielt sich die königliche Familie meist im Spätsommer bis zum Geburtstag des Kronprinzen Friedrich Wilhelm (IV.) am 15. Oktober auf; das letzte Mal im Jahre 1805. Ein Jahr später folgte die Niederlage bei Jena und Auerstedt. Die königliche Familie floh nach Memel und kehrte erst im Dezember 1809 nach Berlin zurück. Am 20. Mai 1810 besuchte die Königin Luise das letzte Mal Paretz. Sie starb am 19. Juli 1810 während eines Besuches bei ihrem Vater in Hohenzieritz in Mecklenburg-Strelitz.
Die große Zeit von Paretz war endgültig vorbei, auch wenn Friedrich Wilhelm IV. gelegentlich, wohl in Anhänglichkeit an seine Mutter, im Obergeschoss des Schlosses wohnte und dort einiges verändern ließ.
Schloss Paretz war mit dem in die Gestaltung einbezogenen Ort ein Musterbeispiel für die Kunst des Klassizismus um 1800 und blieb bis 1945 nahezu unverändert. Um 1900 wurde man wieder auf die Kunst um 1800 aufmerksam, und der Kunsthistoriker Hermann Schmitz schrieb 1919, dass Paretz »einer der in seiner Innenausstattung am besten erhaltenen deutschen Landsitze aus dem Ende des 18. Jahrhunderts ist«.
Bis 1945 war das Schloss im Besitz der Hohenzollern. Friedrich Wilhelm IV. vererbte es an König Wilhelm I., der ab 1871 Deutscher Kaiser war. Von diesem übernahm es 1888 Prinz Heinrich von Preußen, Sohn des 99-Tage-Kaisers Friedrich III. und danach dessen Frau Irene von Hessen und bei Rhein. Das Schloss war über einhundert Jahre in seinem ursprünglichen Zustand und mit seiner originalen Innenausstattung bewahrt worden. Kurz vor dem Ende des Zweiten Weltkrieges wurde es zum Auslagerungsort für Kunstwerke aus Berliner und Potsdamer Schlössern sowie aus den Berliner Museen. Im April 1945 besetzte die Rote Armee das Schloss und nach ihrem

The special feature of Paretz Palace is the wallpaper in the royal chambers. At that time, Schwedt Palace, Machnow House and the palaces of Freienwalde, Friedrichsfelde and Peacock Island had similar wallpapers. While the wallpapers in the other palaces have been lost along with the buildings, they have been preserved in situ on Peacock Island, and in Paretz because they were taken down in 1947 and saved from destruction. The royal chambers of the palace were furnished for the most part with wallpapers manufactured by hand in Berlin by Isaac Joel, Aron Wessely, and Johann Christian, among others. They were especially opulent in the Garden Room with exotic plant motifs, the dining hall with depictions of birds, and the bedchamber, which was decorated with landscapes of the areas around Potsdam, the New Gardens, and Peacock Island. The other rooms had bold monochrome wallpapers with naturalistic borders.
The royal family usually occupied Paretz in late summer, staying until the birthday of the younger crown prince, the later Frederick William IV, on October 15; their last stay was in 1805. A year later, in 1806, the Prussian army was defeated at Jena and Auerstedt. The royal family fled to Memel and did not return to Berlin until December 1809. Queen Louise visited Paretz for the last time on May 20, 1810. She died on July 19, 1810, while visiting her father in Hohenzieritz in Mecklenburg-Strelitz.
The great era of Paretz was over once and for all, even if Frederick William IV, out of devotion to his mother, occasionally lived on the upper floor of the palace and had some changes made there.
Paretz Palace, including the village as part of an overall design, was a prime example of neoclassical style around 1800 and remained almost unaltered until 1945. Around 1900, the art of 1800 again attracted attention. The art historian Hermann Schmitz wrote in 1919 that Paretz was "one of the best-preserved German country residences from the end of the 18th century in terms of decoration and furnishings."
The palace was in the possession of the Hohenzollern family until 1945. King William I, who was German emperor from 1871, inherited it from Frederick William IV. It was taken over in 1888 by Prince Henry of Prussia, son of the 99-day emperor Frederick III, and later by his consort, Irene von Hessen und bei Rhein. As they had no children, they adopted Barbara of Prussia, Princess von Hessen und bei Rhein, who married Christian Ludwig, Duke of Mecklenburg in 1954; she died in 1994, the duke two years later.
The palace was preserved in its original condition with its decoration and furnishings for over one hundred years. Shortly before the end of the Second World War, works of art evacuated from the Berlin and Potsdam palaces and

Abzug Mitte 1946 plante die Provinzialregierung Brandenburg die Errichtung eines Gästehauses. Daraus wurde aber nichts und 1948 gingen Schloss und Gut Paretz in die Zentrale Verwaltung der gegenseitigen Bauernhilfe über. Die nach 1950 erfolgten Umbaumaßnahmen zur Bauernhofschule veränderten das äußere Bild des Schlosses völlig: Die Mittelresalite auf beiden Schlossseiten mit ihren charakteristischen Rundbogenfenstern sowie der Ornamentik wurden beseitigt und durch querliegende eckige Fenster und durch ebensolche Eingänge ersetzt. Der neue Nutzer baute nach 1960 im Inneren die Räume um und veränderte auch die Raumstrukturen.
Die politische Wende 1989/90 brachte auch eine veränderte Nutzung des Schlosses. Anfang 1991 wurde das Haus durch die sogenannte Güterverwaltung Paretz AG agromax übernommen, die jedoch ab 1995 in Liquidation ging. Der 1990 gebildete »Verein Historisches Paretz e.V.« führte seit 1991 mit Unterstützung der Potsdamer Schlösserverwaltung Ausstellungen durch, um das Haus im Bewusstsein der Menschen zu erhalten. Die Potsdamer Schlösserverwaltung, später die Stiftung Preußische Schlösser und Gärten Berlin-Brandenburg, bemühte sich, das Haus in ihre Verwaltung einzugliedern, was im Dezember 1999 auch gelang. Wesentlichen Anteil daran hatte die Cornelsen Kulturstiftung, die die Kosten für die Restaurierung der in Potsdam lagernden Tapeten übernahm und sie wieder in der rekonstruierten Königswohnung des Schlosses anbringen ließ. Das Schloss und die Innenräume wurden ab 1999 mit Mitteln des Landes Brandenburg, des Kreises Havelland und der Stadt Ketzin restauriert.
Seit September 2001 ist das Schloss mit seinen Räumen und den restaurierten Tapeten wieder ganz hergestellt. Ein Hauptwerk David Gillys hat seine Renaissance erlebt, die Berliner Architektur- und Innenraumkunst um 1800 verfügt wieder über ein hervorragendes Beispiel.

also from the Berlin museums were stored there. In April 1945 the Red Army occupied the palace, and after its withdrawal mid-1946 the provincial government in Brandenburg planned to open a guest-house in the palace. Nothing came of this plan, and the manor of Paretz was transferred to the Central Administration for Mutual Aid to Farmers. The rebuilding that followed after 1950 to make it into an agricultural school completely changed the exterior appearance of the palace. The central sections on both sides of the palace, with their characteristic arched windows and ornamentation, were removed and replaced with transverse angular windows and entrances in the same style. The new occupants rebuilt the interior after 1960 and also altered the layout of the rooms.
The end of the GDR in 1989/90 also brought a change in the use of the palace. The house was taken over in early 1991 by the so-called Property Administration Paretz AG agromax, which went into liquidation, however, in 1995. The Historic Paretz Association formed in 1990 organized exhibitions from 1991 with the support of the Potsdam Palace Administration, in order to keep the house alive in people's minds. The Potsdam Palace Administration endeavored to take over management of the house under what was to become the Prussian Palaces and Gardens Foundation Berlin-Brandenburg, an aim that was fulfilled in December 1999. The Cornelsen Cultural Foundation played a decisive role in this, bearing the costs for the restoration of the wallpapers stored in Potsdam and having them installed again in the renovated royal chambers of the palace. The rebuilding of the palace and its rooms was begun in 1999 with funds from the state of Brandenburg, the district of Havelland and the town of Ketzin.
Since September 2001 the restoration of the palace with its rooms and refurbished wallpapers has been complete. A major work of David Gilly has been resurrected; and once again there exists an outstanding example of Berlin architecture and interior design from the period around 1800.

Das Schloss wird seitlich von zwei Gebäuden begleitet. Auf der rechten Seite befand sich der Reitpferdestall, der 1948 abgerissen und durch einen veränderten Bau ersetzt wurde. Östlich befand sich eine Scheune, die schon 1890 durch einen Neubau ersetzt wurde. Nachdem in den 1990er Jahren die späteren Einbauten beseitigt worden waren, ist hier seit 2005 ein Museum für die Kutschen, Sänften und Schlitten des preußischen Königshauses eingerichtet.

The palace is flanked by two buildings at the sides. On the right was the stable for riding horses, which was torn down in 1948 and replaced by a modified building. Eastwards there was a barn that had already been replaced by a new building in 1890. After the removal of later fixtures in the 1990s, a museum for the coaches, sedan chairs, and sleighs of the Prussian royal family has occupied it since 2005.

Da die kostbaren Papiertapeten der Innenräume 1947 durch Abnahme und Deponierung in Sanssouci gerettet werden konnten, wurden sie nach der Restaurierung Ende der 1990er Jahre wieder angebracht. Sie bilden heute den wesentlichen Schmuck der Räume, wie hier des Gartensaales.

The precious wallpapers of the interiors were saved by being removed in 1947 and stored in Sanssouci: they were put up again after restoration in the late 1990s. Today, they constitute the fundamental decoration of the rooms, as here in the Garden Room.

In dem Wohnzimmer und späteren Schlafzimmer zeigen die Tapeten perspektivisch gemalte architektonische Ansichten des Marmorpalais in Potsdam und des Schlosses auf der Pfaueninsel. Sie stammen aus der Fabrik von Isaak Joel in Glienicke.

The wallpapers in the living room and later bedchamber display architectural views in perspective of the Marble Palace in Potsdam and the palace on Peacock Island. They are from the Isaak Joel factory in Glienicke.

Das Mausoleum und der Neue Pavillon im Park von Schloss Charlottenburg Berlin

The Queen Louise Mausoleum and the New Pavilion in the Park of Charlottenburg Palace Berlin

Mit der Thronbesteigung Friedrich Wilhelms III. und der Königin Luise 1797 wurde das Schloss Charlottenburg zu einem der bevorzugten Wohnplätze. Der König bezog die untere, die Königin die obere Etage. Die Eheleute hielten sich gern in Charlottenburg auf. Durch die politischen Ereignisse mussten sie 1806 Preußen verlassen und gingen nach Memel/Ostpreußen. Erst Ende 1809 kehrten sie zurück und hielten am 1. Januar 1810 wieder Einzug in Charlottenburg. Nach ihrer Rückkehr richtete Karl Friedrich Schinkel das Schlafzimmer der Königin in der oberen Etage ein.
Die Königin Luise starb im Juni 1810 und wurde in dem von Heinrich Gentz geschaffenen Mausoleum in Charlottenburg beigesetzt. Das in Carrara gearbeitete Bildwerk schuf Christian Rauch, es wurde aber erst 1815 aufgestellt.
Friedrich Wilhelm III. hielt sich auch in späteren Jahren gerne in Charlottenburg auf und ließ 1824/25 durch Schinkel den »Neuen Pavillon« für sich und seine zweite Gemahlin Auguste Fürstin von Liegnitz errichten. Dem Entwurf Schinkels, der die Bauausführung Albert Dietrich Schadow überließ, lagen Vorbilder der Villa Reale Chiatomone in Neapel zugrunde. Diese Villa hatte der König bei seinem Aufenthalt 1822 bewohnt.
1943 schwer beschädigt, ist der Pavillon bis 1959 wieder aufgebaut worden und seit 1970 der Öffentlichkeit zugänglich. Heute ist er mit Kunstwerken aus der Schinkelzeit, der ersten Hälfte des 19. Jahrhunderts, ausgestattet.

With the accession of Frederick William III and Queen Louise in 1797, Charlottenburg Palace also became one of the royal couple's preferred residences. The king moved into the lower floor, the queen the upper floor, and the royal couple enjoyed staying in Charlottenburg. The political events of 1806 forced them to leave Berlin for Memel in East Prussia. Not until the end of 1809 did they return and, on January 1, 1810, enter Charlottenburg. After their return, Karl Friedrich Schinkel decorated the queen's bedroom on the upper floor. Queen Louise died in June 1810 and was laid to rest in the mausoleum in Charlottenburg fashioned for her by Heinrich Gentz. The sculpture in Carrara marble was the work of Christian Rauch; however, it was not put on display until 1815.
In later years, Frederick William III also took pleasure in staying in Charlottenburg and had the New Pavilion built by Karl Friedrich Schinkel in 1824/25 for himself and his second consort, Princess Augusta of Liegnitz. Schinkel modeled the building on the Villa Reale Chiatomone, which the king had occupied during his stay in Naples in 1822, but left the execution of the work to Albert Dietrich Schadow. Severely damaged in 1943, it had been rebuilt by 1959 and has been open to the public since 1970 to display works of art from the time of Schinkel, the first half of the 19th century.

In dem von Heinrich Gentz von 1810 – 12 errichteten Mausoleum im Schlosspark befindet sich die Grabstätte der Königin Luise und ab 1840 auch ihres Gemahls Friedrich Wilhelm III. Der von Christian Rauch 1811 – 14 in Rom gefertigte Sarkophag ist ein Hauptwerk der Berliner Bildhauerschule.

The mausoleum constructed by Heinrich Gentz from 1810 to 1812 in the palace park holds Queen Louise's tomb and, since 1840, that of her husband Frederick William III as well. The sarcophagus produced by Christian Rauch between 1811 and 1814 in Rome is a major work of the Berlin school of sculpture.

In dem ehemaligen Ankleidezimmer König Friedrich Wilhelms II. war 1810 nach Entwürfen von K. F. Schinkel ein Schlafzimmer für die Königin Luise eingerichtet worden. Die Wände wurden mit weiß gerafftem Voile über einer rosafarbenen Papiertapete bespannt. Bett und Blumentischchen gehören zur ursprünglichen Ausstattung des Raumes.

In 1810, a bedchamber for Queen Louise was fitted out according to K. F. Schinkel's designs in the former dressing room of King Frederick William II. The walls with pink wallpaper were draped with gathered white voile. The bed and flower table were part of the original furnishings of the room.

Rechts: Der quadratische Bau hat in der Mitte ein Vestibül und eine Treppe, die in das obere Stockwerk führt. Die ursprüngliche Malerei nach Zeichnungen K. F. Schinkels, ausgeführt von Julius Schoppe, wurde nach der Bauaufnahme von Albrecht Dietrich Schadow von Klaus Fußmann und Manfred Bleßmann rekonstruiert. Die Büsten zeigen die Kronprinzessin Elisabeth von Preußen, geschaffen von Christian Friedrich Tieck, und rechts den Kronprinzen Friedrich Wilhelm (IV.) von Chr. D. Rauch.

Right: The square building has a vestibule in the middle and stairs that lead to the upper storey. The original painting, executed by Julius Schoppe after K. F. Schinkel's sketches, was reconstructed by Klaus Fussmann and Manfred Blessmann using Albrecht Dietrich Schadow's building documentation. The busts portray Crown Princess Elizabeth of Prussia, by Christian Friedrich Tieck, and on the right, Crown Prince Frederick William (IV) by C. D. Rauch.

Neben dem Knobelsdorff-Flügel baute K. F. Schinkel 1824/25 den »Neuen Pavillon« für Friedrich Wilhelm III. und seine zweite Gemahlin Auguste Fürstin von Liegnitz. Die Ausführung lag in den Händen von A. D. Schadow, einem Schüler Schinkels. Der König ließ beim Entwurf Anregungen von seiner Italienreise verarbeiten. Wie viele Bauten in Charlottenburg, wurde auch der Neue Pavillon 1943 schwer beschädigt, 1959 weitgehend aufgebaut und 1970 wieder der Öffentlichkeit zugänglich gemacht.

In 1824/25, K. F. Schinkel built a New Pavilion for Frederick William III and his second wife, Augusta Princess of Liegnitz, next to the Knobelsdorff wing. The execution was in the hands of A. D. Schadow, a pupil of Schinkel. The king had ideas that he had brought back from his trip to Italy incorporated into the design. As with many buildings in Charlottenburg, the New Pavilion was heavily damaged in 1943. In 1959 it was extensively rebuilt and in 1970 opened again to the public.

Karl Wilhelm Wach

König Friedrich Wilhelm IV., nach 1840, SPSG
King Frederick William IV, after 1840, SPSG

Karl Wilhelm Wach

Königin Elisabeth, nach 1840, SPSG
Queen Elizabeth, after 1840, SPSG

König

Friedrich Wilhelm IV.

King Frederick William IV

reg. 1840–1861

In das sich nach Süden an den Park Sanssouci des 18. Jahrhunderts anschließende Gelände ließ der Kronprinz Friedrich Wilhelm (IV.) nach Entwürfen von K. F. Schinkel ein Schloss bauen. Es wurde schon vor dem Erwerb durch den Kronprinzen nach der ursprünglichen Besitzerin, Charlotte von Gentzkow, benannt.

Crown Prince Frederick William (IV) had a palace built to plans by K. F. Schinkel on the grounds bordering the 18th-century Sanssouci Park to the south. Even before the crown prince had acquired it, it was named after its original owner, Charlotte von Gentzkow.

Schloss Charlottenhof und Römische Bäder. Die Wohnung Friedrich Wilhelms IV. im Schloss Sanssouci. Die Friedenskirche. Die Orangerie Potsdam

Charlottenhof Palace and Roman Baths.
Frederick William IV's Apartment in Sanssouci Palace.
The Church of Peace. The Orangery
Potsdam

Das Belvedere auf dem Pfingstberg Potsdam

Belvedere on the Pfingstberg
Potsdam

Schloss Lindstedt Potsdam

Lindstedt Palace
Potsdam

Schloss Sacrow Potsdam

Sacrow Palace
Potsdam

Schloss Charlottenhof und Römische Bäder. Die Wohnung Friedrich Wilhelms IV. im Schloss Sanssouci. Die Friedenskirche. Die Orangerie Potsdam

Charlottenhof Palace and Roman Baths. Frederick William IV's Apartment in Sanssouci Palace. The Church of Peace. The Orangery Potsdam

Schloss Charlottenhof

Dem Park Sanssouci, der sich im 18. Jahrhundert in schmaler Form von Osten nach Westen erstreckte, wurde ab 1825 ein neuer Parkteil angegliedert, auf dem später das Schloss Charlottenhof entstand. Peter Joseph Lenné, der 1816 nach Potsdam berufen worden war, prägte das Bild der preußischen Parklandschaft entscheidend. Sein Werk ist gekennzeichnet durch die Schaffung großer ungeteilter Rasenflächen, die Bildung von Hainen und die Pflanzungen von Einzelbäumen und Baumgruppen, einer Neuordnung des Wegenetzes nach praktischen und ästhetischen Gesichtspunkten sowie der Umwandlung alter Kanäle in natürliche Wasserläufe. Im Parkgebiet des 18. Jahrhunderts konnte Lenné vorerst nur geringe Veränderungen vornehmen. Erst im Parkbereich von Charlottenhof entfaltete sich sein ganzes Können. Weite, bis zum Neuen Palais reichende Sichtachsen sind gleichsam zum Sinnbild Lennéscher Gestaltungskunst geworden. In diese Parklandschaft eingebettet ist das Schloss Charlottenhof. Das nach Ideenskizzen des Kronprinzen Friedrich Wilhelm (IV.) von Karl Friedrich Schinkel entworfene Schloss ist durchdrungen von der klaren und einfachen Formsprache der Antike. Aus Sparsamkeitsgründen musste Schinkel die Ausmaße des noch aus dem 18. Jahrhundert stammenden alten Gutsgebäudes beibehalten. Das Eingangsportal ist schlicht, aber hoheitsvoll. Durch einen dorischen Portikus tritt man auf der anderen Seite des Hauses in den aufgeschütteten, von einer Exedra abgeschlossenen Hausgarten. Von der Straße verwehrt eine Pergola den Einblick, nur zum Park hin ist die Sicht frei in den Landschaftsraum Lennés. Dem Schloss ordnen sich in seiner unmittelbaren Umgebung geometrisch gestaltete Gartenteile zu, so dass eine Ost-West-Achse entstand, die vom Maschinenteich über den Rosengarten, den unmittelbaren Schlossbereich, den Dichterhain – so genannt nach den Büsten italienischer und deutscher Dichter – bis zu dem in den 30er Jahren des 19. Jahrhunderts angelegten Hippodrom verläuft. War in der Außenarchitektur des Schlosses schon eine bewusst bürgerlich-klassizistische Note angeschlagen worden, so wird dies bei den Innenräumen noch deutlicher. Links und rechts von Vestibül und Speisesaal, die die Mitte einnehmen und deren Raumabmessungen noch aus dem alten Grundriss des Gutshauses herzuleiten sind, liegen neun kleine, an Bürgerstuben erinnernde Räume. Einfach, ja geradezu sparsam ist die Ausstattung mit meist von Schinkel entworfenem Mobiliar. An den oft farbkräftigen Wänden hängen Kupferstiche mit römischen Landschaften und nach Werken von Raffael, Michelangelo und Leonardo. Das Schlafzimmer der Hofdamen bekam durch eine blauweiß gestreifte Tapete, Bespannungen und Vorhänge eine besondere Ausstattung. Derartige Zeltzimmer waren im späten 18. Jahrhundert in Frankreich in Mode.

Charlottenhof Palace

In the 18th century, Sanssouci Park stretched in a narrow shape from east to west. In 1825 a new section of parkland was added, on which later Charlottenhof Palace was built. Peter Joseph Lenné (1789 –1866), who was brought to Potsdam in 1816, not only transformed the appearance of the 18th-century park; his work is characterized by the creation of large, undivided expanses of lawn, groves of trees, the planting of trees individually and in groups, the reorganization of the network of paths from a practical and aesthetic point of view, and the transformation of old canals into natural watercourses. At first, Lenné was only able to make minor changes in the 18th-century park. Not until the Charlottenhof park was added, in 1825, was he able to display all his skill. Broad axes of view reaching all the way to the New Palace have become the symbol of Lenné's art.

Charlottenhof Palace nestles in this park landscape. The palace designed by Karl Friedrich Schinkel (1781–1841) according to ideas sketched by the crown prince (later Frederick William IV) is permeated by the clear and simple forms of antiquity. For reasons of economy, Schinkel was forced to retain the dimensions of the old 18th-century manor house. The entrance is simple but majestic. A Doric portico on the other side of the house leads to an elevated house garden enclosed by an exedra. From the road, a pergola acts as a screen; only in the direction of the park is there an open view of Lenné's landscape. Geometrical elements of the garden in the immediate proximity of the palace relate to the architecture. This creates an east-west axis running from the machine pond through the rose garden, the area directly adjacent to the palace, and the Poets' Grove – so called because of the busts of Italian and German poets standing there – all the way to the Hippodrom laid out in the 1830s.

The bourgeois neoclassical note, already consciously sounded in the exterior architecture of Charlottenhof Palace, becomes even clearer inside. Left and right of the vestibule and the dining hall at the centre, whose dimensions derive from the floor plan of the manor house, are nine small rooms reminiscent of middle-class parlors. The furnishings are simple, almost Spartan, with furniture designed for the most part by Schinkel. Copperplate engravings with Roman landscapes after the works of the great Renaissance masters Raphael, Michelangelo, and Leonardo hang on the walls, many of which have strong colors. The bedroom of the ladies-in-waiting was given a special decor of blue-and-white striped wallpaper, fabric coverings and curtains. Such tent rooms were fashionable in the late 18th century in France.

Karl Friedrich Schinkel

Ansicht des Schlosses Charlottenhof mit dem Vorgängerbau (gz. 1829), 1858, SPSG
View of Charlottenhof Palace with the Previous Building (signed and dated 1829), 1858, SPSG

Römische Bäder

Schloss Charlottenhof war noch im Bau, da entstanden 1826 erste Entwürfe für die Römischen Bäder. Auch diese Baugruppe ging aus der engen Zusammenarbeit zwischen Schinkel, seinem Bauherrn und dem Architekten Ludwig Persius hervor. Im Gegensatz zu Charlottenhof wurde hier jedoch durch die ungezwungene Anordnung der Baukörper eine malerische Wirkung angestrebt, die der unmittelbar heranreichende Maschinenteich – angelegt für die Betreibung der Fontänen – mit seiner Wasserfläche noch unterstrich. Florentinische Villenbauten des 15. Jahrhunderts sowie sizilianische Bauernhäuser mit ihren einfachen Formen und lockeren Gruppierung von Wohn- und Wirtschaftsgebäuden mit flachen Dächern und niedrigen Türmen, Altanen und Loggien sind Vorbilder für dieses Ensemble. Zur sogenannten Italienischen Villa, der Wohnung des Hofgärtners Hermann Sello, gesellt sich 1830, verbunden mit einer Pergola, der am See gelegene Teepavillon in der Form eines griechischen Tempels. Zwei Jahre später wurde das kleine Gehilfenhaus und die zwischen ihm und dem Gärtnerwohnhaus gelegene große Eingangslaube errichtet. Den inneren Garten schloss seit 1833 eine Arkadenhalle ab. Sie diente zunächst als Orangerie bis 1834 der Bau des Römischen Bades und der Räume begann, deren Ausgestaltung erst in den 40er Jahren des 19. Jahrhunderts abgeschlossen wurde. Die Anordnung des Atriums, des Impluviums, des eigentlichen Bades (Thermenhalle), das der Anlage seinen Namen gab, und der übrigen Räumlichkeiten vollzog sich in lockerer Form ohne allzu enge Anlehnung an die Vorbilder antiker römischer Bäder und Häuser.

Schloss Sanssouci

Der Kronprinz Friedrich Wilhelm (IV.) interessierte sich schon seit dem frühen 19. Jahrhundert für die Räume Friedrichs II. im Schloss Sanssouci. Mit dem Bau des Schlosses Charlottenhof war er in dessen unmittelbare Nähe gerückt. Nach seiner Thronbesteigung im Juni 1840 zog er in das Schloss Sanssouci, bewohnte aber mit seiner Gemahlin nur die ehemaligen Gästezimmer. Da sich die Hofhaltung vergrößerte, mussten auch die ehemals niedrigen Seitenflügel des Schlosses durch neue Bauten, entworfen von Persius und ausgeführt von Ferdinand von Arnim, ersetzt werden. Im westlichen Flügel waren Unterkünfte für fremde Damen, Kavaliere und deren Bedienung vorgesehen, im östlichen wurden die neue Küche, der Weinkeller, die Lampenkammer und die Konditorei untergebracht. Außerdem befand sich hier eine Porzellan- und Silberkammer sowie im Obergeschoss Zimmer für die Bediensteten.

Roman Baths

While Charlottenhof Palace was still under construction in 1826, the first plans for the nearby Roman Baths had already been drawn up. This building ensemble was also a result of close collaboration between Schinkel, his royal patron, and Ludwig Persius. In contrast to Charlottenhof, however, here they strived for a picturesque effect through the informal arrangement of the buildings; this is underscored by the water of the adjacent machine pond, which was put in to operate the fountains. The models for this ensemble were Florentine villas of the 15th century and Sicilian farmhouses with their simple forms and loose grouping of residential and farm buildings with flat roofs and low towers, their terraces and loggias. The tea pavilion in the form of a Greek temple set on the lake was joined to the so-called Italian Villa, the home of the court gardener, Hermann Sello, in 1830. Two years later a small cottage for the gardener's assistant and a large entrance arbor situated between it and the court gardener's house were built. Since 1833 a colonnaded hall has bordered the inner garden. It served at first as an orangery until 1834, when construction began behind it of the Roman Baths and rooms that were not completed until the 1840s. The arrangement of the atrium, the Impluvium, the actual bath which gave the complex its name, and of the rest of the premises was carried out informally without following too closely the models of ancient Roman baths and houses.

Sanssouci Palace

In the early 19th century Frederick William IV, when he was still crown prince, had taken an interest in the rooms of Frederick the Great in Sanssouci Palace. With the building of Charlottenhof Palace, he moved into the immediate vicinity of Sanssouci, and after his accession to the throne in June 1840 into Sanssouci Palace itself, but he and his wife occupied only the former guest rooms. Because the court had grown, the low wing of the palace had to be replaced by new buildings, designed by Ludwig Persius and carried out by Ferdinand von Arnim. Accommodations were provided in the west wing for ladies and cavaliers who did not belong to the court and their servants; the new kitchen, the wine-cellar, the lamp room, and the pastry-kitchen were housed in the east wing. Furthermore, there was a porcelain and a silver chamber in this wing. Rooms for the servants were installed on the upper floor. Frederick William IV spent the summer months in Sanssouci Palace and died there on January 2, 1861. His widow, Elizabeth, occasionally used the palace in the summer months until her death on December 14, 1873. After her death, the palace was not lived in again and was just a museum.

Ansicht der Römischen Bäder von Süden (gz. 1832), 1858, SPSG
View of the Roman Baths from the South (signed and dated 1832), 1858, SPSG

Friedrich Wilhelm IV. bewohnte in den Sommermonaten Schloss Sanssouci und starb dort auch am 2. Januar 1861. Seine Witwe Elisabeth nutzte das Schloss gelegentlich im Sommer bis zu ihrem Tod am 14. Dezember 1873. Danach wurde es nicht mehr bewohnt und war nur noch Museum.

Friedenskirche

Schon während seiner Kronprinzenzeit hatte Friedrich Wilhelm (IV.) in der Nähe von Charlottenhof eine antike Villenanlage und bei den Römischen Bädern einen basilikalen Kirchenbau geplant. Dieser Plan wurde beim Bau der Friedenskirche wieder aufgenommen. In Erinnerung an seine Italienreise 1828 und in Anlehnung an Skizzen des Kronprinzen schufen Ludwig Persius, August Stüler, Ludwig Hesse und Ferdinand von Arnim die Entwürfe für die Kirche und das dazugehörige Bauensemble mit Kavalierflügel, Pfarr- und Pförtnerhaus, Schulgebäude, Atrium, Kreuzgang mit Brunnenkapelle und Säulengang. Vorbilder für das Langhaus waren die Kirchen San Clemente und Santa Maria di Cosmedin in Rom. In die Apsis des Innenraumes wurde ein Mosaik aus dem 12. Jahrhundert eingefügt, das beim Abbruch der Kirche St. Cyprianus auf Murano bei Venedig geborgen und vom Kronprinzen erworben worden war. Mit ihrer italienischen Silhouette und den abwechslungsreich ineinander gefügten Baugliedern stellen die Gebäude eine interessante Bereicherung der Architektur im Park Sanssouci dar. Da Persius bereits 1845 starb, übernahmen andere, ebenfalls aus der Schinkel-Schule hervorgegangene, Architekten die Ausführung seiner Pläne. Mit der Bauleitung wurde Stüler beauftragt, während die Bauausführung in den Händen von Hesse und von Arnim lag.
Zinnen, Mauerquaderung und rundbogige Fenster charakterisieren die von der florentinischen Frührenaissance angeregte Fassadengestaltung der Gebäude zwischen der Kirche und dem Grünen Gitter.
Friedrich Wilhelm IV. wurde 1861, seine Gemahlin 1873 in der Friedenskirche beigesetzt.
1846 verwandelte Lenné den ehemaligen Küchengarten, den Friedrich Wilhelm I. in Anlehnung an die französische Anlage spöttisch als seinen »Marly-Garten« bezeichnet hatte, in einen landschaftlich gestalteten Bezirk mit dendrologisch interessanten Gehölzen und ausgeprägten Blumenbeeten. Natur und Bauwerk gehen hier noch einmal eine enge Verbindung ein.

Orangerie

Friedrich Wilhelm IV. hatte für Sanssouci gigantische Baupläne. Nach seinen Vorstellungen sollte sich vom Weinberg am Obelisken bis zum Belvedere auf dem Klausberg eine Triumphstraße erstrecken, in die man zwar die Bau-

Church of Peace

When Frederick William IV was still crown prince, he planned an antique villa complex near to Charlottenhof Palace and a basilica church near the Roman Baths. This plan was revived with the building of the Church of Peace. As a reminiscence of the crown prince's trip to Italy and based on his sketches, Ludwig Persius, August Stüler, Ludwig Ferdinand Hesse and Ferdinand Ludwig von Arnim designed plans for this church and the accompanying ensemble of buildings. It included the Cavalier's Wing, the rector's house and gatehouse, the school building, the atrium, and the cloister with the Fountain Chapel and an arcade. Models included the churches St Clemente, for the nave, and St Maria di Cosmedin in Rome. A 12th-century mosaic decorating the apse of the church interior was salvaged from the demolition of St Cyprian's Church on Murano, near Venice, and acquired by the crown prince. With their Italian silhouettes and variety of interlocking structural elements, the buildings represent an interesting and valuable addition to the architecture of Sanssouci Park. As Ludwig Persius had died in 1845, his plans were completed by other architects of the Schinkel school. August Stüler was charged with supervising the project, while the building work was placed in the hands of Hesse and von Arnim.
The early Florentine Renaissance provided the inspiration for the crenellated roofs, square stone walls, and round-arch windows of the façades of the buildings between the church and the Green Fence.
After their deaths, Frederick William IV (in 1861) and his wife in (1873) were laid to rest in the Church of Peace.
In 1846 Peter Joseph Lenné transformed the former kitchen garden, which Frederick William I had mocking called his "Marly Gardens" in reference to their French layout, into a landscaped area with interesting species of trees and distinctive flowerbeds. Here, too, nature and architecture are closely combined.

Orangery

Frederick William IV had gigantic building plans for Sanssouci. He envisioned a *Via Triumphalis*, a wide avenue stretching from the vineyard at the obelisk all the way to the Belvedere on the Klausberg hill, and although he thought to integrate 18th-century buildings into it, the main emphasis would be on new, architecturally lavish structures. A Greek temple, among other things, was planned for the vineyard, and viaducts were to connect it to Sanssouci Palace and the Historic Mill; this was to be followed by a guesthouse and an orangery, with a Belvedere on the Klausberg hill as the termination. The orangery is the only major part of this project that was built. Construction between 1851 and

Julius Schlegel

Friedenskirche vom Marlygarten aus gesehen, 1858, SPSG
Church of Peace as seen from Marly Garden, 1858, SPSG

ten des 18. Jahrhunderts einzubeziehen gedachte, deren Hauptakzente aber auf neuen, architektonisch sehr aufwendigen Bauwerken liegen sollte. Für den Weinberg war u. a. ein griechischer Tempel vorgesehen, Viadukte sollten die Verbindung zum Schloss Sanssouci und weiter zur Historischen Mühle schaffen. Dem folgten ein Gästehaus und eine Orangerie, den Endpunkt bildete das Belvedere auf dem Klausberg. Nur die Orangerie ist als einziges großes Bauwerk dieses Projektes errichtet worden. Der Ausführung in den Jahren 1851–60 durch die Schinkel-Schüler Stüler und Hesse gingen Skizzen Friedrich Wilhelms IV. und Entwürfe von Persius voraus. Wenn auch die Vorbilder aus der italienischen Renaissance-Architektur – die Villen Pamphili und Medici in Rom sowie die Uffizien in Florenz, entnommen aus Stichwerken von Percier und Fontaine – unschwer abzulesen sind, besitzt das Bauwerk doch eine ausgewogene Proportion und sichere Massenverteilung sowie eine bis in den Park ausstrahlende Monumentalität. Während die beiden über neunzig Meter langen Hallen im Winter die Kübelpflanzen aufnehmen und die pavillonartigen Eckbauten früher Wohnzwecken dienten, befinden sich in dem schlossähnlichen Mittelbau fünf ehemals fürstliche Gästezimmer sowie der Raffael-Saal. Bei den Gästezimmern – bestimmt für die Zarin Alexandra Feodorowna von Russland, Schwester Friedrich Wilhelms IV., und deren Gemahl Zar Nikolaus I. – übernahm man Dekorationsformen der Régence und des Rokoko. Der Raffael-Saal vereinigt 47 Kopien nach Gemälden des italienischen Renaissancemeisters. Angeregt von einer 1814 in Paris veranstalteten Ausstellung, auf der die von Napoleon geraubten Originalgemälde Raffaels gezeigt wurden, beauftragte Friedrich Wilhelm III. in Paris lebende deutsche Maler mit dem Kopieren der wichtigsten Bilder. Friedrich Wilhelm IV. ließ die Sammlung noch erweitern und eigens dafür den Raffael-Saal errichten, der jedoch erst 1858 fertig gestellt wurde.
In der gartenkünstlerischen Auffassung ist für Sanssouci nach 1840 die Hinwendung zur Regelmäßigkeit, die Bevorzugung historischer Stilarten und die Wertschätzung prächtiger Pflanzendekorationen kennzeichnend. In Folge der neuen Bauten nördlich der Maulbeerallee (»Triumphstraßenprojekt«) entstanden Einzelanlagen, bei denen der klassische Landschaftsgarten nicht mehr sichtbar wird.

1860 under August Stüler and Ludwig Hesse – both were students of Schinkel – was based on sketches by Frederick William IV and plans by Persius. Even though the source of inspiration, Italian Renaissance architecture – Villa Pamphili and Villa Medici in Rome as well as the Uffizi in Florence from engravings by Percier and Fontaine – is not difficult to discern, the building possesses a balanced and assured distribution of mass and a monumental character that radiate into the park. While the two ninety-meter-long halls take in potted plants in winter, the pavilion-like corner structures serve as accommodation. The palace-like center section contains five royal guest chambers and the Raphael Hall. Regency and Rococo were adopted as the decorative styles of the guest chambers, which were intended for Empress Alexandra Feodorovna of Russia, the sister of Frederick William IV, and her husband, Tsar Nicholas I. The Raphael Hall holds a collection of 47 copies of paintings by Italian Renaissance masters. Stimulated by an exhibition held in 1814 in Paris, at which the original Raphael paintings stolen by Napoleon were on display, Frederick William III commissioned young German artists living in Paris to copy the most important paintings. Frederick William IV had the collection expanded and the Raphael Hall in the orangery especially built for it. The hall was not completed until 1858.
The artistic approach to garden landscaping in Sanssouci after 1840 is marked by a shift towards formality, a preference for historical styles, and an appreciation of magnificent floral decoration. Individual garden areas, in which classic landscaping was no longer practiced, were created as a continuation of the new buildings north of the Maulbeerallee (*Via Triumphalis* project).

Links: Der Speisesaal hat noch die Dimensionen des alten Landhauses. Die weißen Wände schmücken farbige Kupferstiche nach Fresken Raffaels in den Loggien des Vatikans. Den als Anrichte gedachten Prunktisch entwarf K. F. Schinkel. In den Nischen stehen Statuen des »Ganymed« von A. Wredow, 1830 und »David mit dem Haupt von Goliath« von H. M. Imhof, 1828.
Left: The dining room still retains the dimensions of the old manor house. The walls are decorated with colored copperplate engravings of Raphael's frescoes in the loggias of the Vatican. The center table intended as a sideboard was designed by K. F. Schinkel. In the recesses stand statues of "Ganymede" by A. Wredow, 1830, and "David with the Head of Goliath" by H. M. Imhof, 1828.

Rechts oben: Das Schlafzimmer des Kronprinzenpaares wird durch das Doppelbett bestimmt, das durch einen Vorhang verborgen werden kann. Der Ausschnitt aus dem Gemälde »Die Verhöhnung Christi« von Raffael im Hintergrund weist auf die Verehrung dieses Renaissance-Meisters durch den Bauherrn hin.
Top right: The double bed dominates the crown prince's marital bedchamber, which can be concealed with a curtain. The detail of the painting, "The Mocking of Christ," by Raphael in the background is an indication of the crown prince's admiration for this Renaissance master.

Rechts unten: Dem strengen Risalit auf der westlichen Eingangsseite steht ein offener Portikus an der Ostseite des Schlosses Charlottenhof gegenüber. Er verbindet die Innenräume mit der über dem Gartenniveau liegenden, 1826 aufgeschütteten Terrasse.
Bottom right: The austere architecture of the western entrance stands in contrast to the open portico on the east side of the Charlottenhof palace. It connects the interior rooms with the terrace that was elevated above garden level in 1826.

Rechts: Die Einrichtung des Schlafzimmers der Hofdamen in Form eines Zeltes wurde erst im April 1829 vom Kronprinzen verfügt. Das Potsdamer Zeltzimmer war jedoch nicht das einzige seiner Art, sondern Ausdruck des Zeitgeschmacks, denn derartige Innenräume lassen sich in Frankreich bereits am Ende des 18. Jahrhunderts nachweisen.

Right: The decoration of this bedchamber for a lady-in-waiting in the form of a tent was first commissioned by the crown prince in April 1829. The Potsdam Tent Room was not the only one of its kind but an expression of the tastes of the time, as such rooms are documented in France as early as the end of the 18th century.

Am nordöstlichen Rand des Parks Charlottenhof liegt die Baugruppe der Römischen Bäder, deren Errichtung 1829 mit dem Wohnhaus für den Hofgärtner Hermann Sello begann. Nach einem Entwurf K. F. Schinkels und der Ausführung durch L. Persius entstand ein Bauwerk im italienischen Villenstil, von dem ein großer Einfluss auf die Berliner und Potsdamer Architektur ausging.

On the north-eastern edge of Charlottenhof Park lies the Roman Bath building ensemble. Construction began in 1829 with the domicile for the court gardener Hermann Sello. L. Persius' execution of K. F. Schinkel's design created a building in the style of an Italian villa which exerted a great influence on Berlin and Potsdam architecture.

Links: Den rückwertigen Abschluss des Impluviums bildet das Apodyterium, ein rechteckiger Raum, der in der Mitte und nach den Seiten durch halbrunde blaue Nischen erweitert ist. Dort stehen die Marmorskulptur »Jüngling und Mädchen am Brunnen« nach J. W. Henschel, 1826 und der »Bacchant«, eine Zinkskulptur aus der ersten Hälfte des 19. Jahrhunderts.

Left: The rear of the Impluvium is the Apodyterium, a rectangular room that is extended in the middle and on the sides by semi-circular blue alcoves. The marble sculpture, "Youth and Maiden at the Well" inspired by J. W. Henschel, 1826, and the "Bacchant," a zinc sculpture from the first half of the 19th century, occupy the alcoves.

Das erste, nach 1834 errichtete sogenannte »Römische Bad« ist einem antiken Wohnhaus nachgebildet. Im ersten Raum, dem Atrium, stehen zwei antike Skulpturen – »Dionysos« und »Apoll« – sowie eine Wanne aus grünem Jaspis. Durch eine Öffnung blickt man in den nach oben offenen Innenhof, das Impluvium.

The first so-called Roman Bath constructed after 1834 simulates a classical residence. In the first room, the Atrium, stand two antique sculptures – Dionysos and Apollo – as well as a bath of green jasper. An opening reveals a view of the unroofed inner court, the Impluvium.

Die Küche wurde 1842 für die Hofhaltung Friedrich Wilhelms IV. im Ostflügel von Schloss Sanssouci eingerichtet. Sie wurde nahezu dreißig Jahre genutzt und hat bis heute keine bauliche Veränderung erfahren.

The kitchen was built in the east wing of Sanssouci Palace in 1842 for the running of the court of Frederick William IV. It was used for almost thirty years and no structural changes have been made to date.

Der Name des »Traumzimmers« in Schloss Sanssouci geht auf eine Äußerung Friedrich Wilhelms IV. zurück, die er gegenüber L. Persius gemacht hatte, wonach er bereits »einmal von der Ausstattung dieses Zimmers geträumt habe«. Es gehört mit der grünen Vertäfelung, den versilberten Schnitzereien und Leisten zu den reichsten Räumen im Hofdamenflügel.

The name of the Dream Room derives from a comment made by Frederick William IV to L. Persius, according to which he had already "once dreamt of the furnishings of this room." With its green paneling, silvered carvings, and molded stripping, it is one of the most lavish rooms in the ladies-in-waiting wing.

Links oben: Die Friedenskirche, am östlichen Rand des Parks gelegen, ist der einzige Kirchenbau in Sanssouci; ab 1845 nach Skizzen italienischer Vorbilder Friedrich Wilhelms IV. von L. Persius und anderen Schinkel-Schülern ausgeführt. Das Bauwerk mit dem separaten Glockenturm spiegelt sich in dem künstlich angelegten sogenannten »Friedensteich«.
Top left: The Church of Peace, located on the eastern edge of the park, is the only church building in Sanssouci; construction was carried out from 1845 by L. Persius and other pupils of Schinkel based on Frederick William IV's sketches of Italian houses. The building with the free-standing bell tower is reflected in the artificial so-called Peace Pond.

Links unten: In die Apsis des Innenraumes ließ Friedrich Wilhelm IV. ein Mosaik aus dem 12. Jahrhundert einsetzen, das aus der Kirche St. Cyprianus auf Murano bei Venedig stammt. In der Kirche befinden sich die Gräber Friedrich Wilhelms IV. und seiner Frau Elisabeth.
Bottom left: Frederick William IV had a 12th-century mosaic from San Cipriano Church on Murano near Venice built into the apse of the interior. The tombs of Frederick William IV and his wife Elizabeth are in the church.

Rechts: In dem nach Entwürfen von L. Persius 1846/47 geschaffenen Atrium westlich der Friedenskirche steht die Figur des »Segnenden Christus« von Bertel Thorvaldsen, eine galvanoplastische Replik nach dem Marmororiginal von 1821 aus der Kopenhagener Liebfrauenkirche. Der Sockel symbolisiert die vier Ströme des Paradieses.
Right: To the west in front of the Church of Peace, in the atrium built to designs by L. Persius in 1846/47, stands the figure of the "Resurrected Christ" by Bertel Thorvaldsen, an electroformed replica of the marble original of 1821 in the Church of Our Lady, Copenhagen. The pedestal symbolizes the four rivers of paradise.

Links: Unter dem Eindruck seiner Italienreise 1828 fertigte der Kronprinz Friedrich Wilhelm (IV.) nach 1830 Skizzen für ein großes Orangeriegebäude an, das auf der Hügelkette nördlich des Parks Sanssouci stehen sollte. Später wurde L. Persius mit Entwürfen beauftragt, die nach dessen Tod 1845 A. Stüler weiter ausarbeitete. Die Ausführung von 1851–61 leitete L. F. Hesse.
Left: Impressed by his trip to Italy, after 1830 Crown Prince Frederick William (IV) made sketches for a large orangery that was meant to stand on the range of hills north of Sanssouci Park. L. Persius was subsequently commissioned with the building plans, which A. Stüler completed after his death in 1845. The construction was supervised by L. F. Hesse from 1851 to 1861.

Rechts oben: Das Malachitzimmer, das seinen Namen von den wichtigsten Einrichtungsgegenständen ableitet, war als Schlafzimmer gedacht. Die Formen der Möbel sind dem Rokoko entlehnt. Der Raum ist außerdem mit Gemälden und Skulpturen deutscher Maler und Bildhauer des 19. Jahrhunderts geschmückt.
Top right: The Malachite Room, whose name is derived from its most important piece of furniture, was intended as a bedroom. The forms of the furniture were borrowed from Rococo. In addition, the room is decorated with paintings and sculptures by 19th-century German artists.

Rechts unten: Im Raffael-Saal, dem zentralen Raum des Mittelbaus, sind seit 1858 47 Kopien nach Gemälden des italienischen Renaissance-Meisters ausgestellt. Schon seit 1814 hatte man im preußischen Königshaus Kopien nach Gemälden Raffaels gesammelt. Die Zusammenführung im Raffael-Saal zeugt von der Wertschätzung, die man seinem Schaffen in der ersten Hälfte des 19. Jahrhunderts entgegenbrachte.
Bottom right: In the Raphael Room, the central room of the middle building, 47 copies of works by the Italian Renaissance painter have been on display since 1858. As early as 1814, members of the Prussian royal family had been collecting copies of Raphael's paintings. The gathering of these copies in the Raphael Room testifies to the high esteem in which his works were held in the first half of the 19th century.

Das Belvedere auf dem Pfingstberg Potsdam

Belvedere on the Pfingstberg Potsdam

Der Pfingstberg, wohl die höchste Erhebung Potsdams, war 1683 der Endpunkt einer breiten Allee, die von der heutigen Breiten Straße ausging und mit der im rechten Winkel dazu abgehenden Lindenstraße und der Jägerallee bis auf einen Berg führte, der damals noch den Namen Eichberg trug und auf dem zwei Windmühlen standen. Am südlichen Abhang des Berges lagen im 18. Jahrhundert die Oberweinberge, während das Gelände am Heiligen See (heute Neuer Garten) Unterweinberge hieß. Mit der Anlage des Judenfriedhofs 1743 an der Westseite erhielt der Berg den Namen Judenberg. Seine heutige Bezeichnung soll der Legende nach von einem Besuch der Königin Luise am Pfingstmorgen des Jahres 1804 herrühren. 1817 ging das Gelände in den Besitz des preußischen Königs über und seit dieser Zeit ist der Name Pfingstberg gebräuchlich.
Von der günstigen Lage in der Nähe des Neuen Gartens und der herrlichen Aussicht auf die Havellandschaft angeregt, wollte bereits Friedrich Wilhelm II. 1793 hier ein Schloss in neugotischen Formen errichten lassen. Die Pläne waren von Johann Boumann d. J. schon angefertigt, doch die Ausführung scheiterte wohl an den Geldforderungen der Grundstücksbesitzer.
Das Belvedere, das heute auf dem Berg steht, ist in zwei Bauetappen (1849/52 und 1860/62) errichtet worden. Den Plänen von Stüler und Hesse lagen erste Entwürfe und Ideenskizzen von Friedrich Wilhelm IV. und Persius zugrunde. Das Bauwerk ist das Fragment einer Terrassenanlage, die bis zum Neuen Garten herunterreichen sollte. Wie bei so vielen Bauten, die um die Mitte des 19. Jahrhunderts in und um Potsdam errichtet wurden, stand auch hier die italienische Architektur Pate. Den Kern der gewaltigen Anlage sollte ein Casino, ähnlich dem der Villa Caprarola bei Viterbo bilden, doch sein Bau unterblieb. Man schloss nach 1860 den von einer Doppelturmanlage und einer seitlichen Umfassungsmauer begrenzten Hof durch eine Pfeilerhalle. Bei dem Belvedere handelt es sich um eine reine »Schauarchitektur«, barg doch das Innere nur zwei nutzbare Räume, im Südturm ein »Römisches« und im Nordturm ein »Maurisches« Kabinett. Im Hof befindet sich das Wasserbecken zur Speisung der Fontänenanlage des Neuen Gartens. Die gärtnerische Gestaltung der Umgebung entwarf Peter Joseph Lenné.
Der kleine am Abhang stehende Teepavillon – Pomonatempel – gehörte ehemals zum Oesfeldschen Garten und wurde 1800/01 erbaut. Es ist das früheste ausgeführte Bauwerk Schinkels in Potsdam. Der Pomonatempel hatte zwar den Krieg unbeschadet überstanden, war aber bald danach zur Ruine geworden und konnte erst 1993 wiederhergestellt werden. Das gleiche gilt für das Belvedere, dessen Restaurierung 2004 abgeschlossen wurde. Dies war nur durch die großzügige Unterstützung der Herrmann Reemtsma-Stiftung und von Prof. Dr. Werner Otto möglich.

In 1683 the Pfingstberg, the highest elevation in Potsdam, was the end point of a wide avenue that branched off today's Breiten Strasse and, together with the Lindenstrasse that branched at a right angle from it and the Jägerallee, led to a hill that was then still called Eichberg, upon which two windmills stood. In the 18th century, the upper vineyards lay on the southern slope, while the area on Heiligen Lake (today New Garden) was called Unterweinberge, or lower vineyards. The hill gained the name Judenberg in 1743 from the Jewish cemetery on its west side. According to legend, its present name originates from a visit by Queen Louise on Whitsun (Pfingsten) morning in 1804. In 1817, the area became the property of the King of Prussia and since that time the name Pfingstberg has been customary.
Attracted by the favorable location near the New Garden and the marvelous view of the Havel landscape, Frederick William II wanted to have a neo-Gothic palace built on the hill as early as 1793. The plans by Johann Boumann the Younger were already completed, but the project failed to come about due to the property owner's exorbitant monetary demands.
The Belvedere that today stands on the hill was built in two stages of construction (1849 – 52 and 1860 – 62). The plans by Stüler and Hesse were based on original designs and ideas sketched by Frederick William IV and Ludwig Persius. The building, however, is a fragment of the large terrace that was meant to extend all the way to the New Garden. As with so many buildings constructed around the middle of the 19th century in and around Potsdam, here too Italian architecture was the inspiration. A casino similar to the Villa Caprarola near Viterbo was to form the core of the huge complex, but it was never built. After 1860, the courtyard, bordered by a building with twin towers and an outer wall on both sides, was closed with a colonnade. The Belvedere is purely show architecture; the interior contains only two useable rooms. The south tower contains a small "Roman" room, the north tower a small "Moorish" one. In the courtyard is the reservoir basin to feed the fountains in the New Garden. The landscaping was by Peter Joseph Lenné.
The small Tea Pavilion on the slope of the hill – the Pomona Temple – was formerly part of the garden in Oesfeld and was built in 1800/01. It is the earliest construction work carried out in Potsdam by Karl Friedrich Schinkel.
Although the Pomona Temple and Belvedere survived the war undamaged, they soon became ruins. The temple was restored in 1993, and the restoration of the Belvedere was completed in 2004. This was possible only through the generous support of the Herrmann Reemtsma Foundation and Professor Werner Otto.

Vor dem großen Belvedere steht der bescheidene »Pomonatempel«, 1800/01 erbaut. Es ist das früheste ausgeführte Bauwerk K. F. Schinkels in Potsdam.
In front of the large Belvedere stands the modest Pomona Temple, built in 1800/01. It is the earliest building project carried out by K. F. Schinkel in Potsdam.

Dem Belvedere Pfingstberg, in zwei Etappen 1840/52 und 1860/62 nach Ideenskizzen Friedrich Wilhelms IV. und Plänen von Stüler und Hesse errichtet, liegen, wie bei vielen Bauten des Königs, italienische Vorbilder zugrunde. In den letzten Jahren erfolgte die Wiederherstellung des zum Teil ruinösen Bauwerks. Heute ist es wieder ein beliebter Aussichtspunkt.

The Pfingstberg Belvedere, like many of Frederick William IV's buildings, was based on Italian models. It was constructed in two phases, 1840 – 52 and 1860 – 62, using ideas sketched by the king and plans by Stüler and Hesse. In recent years, the reconstruction of the partially ruined structure has taken place. Today it is once again a popular observation point.

Schloss Lindstedt Potsdam

Lindstedt Palace Potsdam

Das nordwestlich des Neuen Palais gelegene ehemalige Gut Lindstedt hatte Friedrich Wilhelm III. 1828 erworben. Seit dieser Zeit beschäftigte sich der Kronprinz Friedrich Wilhelm (IV.) mit diesem Anwesen, das den Namen des ersten Pächters im 18. Jahrhundert, des Hasenhegers Achatius Daniel Lindstedt, trägt.

In den 1830er Jahren fertigte der Kronprinz über dreißig Skizzen zu Verschönerungen und Um- und Ausbauten des Gutes an. 1840 auf den Thron gekommen, wurden seine Baupläne für das Gutshaus konkreter und er beauftragte anfangs Persius, später Stüler, Arnim und Hesse mit dem Entwurf. Von 1858 – 60 wurde der Bau ausgeführt, wobei sich der Innenausbau noch bis 1863 hinzog. Friedrich Wilhelm IV. hat die Vollendung des Hauses nicht mehr erlebt; er starb 1861.

Der schlichte spätklassizistische Bau wird geprägt durch einen Rundturm mit tempelartiger Bekrönung, eine Tempelfassade mit sehr hoher Freitreppe und einen überlangen Säulengang, der bis zur Straße führt. Diese Architektur ist charakteristisch für die späteren Bauten Friedrich Wilhelms IV.

Peter Joseph Lenné und Gustav Meyer gestalteten den Garten, der nach dem Vorbild antiker Villengärten angelegt ist. Nach 1879 bewohnten Offiziere und Hofbedienstete das Haus; ab 1918 der General Erich von Falkenhayn, dessen Tochter Henning von Treskow heiratete, der eng mit dem Widerstand des 20. Juli 1944 verbunden ist. Das Schloss blieb bis zum Ende des Zweiten Weltkriegs im Besitz der Hohenzollern.

Nach 1945 wurde es von der sowjetischen Kommandantur und von 1953 bis 1983 vom Botanischen Institut der Pädagogischen Hochschule, heute Universität Potsdam genutzt. Von diesem übernahm es 1983 das Institut für Gerichtliche Medizin des Bezirkes Potsdam. Dieses Institut renovierte von 1986 – 88 das Gebäude und rekonstruierte auch den Garten. Als es in ein neues Domizil umzog, kam das Haus 1995 zu den Schlössern und Gärten und wird seit dem für verschiedene kulturelle Veranstaltungen genutzt.

The former Lindstedt estate situated northwest of the New Palace was acquired by Frederick William II in 1828. From that time, Crown Prince Frederick William devoted a great deal of time to this property, which carries the name of the first leaseholder, the rabbit-keeper Achatius Daniel Lindstedt.

In the 1830s the crown prince (later Frederick William IV), who was greatly interested in this house, drew over thirty sketches for the beautification, remodeling and improvement of the estate. When he acceded to the throne in 1840, his building plans for the manor house became more concrete and he commissioned first Persius, then later Stüler, Arnim, and Hesse with the design. Construction was carried out from 1858 to 1860, though the completion of the interior lasted until 1863. Frederick William IV did not live to see the house finished; he died in 1861.

The simple late neoclassical construction is marked by a round tower with a temple-like crown, a temple façade with a very high flight of steps, and an unusually long colonnade that leads all the way to the road. This architecture is characteristic of Frederick William IV's later buildings.

Peter Joseph Lenné and Gustav Meyer designed the garden, whose layout was inspired by classical villa gardens. After 1879, it was occupied by officers and court attendants, and from 1918 by General Erich von Falkenhayn, the father-in-law of Henning von Treskow, who was deeply involved in the act of resistance of July 20, 1944. The palace remained in the possession of the Hohenzollern family until the end of the Second World War.

It was used after 1945 as the Soviet commandant's headquarters and from 1953 until 1983 by the Botanical Institute of the Potsdam University of Education. It was taken over from them in 1983 by the Institute for Forensic Medicine of the District of Potsdam. This institute renovated the building from 1986 to 1988 and also reconstructed the garden. When the institute moved to its new location in 1995, the house was assigned to the Palaces and Gardens Foundation and has been used since then for various cultural events.

Das Schloss, westlich des Parks Sanssouci gelegen, wurde nach Skizzen Friedrich Wilhelms (IV.) und Entwürfen des Schinkel-Schülers F. Stüler als Turmvilla gebaut. Den Garten schuf P. J. Lenné. Das Haus wird heute für Veranstaltungen der Stiftung Preußische Schlösser und Gärten Berlin-Brandenburg genutzt.

The palace, lying west of Sanssouci Park, was built as a tower-villa according to sketches by Frederick William (IV) and building plans from Schinkel's pupil F. Stüler. Today the house is used by the Prussian Palaces and Gardens Foundation Berlin-Brandenburg for events.

Schloss Sacrow Potsdam

Sacrow Palace Potsdam

Auf halbem Wege zwischen Potsdam und der Pfaueninsel liegt in der Nähe der Havel Sacrow; der Ort ist seit 1939 ein Ortsteil von Potsdam.
Bereits 1375 im Landbuch Kaiser Karls IV. genannt, tritt er erst 1764 als Besitzung des schwedischen Grafen Johann Ludwig von Hordt, ab 1776 Gouverneur von Spandau, in die Geschichte ein. Hordt ließ 1773 das heute noch stehende zweigeschossige Herrenhaus errichten. Jahre später, 1779, kaufte es Heinrich Karl de la Motte-Fouqué, der Vater des Dichters der »Undine« Friedrich Heinrich Karl de la Motte-Fouqué, der hier mit seiner Familie bis 1781 lebte. Danach übernahm es wieder ein Schwiegersohn des vorigen Besitzers und erweiterte es durch Wirtschaftsgebäude, eine Ziegelei und eine Kalkbrennerei. 1793 wurde hier eine Schwanenzucht betrieben, die Tiere zum benachbarten Kaninchenwerder, der späteren Pfaueninsel, lieferte.
Das Gut wechselte mehrfach den Besitzer, bis 1828 König Friedrich Wilhelm III. versuchte, Sacrow zu erwerben, um die Potsdamer Parklandschaft um dieses Areal zu erweitern. Doch die Verhandlungen scheiterten an den hohen Preisvorstellungen des Besitzers. Nach der Thronbesteigung 1840 erwarb König Friedrich Wilhelm IV. das gesamte Anwesen. Er ließ große Teile des ehemaligen Ackerlandes in Wald verwandeln sowie Wirtschaftsgebäude, Ställe und Scheune am Schloss abreißen. Auch für das Gutshaus waren Umbaumaßnahmen vorgesehen. Es sollte ein Schloss in »Art des Petzower Hauses« entstehen, wie Ludwig Persius in seinem Tagebuch vom 29. Oktober 1843 vermerkt. Der Umbau unterblieb jedoch, wie auch die Errichtung eines Casinos unmittelbar am Havelufer. Von den vielen Entwürfen zur Veränderung des Schlosses sind nur der Umbau des Fährhauses »Zum Doktor Faust« (im Krieg zerstört und 1970 abgerissen) sowie die Errichtung der Römischen Bank am Ufer der Havel 1842/43 verwirklicht worden. Besonderes Augenmerk richtete Friedrich Wilhelm IV. auf den Bau einer Kirche am Havelufer. Die alte Kirche war schon 1822 wegen Baufälligkeit abgetragen worden. Noch vor dem Erwerb Sacrows skizzierte Friedrich Wilhelm IV. 1832 eine Kirche mit einer Baugruppe aus Pfarr- und Schulhaus. So vermerkte Persius in seinem Tagebuch vom 9. November 1841: »Die Kirche soll im italienischen Styl mit einem Campanile daneben erbaut werden.« Nach mehreren Änderungen ist der Entwurf von Persius 1843/44 ausgeführt worden.
Peter Joseph Lenné hatte Sacrow 1833 in seinen Verschönerungsplan von Potsdam und Umgebung einbezogen. Dieser Park war nun der fünfte und letzte in dem Kranz um dem Jungfernsee. In seinem Plan von 1842 wies Lenné die Zielpunkte der fünf wie Fächer ausstrahlenden Sichtachsen aus.

Sacrow is situated near the Havel River, halfway between Potsdam and Peacock Island; the area has been part of Potsdam since 1939.
Although mentioned as early as 1375 in the land book of Emperor Charles IV, it first enters history only in 1764 as an estate of Johann Ludwig von Hordt, a Swedish count who became governor of Spandau in 1776. In 1773Hordt built the two-storey manor house that still exists today. Years later, in 1779, Heinrich Karl de la Motte-Fouqué, the father of the author of "Undine", Friedrich Heinrich Karl de la Motte-Fouqué, bought it and lived there with his family until 1781. Thereafter, a son-in-law of the former owner took it over again and enlarged it with farm buildings, brickworks, and a lime kiln. Furthermore, he bred swans, and in 1793 delivered animals to the neighboring Kaninchenwerder (Rabbit Isle), which later became Peacock Island.
The estate changed hands repeatedly until 1828, when King Frederick William III tried to acquire Sacrow to expand the Potsdam landscape park. The negotiations failed because of the owner's high asking price, but after ascending the throne in 1840, King Frederick William IV acquired the whole estate in November of the same year. He had large areas of farmland turned into forest and the farm buildings, stables, and barns next to the palace torn down. Rebuilding measures were also planned for the manor house. A palace in the "style of the Petzow house" was intended, as Ludwig Persius noted in his diary on October 29, 1843. The remodeling did not happen, however, and neither did the building of a casino directly on the shores of the Havel. Of the many plans for changes in Sacrow Palace, only the rebuilding of the ferry house "Zum Doktor Faust" (destroyed in the war and demolished in 1970) and the construction of the Roman Bank on the shores of the Havel in 1842/43 were realized.
Frederick William IV gave special attention to the construction of a church on the banks of the Havel. The old church of Sacrow had already been pulled down in 1822 because of its dilapidated state. Even before acquiring Sacrow, Frederick William IV had sketched a church with a group of buildings consisting of a vicarage and a schoolhouse in 1832. Persius made the following entry in his diary on November 9, 1841, "The church is to be built in the Italian style with a campanile next to it." After several changes, Persius' design was carried out in 1843/44.
In 1833, Peter Joseph Lenné had also included Sacrow in his plans for beautifying Potsdam and its surroundings. This park was now the fifth and last encircling the Jungfernsee lake. In his plans of 1842, Lenné identified the terminal points of five lines of sight radiating like a fan. Along with the Kastanienallee, a central avenue that started at the palace and already existed in the 18th

Neben der vom Schloss ausgehenden zentralen, noch im 18. Jahrhundert bestehenden Kastanienallee, sind die Zielpunkte der Jägerhof in Glienicke, der Pavillon in Glienicke (gemeint ist die Große Neugierde), die Mühle auf dem Babelsberg, an deren Stelle heute der Flatowturm steht, und die Garnisonkirche in Potsdam. Der Sacrower Park nimmt damit eine zentrale Stellung in diesem Gebiet ein, das architektonisch bescheidene Schloss hält sich im Hintergrund. Wichtig ist die »Heilandskirche am Port«, wie das Gotteshaus genannt wurde, das zentral an der Spitze der Halbinsel steht. Da ein Pfarrhaus für die Heilandskirche nicht geplant war, wohnte der Pfarrer bis 1848 in dem Schloss, bis er in das neue Haus an der Potsdamer Friedenskirche zog.

Fontane war nach 1870 in Sacrow und hatte 1880 ein Kapitel über den Ort in seine »Wanderungen« aufgenommen. Er besuchte mehrfach seinen Bekannten, den Schriftsteller und Publizisten Werner Hahn, der ab 1870 in Sacrow wohnte. Seit dem Beginn des 20. Jahrhunderts sind wir wieder etwas genauer über die Geschichte der Bewohner und des Schlosses unterrichtet. Kurz nach dem Ersten Weltkrieg bewohnte der damalige demokratische Finanzminister Albert Südekum das Schloss und 1922 bezog es der Flugpionier und Begründer der Deutschen Lufthansa Eberhand Cranz.

Bald nach 1933 mussten die Bewohner das Schlosses verlassen, denn Sacrow wurde 1938/39 mit den Nebengebäuden zum Dienstsitz des preußischen Generalforstmeisters und Staatssekretärs im Reichsforstministerium, Friedrich Alpers, umgebaut. Während der Bau im Äußeren im Wesentlichen die Gestalt des 18. Jahrhunderts behielt, wurde das Innere vollkommen verändert und repräsentativen Ansprüchen angepasst.

Es ist interessant, dass an der Farbgestaltung des Hauses besonders Hinnerk Scheper mitwirkte. Er war 1925 bis 1935 Bauhausmeister und Leiter der Werkstatt für Wandmalerei am Bauhaus in Dessau und Berlin. Seine Mitwirkung in Sacrow ist zwar durch Unterlagen bekannt, aber in der offiziellen Baubeschreibung dieser Zeit wird er nicht genannt.

Nach 1945 wurde das Schloss für kurze Zeit Flüchtlingsunterkunft, dann Erholungsheim für Verfolgte des Naziregimes (VVN) und später Kinderheim sowie in den 50er Jahren kurze Zeit Heim für Schriftsteller. Nach dem Mauerbau 1961 wurde es Sitz der Grenztruppen der DDR und 1973 bezog die Zollverwaltung das Schloss und die Nebengebäude. Im Park wurden diverse Gebäude errichtet, so dass von der Schöpfung Lennés nur wenig übrig blieb. In der Heilandskirche an der Havel, wo 1961 der letzte Gottesdienst vor dem Mauerbau stattgefunden hatte, fand nach der Maueröffnung am Heiligen Abend 1989 nach 28 Jahren wieder der erste Gottesdienst in der zwischen-

century, these terminal points were the Jägerhof, a hunting lodge in Glienicke; the pavilion in Glienicke (known as the Large Curiosity); the mill on the hill of Babelsberg, where Flatow Tower stands today; and the Garrison Church in Potsdam. Sacrow Park thus assumes a central position in this area, although the architecturally modest palace remains in the background. The so-called Church of Our Savior in the Port is an important feature which stands centrally at the tip of the promontory. As a vicarage was no longer planned for the Church of Our Savior, the pastor lived in the palace until 1848, when he moved into the new house at the Potsdam Church of Peace.

Frederick William IV had offered Sacrow to de la Motte-Fouqué as a place for his retirement, but the poet had already died by 1843. The writer Theodor Fontane was in Sacrow after 1870, and in 1880 included a chapter about the place in his “Walking Tours in the Mark of Brandenburg”. He often visited his acquaintance, the writer and publicist Werner Hahn, who lived in Sacrow after 1870. After the beginning of the 20th century, we again have more exact information about the palace and its occupants. Shortly after the First World War, the Social Democratic finance minister, Albert Südekum, lived in the palace and in 1922 the aviation pioneer and founder of Lufthansa, Eberhand Cranz, moved in.

Soon after 1933 the occupants of the palace and the adjacent buildings were forced to leave because in 1938/39 Sacrow, together with its annexes, was converted into the offices of the Prussian General Forestry Superintendent and Under-Secretary in the Reich Forest Ministry, Friedrich Alpers. The alterations essentially retained the 18th-century form of the exterior, but the interior was completely altered and adapted to the needs of official representation.

It is interesting that Hinnerk Scheper was involved in the color scheme of the house. He worked at the Bauhaus between 1925 and 1935 and was director of the workshop for murals at the Bauhaus in Dessau and Berlin. Although his involvement in Sacrow is documented, he is not mentioned in the official building descriptions of the time.

After 1945 the palace was used for a while to accommodate refugees, then as a convalescent home for the victims of persecution by the Nazi regime (VVN), and later as a children’s home as well as a home for writers for a short time in the 1950s. After the construction of the Berlin Wall, it became the headquarters of border troops of the GDR, and in 1973 the customs administration moved into the palace and its outbuildings. Several buildings were built in the park, so that little remained of Lenné’s original scheme.

The last service in the Church of Our Savior on the Havel before the building of the Berlin Wall was held in 1961. The first service after the fall of the wall

Rechts: Der 1773 errichtete einfache Schlossbau wurde besonders im Inneren mehrfach verändert und den verschiedenen Nutzungen angepasst. Nach der politischen Wende 1989/90 wurde auch der von P. J. Lenné gestaltete Park wiederhergestellt.
Right: The simple palace building of 1773 has been altered repeatedly, especially inside, and adapted for various uses. After the political changes of 1989/90, the park that P. J. Lenné had designed was restored.

zeitlich demolierten Kirche statt. Die Restaurierung von 1993 bis 1996 stellte den Innenraum wieder her.
1993 kamen Schloss und Park Sacrow in den Besitz der Potsdamer Schlösserverwaltung, der späteren Stiftung Preußische Schlösser und Gärten Berlin-Brandenburg. Sofort wurde begonnen, den Park wiederherzustellen, indem man Einbauten beseitigte, Wege anlegte und Blicke in die Umgebung öffnete. Die von der Stiftung gedachte Unterbringung der ostpreußischen Sammlung Dohna-Schlobitten konnte nicht realisiert werden. Zurzeit finden im Schloss während der Sommermonate Ausstellungen mit zeitgenössischer Kunst statt.

took place 28 years later, on Christmas Eve 1989. The interior of the church was restored between 1993 and 1996.
In 1993, the palace and Sacrow Park came into the possession of the Potsdam Palace Administration, which later became the Prussian Palaces and Gardens Foundation Berlin-Brandenburg. Immediately, work was begun to restore the park by removing the unsuitable buildings. Paths were laid out again and views of the surrounding area were opened up. The foundation's intention of accommodating the East Prussian Dohna-Schlobitten collection has not been fulfilled. Currently, exhibitions of contemporary art are held in the palace during the summer months.

Franz Krüger

Prinz Carl von Preußen, 1852, SPSG
Prince Charles of Prussia, 1852, SPSG

Julius Schoppe

Prinzessin Marie von Preußen, 1838, SPSG
Princess Mary of Prussia, 1838, SPSG

Prinz Carl

Prince Charles of Prussia

Bruder Friedrich Wilhelms IV. und Wilhelms I.

Brother of Frederick William IV and William I

Schloss Glienicke
Berlin

Glienicke Palace
Berlin

Durch den Umbau eines kleinen Billardhauses entstand 1824 nach Skizzen des Kronprinzen Friedrich Wilhelm (IV.) und Entwürfen von K. F. Schinkel ein kleines klassizistisches Gästehaus. Es war der erste Bau Schinkels in Glienicke. Von der Terrasse hat man einen schönen Blick auf die Havellandschaft, die den Prinzen an Italien erinnerte.

Through the remodeling of a little billiard house in 1824, a small classical guesthouse was created from sketches by Crown Prince Frederick William (IV) and plans by K. F. Schinkel. It was Schinkel's first building in Glienicke. The beautiful view of the Havel landscape from the terrace reminded the prince of Italy.

Schloss Glienicke
Berlin

Glienicke Palace
Berlin

Kurfürst Friedrich Wilhelm, genannt der Große Kurfürst, hatte sich schon 1672 nach Entwürfen von Philippe Dieussart an diesem Ort ein Jagdschloss errichten lassen. Nördlich dieses Schlosses war später ein Gut entstanden, das 1814 in den Besitz des Fürsten Karl August von Hardenberg gelangte. Im gleichen Jahr erhielt das Gutshaus im Äußeren eine neue Gestalt nach Entwürfen des Potsdamer Baumeisters Andreas Ludwig Krüger. Im Jahre 1816 war durch den Fürsten Hardenberg auch der junge Peter Joseph Lenné zur gärtnerischen Gestaltung nach Glienicke gerufen worden. Als der Prinz Carl, ein jüngerer Bruder des späteren Königs Friedrich Wilhelm IV., das ganze Anwesen im Jahre 1824 erwarb, versicherte auch er sich der Dienste des zu Ansehen gelangten Gartenkünstlers. Mit der 1825 bis 1828 erfolgten erneuten Umgestaltung des Gutshauses wurde Karl Friedrich Schinkel beauftragt. So finden wir schon hier beide Künstler mit einer gemeinsamen Aufgabe befasst, wie sie sie wenig später in ähnlicher Art im neuen Parkteil von Sanssouci, Charlottenhof und ab 1833 am gegenüberliegenden Ufer auf dem Babelsberg übernahmen.
Dem streng gegliederten Baukörper des Schlosses fügte Schinkel auf der Rückseite einen Gartenhof an, dessen stimmungsvoll heiterer Charakter in zeitgenössischen Darstellungen häufig wiedergegeben wird. Die angestrebte südländische Wirkung wird durch das angrenzende Kavalierhaus mit dem 1832 angefügten Turm erreicht.
Die Ausführung der umfangreichen Bauvorhaben in Glienicke lag in den Händen des Schinkel-Schülers Ludwig Persius. Der Bau des Maschinenhauses 1837/38 ermöglichte die Anlage und den Betrieb des gleichzeitig entstandenen Löwenbrunnens vor dem Schloss. Mit ihm gab Schinkel, unter Verzicht auf eine ursprünglich geplante Terrasse, dieser Ansicht des Schlosses eine repräsentative Note.
Der erste Bau Schinkels für den Prinzen Carl war 1825 das Casino am Havelufer. Hohe Fenster ermöglichen den Ausblick in die nähere und weitere Umgebung. Pergolen, Treppen und eine kunstvolle Bepflanzung verbinden die Architektur Schinkels mit der Gartenlandschaft Peter Joseph Lennés.
Das Schloss wurde 1935 von der Stadt Berlin erworben. Durch den Straßenbau Berlin – Potsdam in den 1930er Jahren erlitt der Park starke Verluste. Das fast verfallene Schloss wurde 1950 – 52 vereinfacht zu einem Sportlerheim ausgebaut und dabei auch die Schinkelsche Innenraumgestaltung beseitigt. Das in einem beklagenswerten Zustand befindliche Kasino wurde 1963 wiederhergestellt und das Schloss mit den dazugehörigen Gebäuden 1986 vom Berliner Senat der Berliner Schlösserverwaltung zugeordnet.

Elector Frederick William, known as the Great Elector, had a hunting lodge built on this site in 1672 to plans by Philip Dieussart. Later, north of this castle, there was a manor that came into the possession of Charles Augustus, Prince von Hardenberg, in 1814. In the same year, the exterior of the manor house was remodeled externally by Potsdam architect Andreas Ludwig Krüger. In 1816, the young Peter Joseph Lenné was brought to Glienicke by von Hardenberg to design the gardens. When Prince Charles, a younger brother of the future King Frederick William IV, acquired the whole property in 1824, he too secured the services of Lenné, now a renowned landscape gardener. Karl Friedrich Schinkel was commissioned for the subsequent further remodeling of the manor house from 1825 to 1828. We thus find these two artists already involved in a common project similar to those they would soon take on in Charlottenhof, the new section of Sanssouci Park, and from 1833 on the opposite shore on Babelsberg.
To the rear of the clearly structured main body of the palace, Schinkel added a garden courtyard, whose idyllic, cheerful character is often described in contemporary accounts. The desired southern European appearance was accomplished in the adjoining Cavalier House through the addition of the tower in 1832.
The execution of the extensive building project in Glienicke was in the hands of Schinkel's pupil, Ludwig Persius. The construction of the machine house in 1837/38 made it possible to build and operate the Lion Fountain in front of the palace. By dispensing with the terrace that was originally planned in favor of the fountain, Schinkel gave this view of the palace a character of official representation.
The first of Schinkel's buildings for Prince Charles was the Casino on the banks of the Havel in 1825. High windows afforded a view of the surroundings near and far. Pergolas, flights of steps, and an artistic scheme of planting combine Schinkel's architecture with the garden landscape of Peter Joseph Lenné.
The palace was acquired by the city of Berlin in 1935. The park suffered great losses through the construction of the road from Berlin to Potsdam in the 1930s. The palace, which had almost fallen into disrepair, was simplified and expanded into accommodation for athletes from 1950 to 1952 and, in the process, Schinkel's decoration and furnishings were disposed of. The Casino was found to be in a deplorable condition and restored in 1963, and the palace with its accompanying buildings was assigned by the Berlin Senate to the Berlin Palace Administration in 1986.

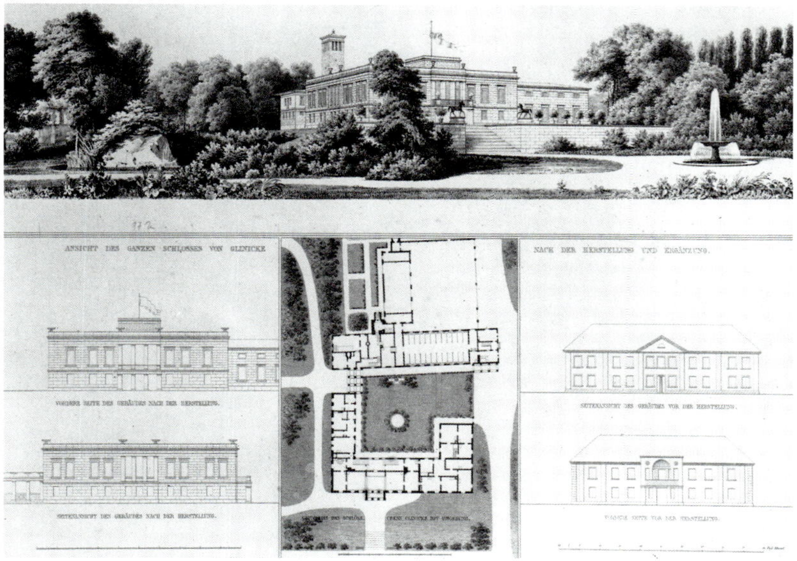

Ansicht des Schlosses Glienicke mit Vorgängerbauten und Grundriss, 1837, SPSG
View of Glienicke Palace with Previous Buildings and Ground Plan, 1837, SPSG

Ende der 1970er Jahre wurde der Betrieb des Sporthotels eingestellt und das Schloss in eine Heimvolkshochschule umgewandelt. 1986 endeten der Lehrbetrieb und 1987 die Übernachtungsmöglichkeiten. Aus dem Haus konnte nun ein Schlossmuseum werden. Die historischen Innenräume wurden rekonstruiert und die Berliner Schlösserverwaltung hatte aus dem Besitz des Prinzen Carl stammende Kunstwerke aus der Stiftung des Barons Cerrini di Montevarchi erworben und wieder nach Glienicke zurückgebracht. 1995 konnte das Haus als Schlossmuseum wiedereröffnet werden.
Angeschlossen ist seit 2001 ein Museum für die Hofgärtner, die seit dem 18. Jahrhundert die Potsdamer Parklandschaft geschaffen und gepflegt haben.

In the late 1970s, the sports hostel ceased operations and the palace was turned into a residential adult education center. In 1986 the teaching program came to an end, in 1987 the overnight accommodation as well. The house could now be made into a palace museum. The historic interior was reconstructed, and the Berlin Palace Administration acquired from the Baron Cerrin die Montevarchi Foundation works of art once possessed by Prince Charles, and brought them back to Glienicke. In 1995, the house was reopened as a palace museum.
In 2001 it was joined by a museum about the court gardeners who have created and cared for the Potsdam park landscape since the 18th century.

Schon von der Straße, die von Berlin nach Potsdam führt, ist der 1837/38 nach einem Entwurf von K. F. Schinkel ausgeführte Löwenbrunnen sichtbar. Zwischen den auf hohen Sockeln stehenden vergoldeten Löwen blickt man auf die Hauptfassade des Schlosses.

The Lion Fountain is visible from the street that leads from Berlin to Potsdam. It was constructed in 1837/38 to a design by K. F. Schinkel. The main façade of the palace can be seen between the golden lions standing on the high plinths.

Rechts: Der Rote Saal nimmt die Mitte des Schlosses ein und ist mit Kunstwerken aus dem Besitz des Prinzen Carl ausgestattet.
Right: The Red Hall takes up the middle of the palace and is decorated with works of art possessed by Prince Charles of Prussia.

Im Grünen Salon ist besonders das Chaiselongue aus dem Wohnzimmer der Prinzessin Marie im Berliner Palais des Prinzenpaares nach einem Entwurf K. F. Schinkels von 1828 raumbestimmend.

The atmosphere in the Green Salon is particularly dominated by the chaise longue designed by K. F. Schinkel in 1828, which is from Princess Marie's living room in the royal couple's Berlin residence.

Paul Bülow

Kaiser Wilhelm I. in seinem Arbeitszimmer, 1883, SPSG
Emperor William I in his study, 1883, SPSG

Minna Pfüller nach/after Franz Xaver Winterhalter

Kaiserin Augusta, um 1880, SPSG
Empress Augusta, c. 1880, SPSG

König und Kaiser

Wilhelm I.

King and Emperor William I

reg. 1861/1871–1888

Schloss und Park Babelsberg mit Flatowturm und Gerichtslaube Potsdam

Babelsberg Palace and Park with the Flatow Tower and the Court Loggia Potsdam

Weithin sichtbar erhebt sich der Flatowturm über die Bäume des Parkes. Als architektonische Vorlage für die Entwürfe von H. Strack diente der Eschenheimer Torturm in Frankfurt am Main. Der Name ist vom Gut Flatow in Westpreußen abgeleitet, das im Besitz des Prinzen Wilhelm war.

Visible for miles around, Flatow Tower rises up above the trees of the park. The tower of the Eschenheimer Gate in Frankfurt am Main served as architectural model for H. Strack's design. The name is derived from the Flatow Estate in West Prussia which belonged to Prince William.

Schloss und Park Babelsberg mit Flatowturm und Gerichtslaube Potsdam

Babelsberg Palace and Park with the Flatow Tower and the Court Loggia Potsdam

Der Park Babelsberg ist die dritte große Gartenanlage Potsdams. Prinz Wilhelm (später Kaiser Wilhelm I.) war durch Lenné wiederholt auf die Schönheiten dieses Gebietes, das gegenüber dem Park seines Bruders, des Prinzen Carl, lag, aufmerksam gemacht geworden. 1833 erhielt er von seinem Vater Friedrich Wilhelm III. einen großen Teil des Geländes geschenkt, das von Lenné durch ein Wegenetz und mit Pflanzungen einheimischer Laubhölzer erschlossen wurde. Das hügelige Gelände des Parks liegt am Tiefen See und der Glienicker Lake. Lenné war darauf bedacht, die schönen Ausblicke auf Potsdam und seine Umgebung, die man von den einzelnen höheren Punkten der Hügel hatte, auch weiterhin zu erhalten. Schinkel wurde beauftragt, Entwürfe für ein Schloss zu machen, das nach den Vorstellungen der Prinzessin Augusta im Stil der englischen Neugotik dort entstehen sollte. Zeitgenössische Architekturschriften, vor allem die des Schlosses Windsor (nach 1824), waren in dieser Zeit beliebt und wurden als Vorlagen verwendet. Im Juni 1834 wurde der Grundstein gelegt und im Oktober 1835 konnte die erste östliche Hälfte des Bauwerks mit der Pergola bis zum Oktogon, dem Speisesaal (Teesalon), eingeweiht werden. Ein zweiter Schlossflügel sollte sich, um die Tiefe des Oktogon zurückgesetzt, nach Westen anschließen, wie auch der erste Bauabschnitt einen Wohntrakt besitzen und mit einem Fahnenturm enden. Der so gestaltete Schlosskomplex hätte sich organisch in die umgebende Landschaft eingefügt. Schinkel hatte diesen ersten Bauabschnitt mit äußerster Zurückhaltung ausgeführt.

1844 – 49 ist der von Schinkel entworfene westliche Baukörper auf Wunsch des Bauherrn um den oktogonalen Tanzsaal erweitert worden. Nach dem Tode Persius 1845, der anfangs den Weiterbau leitete, ist er später von Heinrich Strack zu Ende geführt worden, der dabei eigene Wege ging. Die Innenräume, auch die Schinkelschen, wurden nach 1850 verändert und mit Mobiliar verschiedener Stilrichtungen sowie Erinnerungsstücken eingerichtet.

Für die Gartengestaltung war anfangs Peter Joseph Lenné verantwortlich, der nach 1843 von Fürst Pückler Muskau abgelöst wurde. In den folgenden Jahren wurde der Park im Westen bis zur Grenze der Bebauung von Nowawes (heute Babelsberg) vergrößert und gewann nun erst durch weite Rasenflächen, gerahmt von Baumreihen, den Charakter einer englischen Parkanlage. Für diese Parkgestaltung war eine Bewässerungsanlage notwendig. Dafür wurde an der Glienicker Lake nach Plänen von Persius 1843 – 45 unter der Bauleitung von Rudolf Wilhelm Gottgetreu ein Pumpenhaus gebaut.

Im Lauf der Zeit entstanden neue Bauten im Park, wie das Küchengebäude, erbaut von Strack 1844 – 49, das sogenannte Kleine Schloss an der Havel,

Babelsberg Park is Potsdam's third-largest landscape park. Peter Joseph Lenné repeatedly drew the attention of Prince William (the future Emperor William I) to the beauty of this area that lay opposite the park of his brother, Prince Charles. In 1833, he received a large part of the grounds as a present from his father, Frederick William III, and Lenné developed them through a network of paths and by planting native deciduous trees. The hilly landscape of the park lies on the lakes Tiefensee and Glienicker See. Lenné was also concerned about maintaining the beautiful views of Potsdam and its environs from various higher points of the hill. Schinkel was charged with drawing up plans for a palace there that, according to Princess Augusta's ideas, was to be built in the English neo-Gothic style. Contemporary publications about architecture, especially of Windsor Castle (after 1824), were very popular and were used as sources. The foundation stone was laid in June 1834, and in October 1835 the first, eastern half of the building with the pergola to the octagon and the dining room (tea salon) was dedicated. A second palace wing was intended to be added to the west and was to be set back the depth of the octagon; like the first wing, it was also to have a residential section and end with a flag tower. The palace complex, fashioned this way, would have fitted naturally into the landscape. Schinkel had carried out this first stage of construction with extreme restraint.

Between 1844 and 1849, the western part, though based on Schinkel's design, was extended through the addition of the octagonal ballroom at the prince's wishes. After the death in 1845 of Persius, who had supervised the continued building work, it was completed by Heinrich Strack, who went his own way after 1850 and altered the interior rooms, including those by Schinkel, and fitted them with furnishings of differing styles, as well as keepsakes.

Lenné, who was originally responsible for the garden design, was replaced after 1843 by Prince Pückler-Muskau. In subsequent years, the park was expanded in the west to the boundaries of the built-up area of Nowawes (today Babelsberg), and only then had it gained the character of an English landscape park through wide lawns framed by rows of trees. An irrigation system was necessary for this form of park. A pumping station was built according to plans by Persius on the lake Glienicker See for this purpose from 1843 to 1845 under the supervision of Rudolf Wilhelm Gottgetreu.

In the course of time new buildings were erected in the park, such as the kitchen house, built by Strack between 1844 and 1849; the so-called Little Palace on the Havel in 1842/43 by Eduard Gebhardt for the ladies-in-waiting; and close by – at the same time and by the same architect – the royal stables. In 1842, Strack built the Sailors' House directly on the water. The decorative front

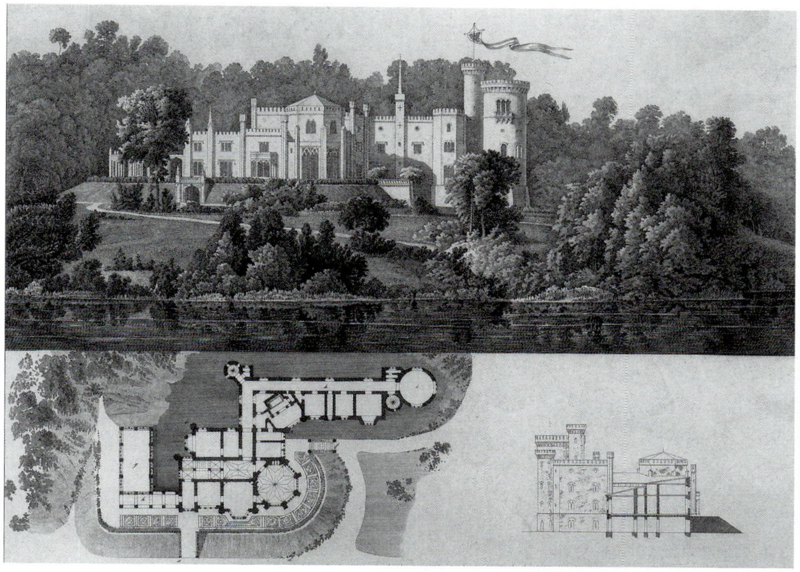

Karl Friedrich Schinkel

Entwurf für Schloss Babelsberg (gz. 1838), 1858, SPSG
Design for Babelsberg Palace (signed and dated 1838), 1858, SPSG

1842/43 von Eduard Gebhardt, und unweit davon der Marstall zur selben Zeit vom gleichen Baumeister. In unmittelbarer Nähe des Wassers baute Strack 1842 das Matrosenhaus. Als Vorbild für die Fassade diente die Schauseite des Rathauses von Stendal. Die hier wohnenden Matrosen bedienten die zum Schloss gehörenden Segelschiffe und Gondeln.

Das Wahrzeichen des Parks Babelsberg ist der auch von Potsdam aus sichtbare Flatowturm. Er erhebt sich anstelle der alten Rehnitz-Mühle (1848 abgebrannt) über die Baumwipfel. Ähnlich einer mittelalterlichen Wasserburg steht er in einem Bassin (notwendig für die Bewässerung des Parks) und wurde durch eine Zugbrücke mit dem Land verbunden. Als Vorbild für den Entwurf von Strack diente der Eschenheimer Torturm in Frankfurt am Main. Seinen Namen erhielt der Turm nach der prinzlichen Herrschaft Flatow in Westpreußen, die die Steine für den Bau 1853–56 lieferte. Die Innenräume wurden seit 1982 wiederhergestellt und zum Teil eingerichtet. Der Turm konnte 1993 wieder als Aussichtsturm eröffnet werden.

Die Gerichtslaube nordöstlich des Flatowturmes stand ehemals am Alten Rathaus in Berlin. Als man dort den heutigen Neubau (Rotes Rathaus) errichtete, wurde sie abgetragen und 1871/72 nach einem veränderten Entwurf von Strack an ihrem jetzigen Ort aufgestellt. Ursprünglich ist das Untergeschoss am Ende des 13. Jahrhunderts, das Obergeschoss 1485 erbaut worden. Der Besucher kann heute unschwer das alte Steinmaterial von dem des 19. Jahrhunderts unterscheiden. Die vier kreuzgewölbten Joche der unteren ehemals nur dreischiffigen offenen Halle werden in der Mitte von einem Pfeiler getragen. Das bemerkenswerte Stuckkapitell versinnbildlicht die menschlichen Torheiten. Während früher im Untergeschoss Gericht gehalten wurde, versammelte sich oben der Rat, fanden Empfänge oder Hochzeiten reicher Bürger statt.

Nach 1945 wurde das Schloss Babelsberg als Richterschule, später durch die Hochschule für Filmkunst und seit 1963 als Museum für Ur- und Frühgeschichte genutzt. Nach dessen Auszug wurden nach 1990 einige Räume wieder eingerichtet und dem Publikum gezeigt. Zurzeit sind sie geschlossen, da das gesamte Haus restauriert werden muss.

of Stendal city hall served as model for the façade. The sailors who lived there served the sailing ships and gondolas belonging to the palace.

The landmark of Babelsberg Park is Flatow Tower, also visible from Potsdam. It rises above the treetops on the site of the old Rehnitz Mill (burned down in 1848). Like a medieval moated castle, it stands in a pond (necessary for the watering of the park) and was connected to land by a drawbridge. The Eschenheimer Gate in Frankfurt am Main served as model for Strack's design. It took its name from the princely manor of Flatow in West Prussia, which supplied the stones for its construction between 1853 and 1856. The interior has been restored since 1982 and partially furnished. The tower was re-opened in 1993 as an observation tower.

The Court Loggia north-east of Flatow Tower formerly stood at the old city hall in Berlin. When the new city hall was under construction, it was removed and re-erected at its present location in 1871/72 according to an altered plan by Strack. The lower floor was originally constructed in the late 13th century, the upper storey in 1485. The visitor today can differentiate without difficulty between the old masonry and that of the 19th century. The four cross-vaulted bays of the open hall, which formerly had only three, are supported by pillars. The remarkable stucco capital symbolizes human follies. In the past, a court of law sat on the lower floor, while the upper storey was used for meetings of the town council, for receptions or the weddings of wealthy burghers.

After 1945, Babelsberg Palace was used for a school for the judiciary, later as a college for cinematic arts and, from 1963, it contained the Museum for Ancient and Early History of Potsdam. After the museum moved out, some rooms were refurnished and after 1990 opened to the public. At present, they are closed because the whole building is in need of complete restoration.

Rechts: Die Vergrößerung geschah 1844 – 49 nach Entwürfen von L. Persius und H. Strack. Die Hofhaltung hatte auch eine Veränderung der Räume im Schloss zur Folge. Nach dem Entwurf von L. Persius entstand deshalb der Tanzsaal.

Right: The enlargement took place between 1844 and 1849 according to the plans of L. Persius and H. Strack. The use of the palace by the court also brought about changes to the rooms, included the creation of the ballroom by L. Persius.

Im Gegensatz zu den Schlössern seines Bruders Friedrich Wilhelm (IV.) (Charlottenhof) und Carl (Glienicke) sollte sich das Schloss auf dem nahen Babelsberg an englisch-gotischen Vorbildern orientieren. K. F. Schinkel entwarf den 1833/34 errichteten Bau, der aber nicht abgeschlossen werden konnte.

In contrast to palaces of his brothers, Frederick William (IV) (Charlottenhof), and Charles (Glienicke), the palace on nearby Babelsberg was to be orientated on English Gothic models. K. F. Schinkel designed the building, which was constructed in 1833/1834 but never completed.

Links: Die Innenräume des Flatowturmes waren mit Kunstgegenständen verschiedenster Art ausgestattet. Von der oberen Aussichtsplattform hat man einen Rundblick auf den Park und die Stadt Potsdam.

Left: The interior of the Flatow Tower was furnished with works of art of various kinds. From the upper observation platform there is a panoramic view of the park and the city of Potsdam.

Durch die gotischen Bögen der Berliner Gerichtslaube aus dem 13. Jahrhundert blickt man auf den Flatowturm. Wilhelm I. hatte die Gerichtslaube nach ihrem Abriss 1871 als Geschenk erhalten und auf einem Hügel im Park Babelsberg wiederaufgebaut.

A view of the Flatow Tower through the Gothic arches of the 13th-century Berlin Court Loggia. William I had received the Court Loggia as a present after it was torn down in 1871 and had it rebuilt on a hill in Babelsberg Park.

Bernhard Zickendraht

Kronprinz Wilhelm, 1932, SPSG
Crown Prince William 1932, SPSG

Philipp von Laszlo

Kronprinzessin Cecilie, 1908, SPSG
Crown Princess Cecilia 1908, SPSG

Kronprinz

Wilhelm

und Kronprinzessin

Cecilie

Crown Prince William and Crown Princess Cecilia

Kronprinz bis 1918 | Crown Prince until 1918

Schloss Cecilienhof im Neuen Garten Potsdam

Cecilienhof Palace in the New Garden Potsdam

Das Schloss Cecilienhof, benannt nach der Kronprinzessin, ist der letzte Schlossbau der Hohenzollern. Er wurde 1913 –17 nach einem Entwurf von P. Schultze-Naumburg im Stil eines englischen Landsitzes errichtet und passt sich mit dieser Architektur sehr gut in die Landschaft des Neuen Gartens ein.

Cecilienhof Palace, named after the crown princess, was the last palace constructed by the Hohenzollern family. It was design by P. Schultze-Naumburg, based on an English country manor, and was built between 1913 and 1917. This architecture fits very well into the landscape of the New Garden.

Schloss Cecilienhof im Neuen Garten Potsdam

Cecilienhof Palace in the New Garden Potsdam

Nachdem sich bereits im 19. Jahrhundert gezeigt hatte, dass das Marmorpalais als ständiger Kronprinzensitz zu klein war und auch zu wenig zeitgemäße Bequemlichkeit bot, wurde 1913 bis 1917 das neue kronprinzliche Schloss Cecilienhof – benannt nach der Kronprinzessin – nach dem Entwurf von Paul Schultze-Naumburg im Norden des Neuen Gartens am Jungfernsee erbaut. Anfangs hatte man daran gedacht, ein entsprechendes Gebäude neben dem Schloss Babelsberg zu errichten, und es waren auch schon Entwürfe von Albert Geyer angefertigt und entsprechende Vorbereitungen im Gelände durchgeführt worden. Aber bald entschied man sich für den Neuen Garten.

In Anlehnung an den englischen Landhausstil mit ornamental verblendetem Fachwerk, vorspringenden Giebeln, mit Torbauten, unterschiedlichen Gebäudehöhen und dekorativen Schornsteinen entstand ein malerisches, sich in die Landschaft einfügendes Bild. Gestalterisches Können beweist auch die Lösung des Grundrisses mit dem quadratischen, allseitig geschlossenen großen Ehrenhof, dem sich mit dem Wirtschaftshof und dem Prinzenhof zwei kleinere Quadrate anfügen. Durch Galerien und Gänge an der Innenseite der Höfe sind alle Gebäude miteinander verbunden.

Die Mitte des Hauses nimmt eine große Wohnhalle ein. Rechts davon schließt sich der Salon und das Schreibzimmer der Kronprinzessin an. Im Obergeschoss befinden sich das Ankleidezimmer und ein Bad sowie das gemeinsame Schlafzimmer. Links von der Halle schließen sich die Suite des Kronprinzen mit einem Rauchzimmer an, dessen Vertäfelung nach englischem Vorbild ausgeführt wurde. Es folgt die Bibliothek des Hausherrn, eine Treppe führt in das Jagdzimmer im Obergeschoss. Im Erdgeschoss ist nach der Bibliothek ein Frühstückszimmer in der Art eines Gartenpavillons angeordnet, von dem aus man in den Speisesaal gelangen kann. Im Obergeschoss liegt neben dem Jagdzimmer die sogenannte Marschalltafel, der zweite Speiseraum, besonders geeignet für die Herrenessen im Schloss. Die sichtbare Fachwerkgliederung der Decke erinnert wieder an englische Vorbilder. Auch die Innenausstattung des Schlosses orientiert sich daran. Aber auch Leistungen der Berliner Kunstgewerbeschule unter Bruno Paul sind in der Ausstattung des Schlosses zu finden. Stuckarbeiten stammen von Joseph Wackerle, einer seiner Schüler, Gustav Weiland, schuf Stuckdekorationen, Kaminvorsätze und Entwürfe für Holzbildhauerarbeiten. Für die Ausmalung des Frühstückszimmers ist Emil Rudolph Weiß mit seinen Schülern verantwortlich. Eine Besonderheit des Schlosses ist ein Zimmer für die Kronprinzessin in Form einer Kajüte mit dem originalem Interieur aus einer alten Kaiserjacht.

After it became clear in the 19th century that the Marble Palace was too small to be the permanent official residence of the crown prince, and also provided too few up-to-date comforts, a new palace for the crown prince, Cecilienhof, was built between 1913 and 1917 in the north of the New Garden on the Jungfernsee lake to a design by Paul Schultze-Naumburg. It was named in honor of the crown princess. The original intention had been to construct an appropriate building next to Babelsberg Palace, and plans had already been drawn up by Albert Geyer and corresponding preparations carried out on the site. But the decision soon fell in favor of the New Garden.

The result, with ornamental half-timbered facing, projecting gables, gatehouses, varying roof heights and decorative chimney stacks, had a picturesque appearance that fitted into the landscape and was inspired by the English country-house style. Creative skill is also demonstrated in the ground plan which adds two smaller squares, the stable courtyard and the Prince's Courtyard, to the large, square, completely enclosed cour d'honneur. All of the buildings are interconnected through galleries and corridors on the inner sides of the courts.

The center of the building is taken up by a great hall. Adjacent to the right are the crown princess's salon and writing room. On the upper storey are the dressing room, bathroom and the common bedroom. Left from the main hall the crown prince's suite begins with a smoking salon fitted with English-style wooden paneling. The crown prince's library follows; a stairway leads to the Hunting Room on the floor above. Behind the library on the ground floor follow a breakfast room and a garden pavilion, which give access to the dining room. On the upper floor next to the Hunting Room is the so-called Marshal's Table, a second dining room especially suited for all-male dinners in the palace. The exposed beams of the ceiling are reminiscent of English models, as is the interior decoration of the palace. However, works of the Berlin Kunstgewerbeschule (School of Applied Arts) under the directorship of Bruno Paul are also to be found in the furnishings of the palace. The moldings were done by Joseph Wackerle, and one of his students, Gustav Weilands, created stucco decorations, fireplace surrounds, and designs for the woodcarving work.

Emil Rudolph Weiss and his students are responsible for the painting of the breakfast room. A special feature of the palace is a room for the crown princess in the form of a ship's cabin with the original interior of one of the old royal yachts.

Crown Princess Cecilia left Cecilienhof on February 10, 1945, with three sons, her brother-in-law, August William, and the crown prince's chief of cabinet, and took the last train from Berlin to Bad Kissingen. At the time, the crown prince had been taking spa treatment since January 3, 1945, in Oberstdorf.

Gottfried Höfer

Schloss Cecilienhof, 1973, SPSG
Cecilienhof Palace, 1973, SPSG

Die Kronprinzessin Cecilie verließ am 10. Februar 1945 mit drei Söhnen, dem Schwager August Wilhelm und dem Kabinettschef des Kronprinzen Cecilienhof und fuhr mit dem letzten Zug von Berlin nach Bad Kissingen. Der Kronprinz befand sich zu dieser Zeit seit dem 3. Januar 1945 zur Kur in Oberstdorf.

Am 27. April 1945 wurde Cecilienhof von sowjetischen Truppen besetzt. Als feststand, dass die Konferenz der drei Siegermächte der Anti-Hitler-Koalition im Juli 1945 im Schloss Cecilienhof stattfinden wird, wurden die Möbel in die nahe Meierei gebracht. Zur Ausstattung des Schlosses wurden Möbel aus anderen Potsdamer Schlössern (Marmorpalais, Babelsberg) geholt. Ein Brand in der Meierei am 18. Juli 1945 vernichtete alle Möbel aus Cecilienhof.

Vom 17. Juli bis 2. August 1945 fand im Schloss Cecilienhof die Konferenz der Regierungschefs der Anti-Hitler-Koalition statt. Am 2. August unterzeichneten Stalin für die Sowjetunion, Truman für die USA und zu Anfang Churchill, später Attlee für Großbritannien am runden Tisch in der als Konferenzraum dienenden großen Halle das sogenannte Potsdamer Abkommen, das zwar keine völkerrechtliche Verbindlichkeit besaß, auf das man sich aber später in der DDR stets bezog.

Bis 1951 gehörte Cecilienhof als Clubhaus zu dem nach der Konferenz im Neuen Garten eingerichteten sowjetischen Kultur- und Erholungspark.

Im Jahre 1952 kam der Neue Garten und damit auch Cecilienhof wieder in deutsche Verwaltung. Im Schloss wurde in den ehemaligen Wohnräumen des Kronprinzenpaares und späteren Konferenzräumen eine Gedenkstätte zum Potsdamer Abkommen eingerichtet. Der überwiegende Teil der Räume wurde ab 1962 in ein Hotel umgewandelt.

Schloss Cecilienhof ist heute im doppelten Sinne interessant: Es setzt den Endpunkt in der vom 17. Jahrhundert ausgehenden Entwicklung der Berlin-Potsdamer Schloss- und Gartenarchitektur und gewinnt in dieser Eigenschaft mehr und mehr an Bedeutung, und zudem ist es ein Ort, an dem nicht nur deutsche, sondern auch folgenschwere Weltpolitik gemacht wurde. Deshalb ist das Schloss auch heute noch für viele Besucher aus dem In- und Ausland interessant.

Cecilienhof was occupied by Soviet troops on April 27, 1945. When it was certain that the conference of the three victorious Allied powers would take place in July 1945 in Cecilienhof Palace, the furniture was taken to the nearby dairy. Furniture was brought from other Potsdam palaces (Marble Palace, Babelsberg) to furnish the palace. A fire in the dairy on July 18, 1945, destroyed all of the furniture from Cecilienhof.

From July 17 to August 2, 1945, the conference of the heads of government of the Allied powers was held. On August 2, the Potsdam Agreement was signed for the Soviet Union by Stalin, for the USA by Truman, and for Great Britain initially by Churchill and later by Attlee, on the round table in the main hall that served as the conference room. Although it had no international binding force, the agreement was later constantly referred to in the GDR.

Until 1951, Cecilienhof was a clubhouse, part of the Soviet cultural and recreation park that was set up in the New Garden after the conference. In 1952, the New Garden, and with it Cecilienhof, again came under German administration. The former living quarters of the crown prince and princess, and later conference rooms in the palace were arranged to commemorate the Potsdam Agreement. The majority of the rooms were turned into a hotel after 1962.

Today, two aspects of Cecilienhof Palace are interesting. It marks the end of the architectural development of the Berlin-Potsdam palaces and gardens, which began in the 17th century, and is gaining more and more significance in this capacity; and at the same time it is a place where not only German, but also momentous world history was made. This is why the palace remains of interest today for many visitors from Germany and abroad.

Links oben: Die hohe Halle in der Mitte des Schlosses diente der kronprinzlichen Familie als Wohnraum. Später war es der Sitzungssaal während der Konferenz der Siegermächte des Zweiten Weltkriegs vom 17. Juni bis 2. August 1945.
Top left: The high hall in the middle of the palace served the crown prince's family as a living room. Later, it was the main meeting room during the conference of the victorious Second World War Allies from June 17 to August 2, 1945.

Links unten: Zu den Besonderheiten der Innenräume gehört das nach einem Entwurf von Paul Ludwig Troost als Schiffskabine ausgebaute Kabinett der Kronprinzessin. Der Zugang zu diesem Raum war auch durch einen Treppenaufgang von den oberen Privaträumen der Kronprinzessin möglich.
Bottom left: One of the special features of the interior is a room that was designed as a ship's cabin by Paul Ludwig Troost for the crown princess. A stairway from her private upper chambers gave access to the room.

Rechts: Der kleine Salon diente der kronprinzlichen Familie als Frühstückszimmer. Während der Potsdamer Konferenz wurde er wohl als Sekretariat genutzt.
Right: The small salon was used by the family of the crown prince as a breakfast room. During the Potsdam Conference it accommodated the secretariat.

Die Deutsche Bibliothek verzeichnet diese Publikation in der Deutschen Nationalbibliografie; detaillierte bibliografische Daten sind im Internet über http://dnb.ddb.de abrufbar.
The Deutsche Bibliothek lists this publication in the Deutsche Nationalbibliografie; detailed bibliographic data is available on the Internet at http://dnb.ddb.de

The Library of Congress Cataloguing-in-Publication data is available.

Auf dem Umschlag | On the cover:
Vorderseite | Front: Vor dem Mittelbau der Orangerie wurde 1873 das Standbild des Bauherrn Friedrich Wilhelm IV. von G. Bläser aufgestellt. | A statue by G. Bläser of Frederick William IV, who commissioned the building, was placed in front of the central part of the orangery in 1873.
Rückseite | Back: Blick in den südlichen Verbindungsgang im Marmorpalais | View of the south connecting corridor in the Marble Palace.

Prestel Verlag
Königinstraße 9
D-80539 München
Telefon +49 (89) 38 17 09-0
Telefax +49 (89) 38 17 09-35
www.prestel.de

Prestel Publishing Ltd.
4, Bloomsbury Place
London, WC1A 2Qa
Tel.: +44 (020)7323 5004
Fax.: +44 (020) 7636 8004

Prestel Publishing
900 Broadway, Suite 603
New York, N.Y. 10003
Tel.: +1 (212) 995 2720
Fax.: +1 (212)995 2733
www.prestel.com

Prestel books are available worldwide. Please contact your nearest bookseller or one of the addresses below for information concerning your local distributor.

Translated from the German by David Andersen, Berlin

Lektorat | Editorial direction: Frauke Berchtig
Copy-editing by John Sykes, Cologne
Gestaltung | Design: tischdreizehn, Büro für Gestaltung und Kommunikation, München
Cover: Cilly Klotz, München
Herstellung | Production: Andrea Mogwitz, München
Reproduktion | Reproduction: Repro Ludwig, Zell am See
Druck | Printing: Passavia Druckservice GmbH, Passau
Bindung / Binding: Conzella Verlagsbuchbinderei, Pfarrkirchen

Gedruckt in Deutschland auf chlorfrei gebleichtem Papier
Printed in Germany on acid-free paper

ISBN deutsch 978-3-7913-3751-7
ISBN englisch 978-3-7913-3801-9

Abbildungsnachweis | Picture credits: Alle Abbildungen stammen von der Stiftung Preußische Schlösser und Gärten Berlin-Brandenburg/Leo Seidel, Berlin mit Ausnahme von: | All photographs by The Prussian Palaces and Gardens Foundation Berlin-Brandenburg/Leo Seidel, Berlin, except for the following:
Stiftung Preußische Schlösser und Gärten Berlin-Brandenburg | The Prussian Palaces and Gardens Foundation Berlin-Brandenburg/Jörg P. Anders, Berlin: S. p. 170/ Hans Bach, 2002: S. | p. 107/Edition Rieger, Neuruppin OT Karwe: S. | p. 52/Roland Handrick: S. | p. 100, 131, 186, 189/Hagen Immel, Potsdam: S. | p. 154/Wolfgang Pfauder: S. | p. 51/Kurt Reutte: S. | p. 6 links/left